Interactive World, Interactive God

Interactive World, Interactive God

The Basic Reality of Creative Interaction

EDITED BY

Carol Rausch Albright

John R. Albright

Mladen Turk

CASCADE *Books* • Eugene, Oregon

INTERACTIVE WORLD, INTERACTIVE GOD
The Basic Reality of Creative Interaction

Cascade Books
An Imprint of Wipf and Stock Publishers
199 W. 8th Ave., Suite 3
Eugene, OR 97401

www.wipfandstock.com

PAPERBACK ISBN: 978-1-4982-9388-4
HARDCOVER ISBN: 978-1-4982-9390-7
EBOOK ISBN: 978-1-4982-9389-1

Cataloguing-in-Publication data:

Names: Albright, Carol Rausch, editor | Albright, John R., editor | Turk, Mladen, editor.

Title: Interactive world, interactive God : the basic reality of creative interaction / edited by Carol Rausch Albright, John R. Albright, Mladen Turk.

Description: Eugene, OR: Cascade Books, 2017 | Includes bibliographical references and index.

Identifiers: ISBN 978-1-4982-9388-4 (paperback) | ISBN 978-1-4982-9390-7 (hardcover) | ISBN 978-1-4982-9389-1 (ebook).

Subjects: LCSH: Physics, Chemistry, Astronomy, Biology, Ecology, Neuroscience, Sociology

—Religious aspects—Christianity | Religion and Science | Creation.

Classification: BL265 P4 I50 2017 (print) | BL265 (ebook).

Manufactured in the U.S.A.   11/06/17

Ad Glorium Maiorem Dei

Contents

Part 3: Interaction in Theology

Preface

O NE COULD SAY THAT this book began with an accident. In 2011, one of its editors, Carol Albright, underwent ankle surgery that accidentally left her sciatic nerve dead from the knee down. Permanent paralysis was predicted. Contrary to expectations, the nerve began to regenerate, top down, growing about an inch a month. After a year and a half she could walk almost normally.

Although this situation was frightening to both Carol and her husband, John R. Albright, it led to new developments, as often happens. Enforced time at home provided opportunity for reading and thinking. Carol and John Albright had worked on the relationship of religion and science for many years, so she explored related issues. New developments regarding complexity and emergence, as presented by Harold Morowitz and others, attracted her attention. She also eavesdropped on conversations conducted on the website of Henry Stapp of the Lawrence Berkeley Laboratory at the University of California.

Morowitz was the founding editor of the journal *Complexity*, a pioneer in exploring emergent systems, in which interactions lead to new and unexpected outcomes.[1] Stapp's work focuses on quantum theory and its significance for the relationship of brain with mind, consciousness, and information transfer.[2] Both thinkers, and their colleagues, pointed the way through reductionistic assumptions to the basic importance of interaction and the emergence of new phenomena.

---

1. See Harold Morowitz, *The Emergence of Everything: How the World Became Complex* (New York: Oxford University Press, 2004). See also John Albright's discussion of complexity in chapter 2 of this volume.

2. See, for example, https://sites.google.com/a/lbl.gov/stappfiles/.

Carol was fortunate that her chief conversation partner was her husband, John, who became coeditor of this book. John has taught quantum physics and learned many other disciplines as well. Once a week we were joined by a group of remarkable people ("the Monday Group") for an afternoon's study: psychiatrist Melvin Gray; theologian/philosophers Jeannette Schmidt and Mary Gerhart; primatologist and emeritus museum director Paul Heltne, and Jim Kolkmeier, an airline founder with a theology degree. We spent some months on Morowitz and emergence across the sciences.

Monthly we were joined by an even wider group: religious studies scholar Mladen Turk, now an editor of this book; the directors of three religion-and-science programs or courses in the Chicago area; a physical chemist; a neuroscience professor, a psychotherapist, a statistician/theologian, and others. This "Chicago Group," including its present and former members, has met at the Albright home for many years. Their varied expertise also convinced us that interactionism is a reality that spans the organization of our world at every level, leading to emergent realities and unpredictable outcomes. Although the basic rules of science are not violated, they are often superseded by quantum effects, top-down influences on simple entities, and exceedingly complex interrelationships.

We were aware that the reductionistic science that characterized the twentieth century had made religious belief untenable for many people. Reductionistic thinking emphasizes material components, not their interaction. It points to results that are quite predictable, and that depend entirely upon simpler components. The current scientific developments reopened windows to admit new understandings of the way the world works, and also new possibilities for divine-human interaction and the unexpected.

A book to sample the possibilities, written for the intelligent nonspecialist, was due. This is our attempt to provide it. The first eight chapters describe interaction in the physical world, at the beginnings of life, in life's development and expression, in its ecological structure, and in the workings of the human brain and human society. The final four chapters cast light on the religious significance of these new understandings. The book could be useful for courses in religion and science, for congregational groups, and for reflective individual study.

The editors thank the members of the Monday Group (Gerhart and Heltne contributed chapters, and John Albright, who leads the group, contributed two). Thanks also to the Chicago Group (Sandra Ham wrote a chapter). We appreciate the continuing work of the Center for Advanced Study in Religion and Science (CASIRAS), which helps support science and religion work at the Lutheran School of Theology at Chicago (LSTC). Chapters were contributed by three members of the CASIRAS executive committee: Grace Wolf-Chase, Mladen Turk, and Carol Albright. Paul Heltne also serves on the CASIRAS board.

We appreciate continuing support from the Zygon Center for Religion and Science (ZCRS) at LSTC, and its directors, Lea Schweitz and Gayle Woloschak (who also chairs CASIRAS). We also express great appreciation to the founding directors of ZCRS, Philip Hefner and the late Thomas Gilbert, and to William Lesher and the late Ralph Burhoe, without whose support it would never have been established.

Other centers for the study of religion and science have also made their contribution to this effort. Ted Peters, who wrote our final chapter, has filled many roles at the Francisco J. Ayala Center for Theology and the Natural Sciences—formerly known as the Center for Theology and the Natural Sciences (CTNS), and he co-edits the journal *Theology and Science*. Joseph Bracken, S.J., has ties to the Center for Process Studies in Claremont, California. Finally, Martinez Hewlett of the University of New Mexico, Philip Gorski of Yale University, and Michael Spezio of Scripps College have brilliantly enriched our understanding of the basic role of interactivity within their own disciplines.

Each of our writers has amazed and enlightened us.

The staff at Wipf and Stock, especially including K. C. Hanson, Jeremy Funk, and Calvin Jaffarian, have all played invaluable roles in bringing this book to fruition. We are grateful to all of them.

—Carol Rausch Albright, John R. Albright, and Mladen Turk

Contributors

Carol Rausch Albright has been Executive Editor of *Zygon: Journal of Religion and Science* and an award-winning medical writer. As regional codirector of the Templeton Religion and Science Course Program, she worked with John Albright to arrange twenty national and regional conferences, where faculty planning science-and-religion courses could learn from one another and hear speakers. She is Past President of the American Theological Society (Midwest Division) and Visiting Professor at the Lutheran School of Theology at Chicago. Her books include *Beginning with the End: God, Science, and Wolfhart Pannenberg* (Open Court, 1997), and *The Humanizing Brain: Where Religion and Neuroscience Meet* (Pilgrim, 1997) coauthored by James G. Ashbrook.

John R. Albright is Visiting Professor of Religion and Science at the Lutheran School of Theology at Chicago as well as Emeritus Professor of Physics at Purdue University and at Florida State University. He did research at Brookhaven and Fermi National Laboratories, published *Introduction to Atomic and Nuclear Physics,* and taught prizewinning courses in religion and science. With his wife, Carol Rausch Albright, he directed the Southern and Midwest regions of the John Templeton Foundation Religion and Science Course Program. He currently serves on the Evangelical Lutheran Church in America's Alliance for Faith, Science, and Technology, and on the Ecumenical Roundtable on Science, Technology, and the Church.

Joseph A. Bräcken, S.J., Professor Emeritus of Theology at Xavier University in Cincinnati, Ohio, has specialized over the years in linking the metaphysical scheme of Alfred North Whitehead with classical Roman Catholic Church doctrine. Above all, he deals with the philosophical presuppositions of interreligious dialogue and the proper relation between religion and science. His latest books are *Does God Roll Dice? Divine Providence for a World in the Making* (Liturgical, 2012) and *The World in the Trinity: Open-Ended Systems in Science and Religion* (Fortress, 2014)

Mary Gerhart is Professor Emerita of Religious Studies at Hobart and William Smith Colleges where, among others, she taught bidisciplinary courses in science and religion with physicist Allan Russell. They coauthored *Metaphoric Process: The Creation of Scientific and Religious Understanding* (Texas Christian University Press, 1984) and *New Maps for Old: Explorations in Science and Religion* (Continuum, 2001). She was awarded a Fulbright scholarship in Berlin and held Visiting Professorships at the University of Houston, Syracuse University, and the University of Notre Dame. She was the Senior Fellow at the Martin Marty Center for the Advanced Study of Religion at the University of Chicago (2007–8) and editorial chair of *Religious Studies Review* (1979–1987). Her publications include *The Question of Belief in Literary Criticism: An Introduction to the Hermeneutical Theory of Paul Ricoeur* (Heinz, 1979), *Genre Choices, Gender Questions* (University of Oklahoma Press, 1992), and *The Christianity Reader* (University of Chicago Press, 2007), edited with biblical scholar Fabian Udoh. Her primary recent interest is the work of Hildegard of Bingen.

Philip S. Gorski is Professor of Sociology and Religious Studies at Yale University. His research focuses on religion and politics in western Europe and North America during the early modern and modern periods. He also has a long-standing interest in the philosophy of science and social science. His most recent book is *American Covenant: A History of Civil Religion from the Puritans to the Present* (Princeton University Press, 2017).

Sandra A. Ham is a Senior Statistician in the Center for Health and the Social Sciences at the University of Chicago. She has worked in government and industry with sciences and engineering related to human interactions with the environment. She is a generalist in science and religion. Her scholarly work aims to develop a Christian ecosystem theology that is the nexus of old religion and new science, meeting at a common understanding of Nature. This transdisciplinary, constructive work reflects on historical and modern approaches to the responsibility to protect the integrity of life, both human and nonhuman. She believes that ecology, more than any other science, can be shown to facilitate the constructive work of letting authoritative religious texts and traditions speak again. By doing so, Christianity may develop improved tools for guiding future ethical

decisions about how to conduct a society with fast-changing social, political, and environmental issues.

Paul G. Heltne holds a Ph.D. from the Division of Biological Sciences at the
University of Chicago. After graduation, he accepted an appointment at the
Johns Hopkins School of Medicine with a joint appointment in the School
of Public Health. While an undergraduate, he did field work in South Africa
and Namibia working with Dr. Ronald Singer on the physical anthropology of Hottentots and Bushmen. He also studied New World primates in a
captive setting and began a series of studies on the distribution and abundance of *Aotus* in the field and learning how to breed the night monkeys
in captivity, both for studies of developing a vaccine for malaria. Heltne
then accepted an invitation to head the Chicago Academy of Sciences. He
established an educational enrichment program for public schools, which
included teacher training and in-classroom coaching. The Academy is the
leading provider of enrichment for students and teachers at their Chicago
schools. Heltne also obtained permission to build the new Peggy Notebaert
Nature Museum adjacent to the North Pond in Lincoln Park, thanks to the
generosity of many wonderful people.

Martinez Hewlett is a molecular virologist, a philosopher, and a novelist,
and is currently serving as Research Scholar and Interim Branch President
of the University of New Mexico, Taos. He has been awarded research grants
from the National Institutes of Health, the National Science Foundation, the
Kroc Foundation, the American Cancer Society, and Fogarty International.
Dr. Hewlett is facilitator for Philosophy of Medicine at the University of
Arizona College of Medicine. He is a founding board member and past co-
ordinator of the Saint Albert the Great Forum on Theology and the Sciences
at that university. With Ted Peters, he authored *Evolution: From Creation to
New Creation* (Abingdon, 2003), and *Can You Believe in God and Evolution?
A Guide for the Perplexed.* (Abingdon, 2006).

Ted Peters is a systematic theologian and ethicist who concentrates on
Reformation theology as well as the dialogue between faith and science,
and currently works in astrotheology, cosmology, and divine action. He is
Emeritus Professor of Systematic Theology and Ethics at Pacific Lutheran
Theological Seminary and California Lutheran University, as well as at the
Graduate Theological Union in Berkeley, California. Along with Robert
John Russell, he coedits the journal *Theology and Science* at the Center for
Theology and the Natural Sciences. He is author or coauthor of four books

and numerous articles in religion and science. He serves on the Standards Working Group of the California Institute of Regenerative Medicine.

Michael Spezio is Associate Professor of Psychology and Neuroscience and directs the Laboratory for Inquiry into Valuation and Emotion (the LIVE lab) at Scripps College. He also holds a visiting scientist position at the Institute for Systems Neuroscience at the University Medical Center in Eppendorf, Hamburg, Germany. He was a resident fellow and is a member of the Center of Theological Inquiry in Princeton, New Jersey. His articles on virtue science include those published in *Theology and the Science of Moral Action* (Routledge, 2012) and *Habits in Mind* (Brill, 2017).

Mladen Turk is Niebuhr Distinguished Service Chair and Associate Professor of Religious Studies, at Elmhurst College. He is a past President of the American Theological Society (Midwest Division) and is Secretary of the Board of the Center for Advanced Studies in Religion and Science (CASIRAS). Currently he is the Book Review Editor of *Zygon: Journal of Religion and Science.*

Grace Wolf-Chase is an Astronomer at the Adler Planetarium, an Associate at the University of Chicago, and an Affiiated Faculty member of the Zygon Center for Religion and Science in Hyde Park. After receiving a Ph.D. in astronomy from the University of Arizona, she studied star formation at NASA's Ames Research Center in Moffet Field, California, and the University of California, Riverside on postdoctoral fellowships. Wolf-Chase's primary research interests include all aspects of the earliest stages of star formation in our galaxy, about which she publishes prolifically. Concurrently, she is a member of the science team for the Milky Way Project, a citizen science initiative that is part of "Zooniverse," the world's largest and most popular platform for people-powered research. Wolf-Chase is Vice President of the Center for Advanced Study in Religion and Science (CASIRAS). She resides in suburban Chicago with her spouse, and she has three adult children.

Introduction

Carol Rausch Albright

THE RELATIONSHIP BETWEEN RELIGIOUS and scientific beliefs is clearly not a settled issue in Western societies. Religious believers don't deny that science exists, although some deny its conclusions; some scientists deny the very existence of religious reality. Many take the easy way out and ignore the issue. They may not deny theological assertions, but they think mainly in popular terms of materialistic cause and effect. Religious perspectives may have little relevance as people adopt values and consider life's meanings; the connections are too hard to discern. This is a commonplace situation today.

Through many centuries, the doctrines of the various religions have not changed a great deal, but their real meaning has consistently been colored by all the other assumptions of the era. When the Renaissance reached various parts of Europe, for example, new educational institutions were built, and traditions were debated. When the printing press was invented, many people learned to read, and they sometimes interpreted Scripture for themselves; this development played an important role in the Reformation. With the Enlightenment came the beginnings of scientific exploration, and logical evidence reigned. When the Romantic era brought back emphasis on emotion, religion followed suit. For more discussion of relationships between theological and cultural beliefs, see chapter 9, by Mladen Turk.

The Age of Technological Development: 1850–1980

In 1907, my grandfather, Emil Rausch, was a young pastor who took time to study philosophy at the University of Michigan. In one paper that he wrote, he predicted that the relationship between religion and science would become the prevailing issue of the coming twentieth century. This piece of work was saved in family papers, which I eventually inherited. Emil Rausch's paper was dated January 30, 1907. I happened to read it just a century later, on January 30, 2007. I think he predicted well.

When he wrote, telegraphs had been whizzing information from place to place for half a century. The railroads were moving both people and freight, including coal to warm buildings and to power the burgeoning steel industry. Automobiles had begun to appear, and roads improved. Before long, many people replaced oil lamps, gaslights, and wood stoves with electric lights and cook stoves—although many did not acquire indoor plumbing until the 1940s or later. Farmers sold their horses and bought tractors and harvesters, and some went to work in factories. Hand-cranked—or even automatic—telephones kept families and friends connected. The radio brought the news, and after World War II, television brought even more entertainment.

During that century, understandings of the world became more materialistic. Life was being shaped by technology of all sorts, and this rested upon scientific logic. Such logic could then be used as a basic approach to understanding all of reality.

Religious creeds may not have changed, but quietly, people wondered about miracles. Diseases were addressed with prayer but often cured with antibiotics. No more was heaven just above the blue sky. Spaceships went there instead.

So my grandfather was correct. During the twentieth century, religious creeds did encounter scientific findings, and some people struggled to reconcile the two.

The Electronic Revolution

Toward the end of the twentieth century, society took a new turn, which was actually based on advances in physics and electrical engineering. The first computers, huge devices equipped with vacuum tubes, worked out complex scientific problems which previously could not have been analyzed. Then smaller electronic computers did some similar work, and by the 1990s, e-mail sent information around the world, dramatically increasing knowledge and communication. Even recreation and relationships changed: many games and friendships and even romances depended on the new devices.

The science that fostered the electronic revolution led to other important activities as well. It enabled scientific research of a sort that previously had not been possible. Physicists, for example, had long posited the existence of subatomic particles, joined together to form atoms, molecules, and larger substances. They had also suggested quantum mechanics, in which interactions among particles are random, not completely predictable. Many of these theories date as far back as Werner Heisenberg, Paul Dirac, and Erwin Schrödinger during the 1920s, but they could be tested only by observing their effects. With huge accelerators, subatomic particles could be studied directly. Their interactions were seen just as they had been at the very beginnings of the universe, small fractions of a second after the Big Bang, when almost all that existed was energy—light.[1] (The book of Genesis is strangely accurate with its report that God's creation began with the command, "Let there be light.")

Complexity and Emergence

With one set of interactions after another, the organization of matter became more complex. The most basic material substances were created through the interactions of particles of energy. Even today, only about 5 percent of all that exists has become a material substance—except, perhaps, for dark matter, which demonstrates its existence through its interactions but has never been detected otherwise. For more discussion of these issues, see chapter 1, by John R. Albright.

The world is coming to be seen as interactive all the way down—or all the way up—from the tiniest of realities to the largest. As we see in chapter 2, also by John R. Albright, interactions have given rise to all of material reality. They led to subatomic particles, atoms, molecules, compounds, and more complex material substances, interaction after interaction, from one level to the next. Even the cosmos has become enlarged and complexified beyond the reach of human imagination, as we learn from Grace Wolf-Chase's fine description in chapter 3.

As the organization of matter became more complex, the *rules* of interaction changed. Molecules behave differently than subatomic particles

---

1. See Weinberg, *The First Three Minutes.* Although this book was first published more than thirty-five years ago, its basic conclusions have stood up to intensive investigation.

do. Through eons of interaction, even cosmological bodies—stars, planets, black holes, and so on—have changed over time, with a large increase in chemical complexity.

The early study of such processes was fostered especially at the Santa Fe Institute, in New Mexico, founded in 1984 by a group of scientists who wished to work together outside of traditional scientific boundaries. They had become aware that, as complex interactions take place, unexpected outcomes occur. Substances turn out to be organized in unprecedented ways; even the rules of interaction may change. So they set out to study nonlinear processes—those that work in unexpected modalities and have surprising consequences.[2] These processes occur not only at the level of physics and chemistry, but also in the experiences of living things, as we will see in chapters 4 through 8.

At the Santa Fe Institute and other labs, burgeoning computer capability enabled scientists to track these emergent phenomena, especially as related to processes called *chaos* and *complexity*.

In chaos theory, interactions follow the ordinary laws of nature, but there are so many interactions going on at once, and so many variables, that it is impossible to foresee their outcomes. That is why weather is not predicted more than a week in advance, and forecasts a week out are not very reliable.

Complexity deals with developments that—unlike chaos—actually change the rules. Studies of complexity concern the appearance of new modes of action and organization that are unlike those seen in predecessors. However, as Kirk Wegter-McNelly points out, these new properties "emerge out of the possibilities offered by the underlying property," by which he means quantum mechanics. This is not the place for a long discussion of a very complex form of physics. However, it is safe to say that interactions involving quantum mechanics have random, basically unpredictable outcomes. Robert John Russell believes that this quality affords an opportunity for God to interact with human life without breaking laws of nature.[3] Quantum physics is also associated with lasting linkages among subatomic particles—even after they are separated. Some, including Wegter-McNelly, have interpreted such "quantum entanglement" as a "hint that the universe is a place of subtle interconnections in the midst of bewildering diversity."[4]

2. See, for example, Morowitz, *The Emergence of Everything*.

3. Russell, "Quantum Physics and the Theology of Non-Interventionist Objective Divine Action," 583.

4. Wegter-McNelly, "Fundamental Physics and Religion," 166.

In chapter 3, Grace Wolf-Chase discusses consequences of all these interactions for the cosmos. The universe is thought to have existed for some 13 billion years. Over time, it continues to grow larger, for reasons not well understood. Interactions in space have led to a first generation of stars, which eventually exploded; scattered material formed new stars as well as black holes, where matter is so concentrated that gravity overwhelms all other forces. Our sun is probably a second–generation star.

With better equipment and the help of many volunteer astronomers in a process called "crowdsourcing," professional astronomers are learning more about the extent and complexity of galaxies. They have discovered various planets that may well be hospitable to life—adding enormous dimensions to human understandings of a Creator.

Life Arrives

Planet earth was a relative latecomer to the cosmic scene, appearing perhaps 4.5 billion years ago.[5] Life may have appeared here as early as 3.8 million years ago,[6] but those early life forms lived on carbon dioxide and natural minerals. By 3 billion years ago,[7] one-celled plants containing chlorophyll had appeared. These simple green organisms could make their own food from oxygen, water, and sunlight, and then store it for later use in the form of carbohydrates.[8]

Finally, about 1.8 billion years ago, some of these simple sorts of cells interacted, and they merged to form complex cells and multicellular organisms called eukaryotes, as Martinez Hewlett describes in chapter 4. This event was an enormous breakthrough. Eukaryotes include more than one carrier of DNA, and they reproduce by breeding with one another. For this reason, their descendants vary; they eventually gave rise to plants, animals, and fungi. Through natural selection, most of the new variants did not survive, but some thrived and developed further. If one sort of life was wiped out by a natural disaster, another soon occupied its niche, proliferating and forming new variations, as happened with dinosaurs and mammals.

Because many sorts of life forms share a habitat, they begin to depend upon one another for nutrition, protection, hiding places, and shade. Eventually, such interactions become necessary in order for the participants to thrive. In chapter 5, Paul Heltne describes healthy interactions among the

5. www.bbc.co.uk/nature/history-of-the-earth.

6. Ibid.

7. https.www.ScientificAmerican.com/article/timeline-of-photosynthesis-on-earth.

8. www.bbc.co.uk/nature/history-of-the-earth.

millions of tiny life forms found in only a cubic meter of fertile soil: bacteria, worms, insects, a few mammals, and others. In chapter 6, Sandra Ham describes ecological interaction on a large scale, in a tropical rainforest of large and small trees and plants, birds, reptiles, insects, various mammals, even monkeys. Both Heltne and Ham also describe the destruction that results when these interactions are disturbed by human intervention for the sake of agriculture, habitation, or convenience.

Of all the earth's creatures, human beings are not the largest or strongest, but we are surely the most complex. Like simpler creatures, we rely entirely on interaction for our survival: within the cosmos, to produce the atoms and molecules that compose our bodies; and, within our bodies, to regulate the digestive system that supplies our fuel, the intake of oxygen to interact with the food, the metabolism of the cells using these nutrients, the hormones that regulate metabolism and other systems, the blood that transports these substances, and the heart that pumps the blood where it needs to go.

By far the most complex interactions in human beings—and, in fact, anywhere on earth as far as we know, involve the nervous system—in particular the brain. There are billions of neurons in the "elegant human brain," which "interfaces with the world on many fronts."[9] Although some neurons are closely situated, there are also communication paths among sectors of the brain, which are receiving information from the body, the senses, and other parts of the brain. And to make communications even more complex, none of these connections are hardwired; they are carried by reactions among chemicals called neurotransmitters.

The outcome of an interaction among neurons may differ from one time to the next, which may be one reason why our minds follow different tracks of thinking on different occasions. For consciousness itself is often seen as an emergent process, not entirely predictable from the interactions of the neurons on which it depends.

Some neuroscientists still insist that all of the brain's functions are material. Others see consciousness as a different level of reality, entirely dependent upon interaction.[10] In chapter 7, Michael Spezio makes important points about the nature of interaction in the process of consciousness; his suggestions are likely to elicit new discussions in the field of neuroscience.

Even beyond the critical nature of interaction within a human being, it is also true that we cannot live truly human lives without intensive and extensive interactions with other people. Sociologists have spent considerable

9. Ashbrook and Albright, *The Humanizing Brain*, xxxii.
10. Stapp, *Mindful Universe*.

effort in tracing human interactive processes, with emphasis on epistemology. Philip S. Gorski addresses the new task of developing an interactive ontology that structures the basic nature of human social interaction. His analysis comprises three parts. The first concerns social substance. He argues that an adequate account of social structure must minimally include persons, symbols, and artifacts. These three building blocks are connected by several types of relationships, and interaction takes place through several principal types of social process, all of which Gorski names and discusses. These understandings are vital to our discussion, because interaction among people is absolutely essential to human thriving, whether it involves care of the young, teaching, invention, provision of resources, distribution of property, or other activities.

In sum, for human beings, interactions of all sorts are basic to existence. They produce the atoms in our bodies and knit them together. Interactions are basic to the processes of life—respiration, nutrition, circulation, and neurological coordination. They encode thought and consciousness. They build relationships.

Ten minutes after a person's death, virtually all the material components that made up the person are still present. But the interactions have ceased. The person is gone.

Larger Realities

As our studies have progressed through descriptions of current research in many scientific disciplines, we have consistently seen at least two things. First, the interactive nature of the world at every level is seen to give rise to unexpected and basically unpredictable consequences, in which new modes of interaction emerge. Second, we have seen that clear predictions may in some cases be simply impossible, because of enormous complexity, or because of basic randomness in the outcomes of interactions. With new levels of organization come new rules of interaction. Emergent realities may turn around and influence simpler processes that had preceded them.[11]

Although the popular views of science in our culture are still quite reductionistic, these views may change. The interactive nature of reality is becoming more widely understood, and not only by physicists. For example, writers on health expend considerable effort in explaining the complex interactions that play a role in health outcomes. Perhaps such insights can lead to more intuitive understanding of the basically interactive nature of all that is—even God.

11. See Peacocke, *Theology for a Scientific Age.*

Danish theologian Niels Henrik Gregersen, speaking at a 2017 conference,[12] addressed this issue, and surprisingly, began by looking back five hundred years. Martin Luther, he said, observed that God's work of creation is active at every moment, and is more concerned with novelty than with maintenance. And, Luther said, God is continually addressing creatures by way of other creatures.

If so, Gregersen observed,[13] God is present not only as a spiritual principle alongside of the material world, but is actually a part of it. Thus, the "deep incarnation" of the Logos in Jesus includes materiality. In this event, God was "taking on board the full weight of material existence." This materiality includes not only physical existence, but underlying it, the energy of matter and its information structures.

Information, said Gregersen, is at the "rock bottom of physical reality, and it reflects the generative capacities of quantum effects. These make a difference and that which makes a difference is real. This finding discourages old-style reductionistic claims.

The old concept that the corpuscular is matter has been replaced by the informational structures of matter, Gregersen said. In our time, we must begin to think of God as an interactive agent. And, as God is continually involved in material events, "there is a deep coherence of all that is." We can say that interaction is reality, God is interactive, interactivity leads to physical reality, and God has a role in physical reality. God has specific transformative goals for different persons, and they oppose the trends of entropy, which as Robert John Russell observed, is a precursor of evil. God did not create stasis.[14]

Thus, Gregersen clearly asserted God's interaction with the material world. He mentioned the work of Russell, but did not address it deeply. Now is the time to have a look. Russell, a physicist as well as a theologian, is concerned with scientific aspects of God's interaction with the material world. In a recent publication, he addresses this issue at length. His methodology is to seek a concept called noninterventionist objective divine action, abbreviated as NIODA. Russell asserts that the principles by which the universe operates are God-given, and not broken by God. Like Gregersen, he addresses the possibility that God may work through the uncertainties and basically unpredictable nature of quantum mechanics. This scientific

12. Niels Gregersen, speaker at a conference titled Deep Incarnation: From Cosmos to Commitment, at Goshen College on April 7–9, 2017. Gregersen's remarks, cited here, are from his lecture, "The Cosmic Christ: God in a World of Mass, Energy, and Information."

13. Ibid.

14. Gregersen in "The Cosmic Christ."

discipline is far from reductionism, for it has found that, on the level of subatomic particles, identical interactions do not always have identical outcomes. There is an inescapable element of randomness in the behavior of these particles, which sometimes appear instead as waves, and which interact with different results at different times. Yet there are also inexplicable linkages among them. When two are linked in their means of rotation, they will continue to act in synchrony over a long distance. This phenomenon is known as quantum entanglement.

God, says Russell, does not manipulate these effects, but works through them without violating natural law. Certainly, as mentioned in earlier discussion of the functioning of the human brain, quantum effects seem to be in play, and in the brain they may account for the variability of thought patterns from one occasion to another.

Thus quantum effects seem to offer a fine window for divine action. Since they have consequences at many levels of physical reality, broader assertions may be made as well. As Wegter-McNelly observes, quantum entanglement leads to various interconnections with subtle consequences.[15]

Theologians Comment

Beliefs in direct interaction between human beings and God have never been entirely absent, as Mary Gerhart describes in chapter 10, which deals with mystical experience. Mysticism was known and discussed early in Christian history, and it was powerfully invoked by Hildegard of Bingen in the twelfth century. Hildegard, an abbess, is remembered as a writer of visionary theology, a composer of liturgical music, a preacher, and an authority on natural medicine.

Enlightenment rationalism undermined mystical thought, but it was alive enough in the nineteenth century for William James to discuss it in his classic book *Varieties of Religious Experience*.[16]

It may come as a surprise to many readers that mystical experience was discussed by Albert Einstein and Paul Dirac, leaders of twentieth-century physics. As Gerhart notes, they seem to have experienced "perceptions of new relationships in what exists, new ways of understanding, relating to, and familiarity with the empirical and extra-empirical natural powers of divine things." For a number of people, interaction with the divine has become "a surprising alternative to a philosophy of materialism."

15. Wegter-McNelly, "Fundamental Physics and Religion."
16. James, *The Varieties of Religious Experience*.

Joseph Bracken, in chapter 11, writes of interaction's role in spiritual life in an encompassing way, including a discussion of the problem of life after death unless one is seen as merely a by-product of the other. Initially, he says, one may believe that "the dichotomy between matter and spirit will never be overcome"; rather, "either Spirit is to be perceived as a by-product of interaction on the material level, or . . . on the contrary, matter is to be perceived as a by-product of interaction on the spiritual level."[17]

In order to avoid this forced choice, Bracken turns to the work of Alfred North Whitehead, a philosopher and mathematician of the late nineteenth and early twentieth centuries. Whitehead was early to intuit the philosophical consequences of scientific work that was taking place in Oxford and Cambridge at the same time that he was shifting his own focus from mathematics to philosophy. Whitehead's insights seem today to reflect developments in quantum mechanics on the part of Heisenberg and Dirac in the 1920s, with which he had some familiarity through shared friendships. Whitehead invented his own vocabulary to describe the concepts that he developed, and this language often needs some translation for nonspecialist readers.

Whitehead proposed that "the final real things of which the world is made up" are not material objects but immaterial subjects of experience. Always in interaction, always changing, these "actual entities" develop "prehension"—a form of knowledge—of their own predecessors and of other "actual entities," and are aware of the explicit or implicit patterns of behavior operative among them over time. They formulate and reformulate themselves through dynamic interaction with the other "subjects of experience," creating their own patterns of interrelation at every moment. Each pattern that occurs is called an "actual occasion."[18]

Whitehead's terminology and references to "actual occasions" has been baffling to many who are not familiar with his work. In fact, although Bracken does not say this, Whitehead's "actual occasions" seem today to closely resemble the interactions among particles of energy in the universe, which do give rise to matter, as John Albright writes in chapter 1. Bracken adds that God provides a "field" in which all these interactions may take place. He adds some further modifications of Whitehead's proposal in order to help to explain life after death as a persistence of individual patterns.

Ted Peters uses the metaphor of a tower to describe the experiences of the human self. At the ground level, an individual perceives reality; at increasing levels, one gains conscious access to the experience, and describes

17. See footnote 17, p. 197.
18. Whitehead, *Process and Reality*, 18.

it in language. Moving ever higher, the climber describes perceptions using language and other symbolism inherited from centuries of culture, engages in reasoning about the experiences, and finally, at the top level, arrives at abstract ideas about the nature of the reality perceived.

As he leads this tour, Peters encounters reductionistic beliefs that describe mind or consciousness as delusions and claim that all decisions are made by the material brain with no human will involved, or that evoke the "explanatory gap"—the impossibility for immaterial consciousness to result from activities of a material brain. Peters decides to presuppose the reality of subjectivity, and to understand free will on the basis of quantum indeterminacy. He describes consciousness as system-wide information sharing capable of self-determination.

Choices are available to a truly conscious person, and one choice is Christian freedom—the decision to love God and love others, rather than live only for self. Loving actions may become habitual, thus altering one's neurology. As one descends the tower, these habits persist. This orientation, says Peters, is a gift given to us by God—for love is the ultimate form of interactivity.

Conclusion

In the following text, we will explore an ontology of interaction, beginning with the very bases of physical reality and the nature of the cosmos, through the origins and interactions of living things. As interactions become increasingly complex, we will speak of the human brain and the society that results from the interactions of human beings with one another.

We will learn that human religious beliefs are in continual interaction with the societies in which people spend their lives. Yet, for millennia, people have reported mystical encounters with God, and we will learn something about them.

Alfred North Whitehead's early suggestion of a basic ontology of interaction—and the nature of God that is thereby implied—will be explored and discussed. The parallels between such insights and some very recent findings in physics will be noted. Implications for life after death will be explored.

Finally, we will track a description of the human journey—through sensory experience, consciousness, language, understanding, reasoning, abstract thought, and choice. Choosing to live a life of love, for God and for others, can enable us to transcend the boundaries of love of self.

God is free and powerful to interact with us; we define ourselves by our choices of interaction with others and with God.

References

Ashbrook, James B., and Carol Rausch Albright. 1997. *The Humanizing Brain: Where Religion and Neuroscience Meet.* Cleveland: Pilgrim.

British Broadcasting Corporation. *Nature. History of Prehistoric Life.* "History of Life on Earth." www.bbc.co.uk/nature/history_of_the_earth/.

Clayton, Philip, and Zachary Simpson, eds. 2006. *The Oxford Handbook of Religion and Science.* Oxford Handbooks in Religion and Theology. New York: Oxford University Press.

Gregersen, Niels Henrik. 2017. "The Cosmic Christ: God in a World of Mass, Energy, and Information." Lecture presented at the conference Deep Incarnation: From Cosmos to Commitment at Goshen College Annual Science and Religion Conference, Goshen, Indiana.

James, William. 1902. *The Varieties of Relgious Experience: A Study in Human Nature.* Gifford Lectures on Natural Religion 1901–1902. New York: Longmans, Green.

Morowitz, Harold. 2004. *The Emergence of Everything: How the World Became Complex.* New York: Oxford University Press.

Peacocke, Arthur. 1993. *Theology for a Scientific Age: Being and Becoming—Natural, Divine, and Human.* Theology and the Sciences. Minneapolis: Fortress.

Russell, Robert John. 2006. "Quantum Physics and the Theology of Non-Interventionist Objective Divine Action." In *The Oxford Handbook of Religion and Science,* edited by Philip Clayton and Zachary Simpson, 579–95. Oxford Handbooks. Oxford: Oxford University Press.

Scientific American. 2008. "Timeline of Photosynthesis on Earth." https://www.scientificamerican.com/article/timeline-of-photosynthesis-on-earth/.

Stapp, Henry P. 2007. *Mindful Universe: Quantum Mechanics and the Observer.* The Frontiers Collection. New York: Springer.

Wegter-McNelly, Kirk. 2009. "Fundamental Physics and Religion." In *The Oxford Handbook of Religion and Science,* edited by Philip Clayton and Zachary Simpson, 156–71. Oxford Handbooks. Oxford: Oxford University Press.

Weinberg, Steven. 1997. *The First Three Minutes: A Modern View of the Origin of the Universe.* New York: Basic Books.

Whitehead, Alfred North. 1978. *Process and Reality: An Essay in Cosmology.* Corrected ed. Edited by David Ray Griffin and Donald W. Sherburne. New York: Free Press.

Part 1

Interaction in the Physical Sciences

1

Interactions in Physics

John R. Albright

FOR MUCH OF INTELLECTUAL history, the hegemony of materialism and straightforward cause-and-effect has been assumed, on the popular level and in scholarship as well. In recent centuries, however, there has been a series of attempts to give proper recognition to interaction as a basic reality. This book explores these developments in various sciences and considers the significance of interactions of many sorts. For clarity, we assume that

> **two objects interact if they exert mutual influence on each other.**

In the physical sciences, *influence* often means *force*. As we shall see, the connection between force and motion was widely misunderstood in ancient and medieval times. The popular perception is not always lucid even today, although physicists have mostly been clear on the subject since Newton's time.

It is important here at the outset to draw a distinction between interaction and causality. The concept of causality by long tradition does not have mutuality built into it, the way that interaction does. What causality does have is a long history of connection to determinism, predictability, and even predestination. The validity of these somewhat fatalistic concepts has been argued for centuries in both science and religion. It is one of the great glories of the twentieth century that science has achieved the overthrow of determinism: first by quantum mechanics (this chapter) and then by chaos theory (chapter 3). In each case a small interaction can produce large and unexpected consequences.

Ancient Greek Thought

It has often been claimed that no new ideas in science or philosophy are possible because the ancient Greeks thought of all the variations that could be imagined. This may be true (although I doubt it), but in most cases their ideas were conjectures that could not be subjected to comparison with experiment or observation. Sometimes the lack of comparison came from a certain disdain for such mundane activity, but more often it was a lack of the technology and equipment needed to put hypotheses to the test.

Of all the ancient Greek thinkers, the most celebrated is surely Aristotle. His wide-ranging mind considered an enormous variety of subjects and handled most of them with skill, even when the topic turned out to be wrongheaded. But his most important claim to fame arose from the reverence that his ideas inspired for millennia. Even today, it is possible for a serious scientist to suffer occasional rebuke from someone quoting Aristotle.

Like others of his time and later, Aristotle based his efforts to understand the workings of the physical world on causality. For our purposes, it is most useful to focus on Aristotle's categories of causality: *material, efficient, formal,* and *final.* To illustrate these types, the customary example is a house being built. Material (*causa materialis*) refers to the things that are assembled to form a house, such as concrete, bricks, wood boards, and roof tiles. Efficient (*causa efficiens*) refers to the activities of the workers as they assemble the material pieces. Formal (*causa formalis*) refers to the blueprints and specifications of the pieces. Final (*causa finalis*) is the desire for shelter from the weather. The notion of a final cause is related to teleology.

These understandings of the nature of causation remained basic to philosophy and science for too long. For understanding the relationships of events, they have at least three flaws that must be dealt with.

First, *causes* act in only one direction. If A and B are events, and A precedes B in time, then A is a possible cause of B, but not the reverse. However, many relationships of A and B are *interactions,* in which each event influences the other.

Second, the classic dictum that "every event must have a cause," subject of long debate in philosophy, is dramatically challenged by quantum physics.

Third, in relation to efficient cause, Aristotle held that motion requires a cause (force) to be maintained. This incorrect idea was eventually demolished by Isaac Newton, who saw that motion continues unless something stops it.

Aristotle was not always revered to the extent claimed by some writers.[1] In classical times there were those who disagreed with him and got away with it. First there was Aristotle's teacher, Plato; later, there arose the school of Neoplatonism, led by Plotinus. Saint Augustine, who admired Plotinus, was no Aristotelian, and this is part of his appeal to readers in the twenty-first century.

The Middle Ages

Aristotle's thought as originally written was lost to Western Europe with the collapse of the western half of the Roman Empire in the 400s. What remained in the West were commentaries on Aristotle, written in Latin and of highly variable quality. In the Eastern Roman Empire, his writings did survive in Greek (the local language), and they were also preserved in Arabic translation through centuries of Islamic civilization.

Aristotle's ideas in direct translation made their way to the West, partly through Islamic scholars in Spain, partly from manuscripts carried westward by Crusaders and subsequent traders, and finally by Greek refugees from Byzantium when it fell to the Ottoman Turks in 1453.

Saint Thomas Aquinas (1224–1274) built a theological edifice with the intent of reconciling Christian dogma with the teachings of Aristotle. As a member of the Dominican order, he was esteemed by his confreres; he and Aristotle are still revered by Dominicans today. His Aristotelian notions of cause and effect are cornerstones in his proofs for the existence of God.

The Seventeenth Century: Pre-Newtonians

The teachings of Aquinas regarding cause and effect remained in use for centuries. However, important changes began in the early seventeenth century. In the early 1600s, Galileo (1564–1642) discovered a prodigious amount of scientific truth. He is most famous for his findings in astronomy: the four moons of Jupiter, the phases of Venus, sunspots, the discrete nature of the Milky Way, and championship of Copernicus's heliocentric arrangement of the sun and planets. None of these has much to say about interaction.

However, Galileo made major contributions to mechanics as well. He made clear the distinction between velocity and acceleration, a necessary clarification for any mathematical theory of force and motion. In this, as in astronomy, Galileo was bold in his rejection of Aristotelian errors, leading

1. Dyson, *Birds and Frogs*, 63–66.

in no small measure to the enmity of the Dominicans, who controlled the Inquisition. Acceleration does involve interaction of forces. Galileo did not clearly spell this out, but he began the conversation.

Christian Huygens (1629–1695) carried the science of dynamics forward with his work on the pendulum and his realization of the importance of *vis viva*, the name in the seventeenth century for what we call *kinetic energy*, which is central to understanding the relationship between velocity and acceleration. Huygens is justly famous as well for his theoretical treatment of waves, including light waves, and his related understanding of optics. But the connection between light waves and interaction was not yet understood in his time.

René Descartes (1596–1650) was such a prolific and important intellect that it would take us too far afield to review all of his ideas. We shall limit the discussion to three of his advances most relevant to development of ideas of interaction.

First, Descartes invented analytic geometry, which provides a coherent way to combine algebra and geometry. Algebra is a numeric discipline, which is processed by the left hemisphere of the human brain. Geometry, being pictorial, is a right-brain function. Analytic geometry allows both hemispheres of the human brain to collaborate in supporting the progress of mathematics. Through the invention of analytic geometry, Descartes provided important foundational work for the introduction of calculus, without which the development of theoretical physics could not have happened. It also allows the clear definition of *function*, which is essential to calculus.

Second, Descartes worked toward a comprehensive understanding of mechanics. He did not establish all of Newton's laws, but he stated clearly the essence of the first law: a body at rest remains at rest unless acted on by an external force; a body in motion remains in motion in a straight line at the same speed unless acted on by an external force. The second part of this principle is in violation of the precepts of Aristotle, particularly the assumption that causes act in only one direction. Descartes knew that, and he was aware that he was in a certain amount of danger from his church. Aristotle's work had provided foundations of thought for centuries, and the suggestion of such major change was disturbing and may even have seemed evil.

Third, Descartes based his mechanics on the notion of vortices: that all matter is made up of such rotating objects. This model was in vogue for about twenty years but has been thoroughly rejected by scientists since then. Vortices are not well suited to help people understand interaction.

Isaac Newton

The realization of the importance of interaction in understanding physical reality originates with Isaac Newton (1642–1727), the English mathematician and scientist who invented calculus and who systematized mechanics. Newton summarized the principles governing any sort of motion by means of three laws:[2]

1. Everybody continues in its state of rest, or of uniform motion in a straight line, unless it is compelled to change that state by forces impressed upon it. This principle was already in place in the work of Descartes, as noted above.

2. The change of motion is proportional to the motive force impressed, and is made in the direction in which that force is impressed.

Here is a fertile source for set-piece problems that physics teachers can assign to their students. The second law is very practical, but it does not really address interaction.

3. To every action there is always opposed an equal reaction—that is, the mutual actions of two bodies upon each other are always equal, and directed to contrary parts. Newton's third law is in a category by itself. It does not enable you to predict the motion of a body on account of an external force; the second law does that. In elementary physics courses, teachers tend to spend little time on the third law because it does not lead to tricky questions that are so valued by teachers (and hated by students). But the third law is crucial for interactions.

The reason for the subtlety of the third law is that the two equal and opposite forces that it mentions do not act on the same body. Herein lies the resolution of paradoxes that come up from the misuse of the third law. In Newton's *Principia,* he writes of a horse pulling on a rope tied to a stone. The horse pulls with a certain force, and the rope pulls back with an equal and opposite force. So the unwary person might conclude that no motion is possible, since the forces add to zero. But the forces act on different bodies, and it is not legitimate to add them. To avoid being caught in a paradox, it is necessary to consider the system of horse, rope, and stone as three separate subsystems and analyze the forces on (not by) each subsystem separately. It is important not to forget the force that the earth exerts horizontally on the hooves of the horse.

2. Newton, *Mathematical Principles of Natural Philosophy,* preface. The three laws are on pp. 13–14 of the 1726 edition.

Newton's three laws of motion are perfectly general for motion or stasis of human-sized objects over a broad range. They have a wide range of applicability: they work well for a great variety of forces and interactions.

Newton is also famous for an additional law of nature, that of gravity. This law is more specific than the general laws of motion. It states that two massive bodies exert a mutual gravitational attraction that is proportional to the product of the masses and inversely proportional to the square of the distance between them. In symbols,

$$F \text{ (by m on M)} = GmM / R^2$$

where m and M are the two respective masses, R is the distance between them, and F is the force of gravity. The quantity G is a constant of nature; Newton did not know its value, although he understood that it is a small number. Its measurement was not made until early in the nineteenth century.

It is evident that the gravitational force of F (by M on m) is numerically equal to the value of F (by m on M). This is what Newton's third law of motion would lead you to expect. The two forces are directed oppositely and act on two different objects. So we have here an explicit example of an interaction—the gravitational interaction of two massive objects. From this interaction one can understand the motions of the planets in the solar system.

There is a serious philosophical problem with gravitation as presented by Newton: it posits action at a distance. Such an interaction was a horror to the rational mind in the age of reason. Descartes went to great lengths to construct a system of vortices to avoid this problem. Newton was well aware of the vortex concept, and it took him a long time to conclude that he did not need it.[3] Newton's gravitational interaction theory worked so well that scientists swallowed hard and used it in spite of their desires for contiguity of interaction.

Energy of Interaction

Newton did not use the concept of energy. He preferred to describe motion by means of force and momentum. Newton used "quantity of motion" to denote what English speakers in subsequent centuries have called "momentum," namely the product of the mass and the velocity. Newton's second law states that the force on an object is equal to the time rate of change of its momentum. This statement remains true even in Einstein's special theory of relativity, provided you define momentum in a particular way.

3. White, *Isaac Newton*, 205ff.

A rival school of mathematical and scientific thought arose on the continent of Europe in Newton's time. Its leader was Wilhelm Gottfried Leibniz (1646–1716), who invented calculus at the same time that Newton did. The German and the Englishman used rather different notations to write their mathematics. Newton's notation is more compact and easier to set into type. That of Leibniz is more spread out, but more intuitive. Although the followers of these great leaders argued for a generation about which version of calculus is correct, the verdict is that they are both right. Students today need to be fluent in both written forms.

A controversy also arose over the best way to refer to, understand, and describe the motion of a body. Newton preferred mass times velocity, as we have seen. Leibniz used the mass times the square of the velocity to define what he called *vis viva* or live force; the more modern term is *kinetic energy*. Once again, there was unseemly competition between the two camps until it was finally realized that both concepts are correct and indispensable; even as they are different, they have different and important uses.

From what has been said, it seems apparent that Newton's ideas of force are better suited to describe interactions than are the ideas of energy. First appearances can be deceiving. After a troubled start by Pierre Moreau de Maupertuis (1698–1759) to address this problem, the form of mechanics by Joseph-Louis Lagrange (1736–1813) arrived and made it possible to present motion—including interactions—by means of energy. Such concepts of energy, as we shall see, proved critical to understanding interaction even into the twenty-first century. See appendix A for a discussion of Lagrange's method.

Why would one wish to bother with Lagrange's formalism, since it is equivalent to Newton's? Some systems are not so simple, and you can gain insight more readily through Lagrangian methods. They also lead to a more systematic way of organizing the analysis. Perhaps the most important philosophical point is afforded by the case where the Lagrangian function is insensitive to a change in the value of a coordinate.

When a system in classical mechanics is described using a Lagrangian approach, it is often insightful to consider the symmetry of the system. The formal definition of symmetry in this connection is more specific than the everyday use of the word. If the Lagrangian function $(T-V)$ does not change when you change a particular physical quantity, then the system is said to be symmetric with respect to that quantity. The quantity in question may be a space coordinate, an angle, time, or some other entity.

By way of example, suppose the Lagrangian function does not depend on a particular horizontal coordinate, say x. Then the system has translational symmetry with respect to the x-coordinate.

Why do we care? The symmetry of the Lagrangian function implies a conservation law. In the case just mentioned, translational symmetry of the *x*-coordinate implies that the *x*-component of momentum will be conserved. *This will be true in spite of interactions that may be present.*

1. If the Lagrangian is constant under rotation about some axis, then the angular momentum about that axis is conserved, again despite interactions.

2. If the Lagrangian does not change in time, then the energy of the system is conserved.

Conservation laws are cherished by physicists for many reasons:

1. There is inherent beauty in conservation laws. They often tie together ideas that are not so obviously connected. For example, conservation of angular momentum is equivalent to Kepler's second law of planetary motion (a planet in orbit sweeps out equal areas in equal time intervals).

2. Physics teachers emphasize conservation laws because they facilitate the solving of problems that look difficult.

3. Conservation laws enable one to ignore details of interactions. This property leads toward ignoring interactions altogether—hence the need for this book.

4. The robustness of conservation laws is more evident as one goes to areas other than classical mechanics. Thermal physics, electricity and magnetism, and atomic and nuclear physics are all areas where conservation laws provide valuable insights.

5. In quantum mechanics, the connection between symmetries and conservation laws is maintained. This realization was due to Emmy Noether in 1918, and it is explained in detail by Dwight Neuenschwander.[4]

The Nineteenth Century: Classical Fields

As noted above, the Newtonian law of gravitation involves an interaction between two bodies that are separated in space. David Hume, the epitome of eighteenth-century rationalism, set out a set of criteria for causality, among which was *contiguity*. Telekinesis, spoon bending, and similar claims were not to be allowed. Yet Hume should have realized that action at a distance is

4. Neuenschwander, *Emmy Noether's Wonderful Theorem.*

fact, not fiction. Not only is there gravity, but also the early discoveries about electricity and magnetism involve explicit action at a distance.[5]

The attraction and repulsion that come from electricity and magnetism are clear examples of interaction over a distance that separates the interacting objects. In 1785 Charles Augustin Coulomb showed that electric forces obey an inverse square law of force just like the law of gravity. The conceptual problem of interaction at a distance was thereby exacerbated, not solved.

Michael Faraday contributed powerfully to the understanding of interactions by introducing the field concept. In mathematics and physics, the concept of *field* makes it possible to calculate the value of a particular quantity. If there is just one such quantity, it has only one dimension: this is called a scalar field. Potential energy is an example of a scalar field. On the other hand, electricity has a field with three components. Fields with more than one dimension are known as vector fields. An electric field is three-dimensional. To describe such a field, you have to be able to calculate three numbers at each point in space, corresponding to the three components of the field.

The magnetic field is similarly a vector field quantity. Faraday illustrated the magnetic field by sprinkling iron filings onto paper held above a magnet. The paper interrupted the three-dimensional magnetic field, turning it into a two-dimensional field. The magnetic forces moved the filings, and they arranged themselves on the paper into a shape that followed the field, thus making it visible.

The field concept is of paramount philosophical importance for science. It gets rid of the problem of action at a distance because it transforms these actions into local interactions. For example, a mass *A* sets up a gravitational field that extends through space. Another mass, *B*, meanwhile, seems to interact with *A*. The two are separated in space; yet, the two masses influence each other. This takes place because gravitational fields of *A* and *B* interact with one another at various points in space.

Newton's third law is still valid because the two gravitational fields interact locally. By now, physicists scarcely know how to talk or think about interactions without using the concept of a field.

Although we have been discussing electric and magnetic interactions independently, they are actually independent only if nothing changes in time. Hans Christian Oersted showed that *moving* electric charges—electric currents—give rise to interactions with magnets. (Conversely, Michael Faraday and Joseph Henry separately showed that time variation in magnetism gives

5. *Encyclopedia Britannica* (1771, 1st ed.), 3:34.

rise to electrical effects. Faraday recognized this by using the term "electro-magnetic" in his writings to describe the various interactions that he observed and measured. (In our day it is customary to omit the hyphen.)

Electric motors operate on this basis; electric charges move through wires inside the motor and interact with the magnetic field there. The result is a force by the field on the wire, producing a current that make a shaft rotate.

It was the glorious achievement of James Clerk Maxwell to collect all the relevant attributes of the electric and magnetic interactions—including their dependence on time—into a set of interlocking equations: Maxwell's equations.[6] The Maxwellian theory of electromagnetism proved immensely fertile when it was extended and its consequences were explored.

1. Interactions of electric and magnetic nature were shown to be the result of stresses in the fields. Faraday had undestood this fact intuitively and qualitatively. Maxwell made it quantitative and supplied mathematical rigor.

2. Energy relations of the electric and magnetic fields were elucidated. It was this point that led Maxwell to the realization that prior equations on the subject were missing a term, which Maxwell supplied in the final form of his equations. It is called Maxwell's displacement current; it expresses the time variation of the electric field.

3. Maxwell's equations admit a wave solution for the electric and magnetic fields, i.e., the mathematics describe a disturbance that propagates in space and time. Electric and magnetic fields, which obey this wave equation, propagate *in vacuo* at a speed equal to the speed of light. Because they behave as light does, the rules that describe electromagnetic behavior apply to all of classical optics—both its geometric description and its physical behavior.

These results were so revolutionary that they called for experimental testing. A most convincing experiment was performed by Heinrich Hertz in 1887. An electrical discharge in one circuit caused a discharge in a second circuit on the other side of the laboratory, unconnected to the first circuit.

This became the basis of an entire technology of communication, from wireless telegraphy to radio to television to wireless connection of computers to the Internet. These developments have certainly led to new possibilities for interactions among humans! They have also opened new windows for astronomy: radio telescopes, infrared telescopes, and microwave detectors, to name a few, as described by Grace Wolf-Chase in chapter 3.

6. Maxwell, *Electricity and Magnetism*.

As the nineteenth century approached its close, a profound electrical discovery occurred. In 1897, J. J. Thomson in Cambridge, England, established the fact that an electric current is not a continuous fluid, but rather consists of a large number of discrete electric charges in motion. These particles are called electrons. They have electrical charge and mass. Their existence and interactions are essential to the scientific scene of the twentieth century and beyond.

The Twentieth Century: Relativity

In 1905, Albert Einstein published two papers that established the special theory of relativity. There has been a certain amount of confusion about the origins of special relativity in Einstein's thought. From some of his own accounts of it, he was pondering the properties of electromagnetic fields as viewed from different frames of reference.

Consider two frames of reference: one at rest, the other moving at a constant speed in a constant direction. The laws of mechanics as laid out by Galileo—and especially Newton—look exactly the same in these two frames of reference. If the two frames are typified by two railroad passenger cars riding on a smooth track, a person riding in one of them can sometimes be confused as to which one is moving and which one is at rest. This situation is called "Galilean relativity." Einstein saw the need for something better because he wanted the laws of electromagnetic interaction—i.e., Maxwell's equations—to look the same in both frames of reference: the one that is at rest and the one that is moving.

The sad fact is that if you use Galilean ideas to look at Maxwell's equations in a moving frame, you get a mathematical mess. Adding velocities, as Newton prescribed, will not suffice. You need a different procedure to get from one frame to another: Einstein correctly determined that such a procedure had already been discovered by Hendrik Antoon Lorentz. Einsteinian relativity uses this newer form to obtain the following results:

1. Space intervals change size as viewed from different frames of reference.

2. Time intervals change duration as measured in different frames.

3. Maxwell's equations keep the same form when you change frames.

4. The speed of light is the same in all frames.

5. Space and time are treated on a symmetrical footing in all frames.

Other and more subtle consequences arise from this theory:

1. It is not possible—even in principle—to denote a system absolutely at rest.

2. Space coordinates and time form a four-dimensional continuum, called space-time . . . . In this non-Euclidean space a four-vector has three space components and a time component.

3. Similarly, the total energy of an object and its three components of momentum form a four-vector.

4. Again, the density of an electric charge and the three components of the density of the current form a four-vector.

5. The electric and magnetic fields are blended together to form a four-by-four tensor in space-time.

From all of these entities, one can try to form a Lagrangian, after the fashion of classical mechanics, as in Appendix A. Two conditions must be satisfied: space-like and time-like quantities must be on an equal footing, and the Lagrangian must not reduce to zero. With these two constraints, there are still very many possibilities. The simplest of these, when used with the Euler-Lagrange formalism, provides the equations of motion for the electromagnetic fields; they are just Maxwell's equations.

Thus, special relativity began with the electromagnetic interactions, and now we see that it concludes with them.

The Twentieth Century: Quantum Theory

The need for a quantum theory in physics was made clear by Max Planck in 1900, with his use of energy quantization to obtain the spectrum of light radiated from a hot object. He found that the hottest objects emitted light at a higher frequency than objects not quite so hot. A piece of white-hot iron is hotter than one that is red hot, and the emitted light has higher frequency. The relationship between heat and frequency of light pointed to the role of energy in determining frequency.

This idea was used by Albert Einstein in 1905 to explain the phenomena associated with the photoelectric effect—that is, the effect of the interaction of energy with matter, which in this case involved phenomena of light.

Niels Bohr used ideas from both Planck and Einstein to construct another theory addressing the interaction of energy and matter. It involved a theory about the relationship of energy with the structure of the atom. Bohr proposed that the atom is arranged like the solar system, with the nucleus at the center, like the sun, and the electrons in orbit around it, like the planets. (This theory, taught to many in school, proved to be inaccurate, as we shall see.)

This model—called the "old quantum theory"—has the electrons in orbit with no emission of light except when an electron changes from one orbit to another. (The orbit would continue in the same direction, but at a greater or lesser distance from the nucleus.)

Such behavior would be at odds with Maxwell's equations, which require a charged particle to emit light whenever it executes circular motion. Bohr's theory simply denies such radiation by fiat. Apart from quantized orbit, the Bohr theory is essentially based on Newtonian mechanics, and has nothing new in it about interactions. It does have certain advantages—and disadvantages:

1. It predicts the spectrum of the hydrogen atom to good accuracy.

2. It is based on familiar physics.

3. It does not say much about how atoms interact to form molecules.

4. Attempts to merge relativity to the Bohr theory are difficult and lead to incorrect results.

These difficulties became evident, and three men separately proposed solutions to the issues; these proposals together came to form the new quantum theory. See Appendix B for details.

All three versions of the new quantum mechanics base their dynamical theory on a Hamiltonian form, as described in Appendix A. The question of how to represent interactions is readily answered. The standard subjects of classical mechanics are handled in great style by the new quantum mechanics, with additional and deeper insight included. One by one, the disturbing defects of Bohr's old quantum theory were cleared away, and the interactions were turned from a barrier into items of fascination.

What was the essential novelty that Bohr and others missed? The answer in brief is that the new quantum theory changed the requirements needed to specify the state of a system.

In detail, the old quantum theory—in agreement with Newtonian physics—says that for a system of one particle, complete information consists in knowing the position of that particle at every instant of time, i.e., the trajectory of the particle. Heisenberg points the way to the new quantum theory by insisting that the theory should be based only on entities that are observable, at least in principle.[7] Thus the orbit of an atomic electron does not enter the discussion.

7. Heisenberg, "Über quatentheoretische Umdeutung kinematischer."

Wave Function

For a quantum system, complete information consists in knowing the wave function of an object for all points in space and at all times. This requirement is very different from the Newtonian case, and it leads to different types of knowledge at the atomic level.

In the Schrödinger version of quantum mechanics, the fundamental equation that describes a system at the microscopic level is the Schrödinger equation. It contains the Hamiltonian $(T + V)$ for the system, which is assumed to be known, and an unknown function, *psi*, which depends on space and time coordinates. The equation is a partial differential equation, which can be solved (you can find *psi* as a function of its variable). The *psi* function is spread out over space-time. For many important cases, it oscillates in time and space, just like sound waves, water waves, and light waves: hence *psi* is often called the wave function.

In all forms of the new quantum mechanics as an inescapable consequence is Heisenberg's uncertainty principle of 1927, which imposes limits on the experimenters' ability to measure both the position and the momentum of a body to complete accuracy. Hence the conditions for Newtonian determinism cannot be met. This restriction applies whether or not there are interactions.

The ironic thing about the way quantum mechanics has become standard in microscopic physics is that Heisenberg's requirement of observability is no longer viable. It is not possible to measure a wave function! What you can do is measure the square of the wave function (it is the probability of observing an article in a small region of space). You can measure other things such as averages of physical quantities that involve two appearances of a wave function (*psi*). Another very important example is the calculation of a rate of transition from one state to another. For this you need the wave functions of the initial and final states respectively and the mathematical form of the interaction that serves to drive the transition.

The correct theory that merged quantum mechanics with special relativity was introduced by P. A. M. Dirac in 1928. In his paper of that year, Dirac (1) introduced what the world now knows as the Dirac Equation[8]; (2) showed that the spin of the electron arises in a natural way; (3) showed the existence of negative-energy states (later to lead to theories of antimatter); (4) explicated the interaction of an electron with a magnetic field; and (5) showed that this interaction requires the magnetic dipole moment of the electron to have nearly the correct experimental value.

---

8. Preserved on Dirac's monument on the floor of Westminster Abbey; his tombstone reads, "Because God made it that way."

Quantum Field Theory

Quantum mechanics, as described in the preceding section, applies to systems where the number of particles is constant. Many very important systems require a more general approach.

A good example of such a system is afforded by a sodium vapor lamp, where an electric current raises valence electrons of sodium atoms to an energy level higher than the ground state. The excited atom relaxes to the ground state by emitting a photon (a quantum of light) that has energy equal to the energy difference between the excited state and the ground state. Ordinary quantum mechanics is not equipped to handle the creation of the photon, which is perceived as the characteristic yellow-orange light so often used to light city streets at night. To describe creation and annihilation of particles one needs quantum field theory.

The subject of quantum field theory is so vast that we must limit the discussion to the concepts associated with interactions. In the 1920s, P. A. M. Dirac (private communication with the author) imagined the electric force between two charged particles to come about through the exchange of photons.[9] One charged particle emits a photon, which is absorbed by the other charged particle. In this way, a force of interaction occurs between the two. Since the exchanged particle (the photon) is massless, the force is inversely proportional to the square of the separation distance, as Coulomb stated in 1785.

In the 1930s, it was recognized that something other than photon exchange was needed to account for the interactions that keep the nucleus of the atom from flying apart, since so many positive charges are confined in a very small space. Hideki Yukawa suggested that the strength of the interaction and its limitation to short distances could be explained if there were a new particle—later called the meson—to be exchanged among protons and neutrons in a nucleus.[10] Knowledge of the range of the interaction enabled Yukawa to estimate the mass of the meson; later, experimental work corroborated the calculation. A more mature understanding of the strong nuclear interaction arose later when quarks and gluons came into the discussion.

In 1942, Richard P. Feynman finished his doctoral dissertation, in which he presented a different approach to quantum field theory.[11] During World War II, Feynman worked on the nuclear bomb at Los Alamos, New Mexico, but he resumed his work on field theory at the end of the war.

9. Dirac told this to the author during one of the many lunches they shared during the 1970s.

10. Yukawa, "On the Interaction of Elementary Particles."

11. Brown, *Feynman's Thesis*.

He introduced a fertile way of looking at quantum field theory, especially for dealing with the details of interaction at the atomic level. The stick-like structures that he introduced have become universally known as Feynman diagrams, or sometimes Feynman graphs. They provide a way of organizing the calculations and specifying a set of rules to follow. A succinct summary of the Feynman rules is collected in Bjorken and Drell.[12] A more elaborate explanation was presented by Weinberg.[13] An illustration of a Feynman diagram appears in Figure 1.1, which shows the interaction of an electron and a positron that results from the exchange of a photon.

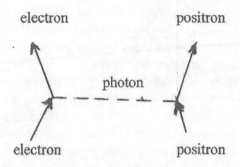

Feynman Diagram
© 2017 John R. Albright

Uses of Feynman's techniques led to the refinement of quantum electrodynamics (mostly abbreviated as QED) to the point that the theory can calculate results that agree with experiments to many significant figures.

Quantum field theory is more than just a very accurate calculational device. The idea that interactions are the result of the exchange of particles has become pervasive.

Fundamental Interactions:
Particles and Fields

By the late 1970s the discipline of particle physics had arrived at a consensus of how to organize discourse in that subject. The name "standard model" has become the usual way to refer to this consensus. There were missing pieces in the picture, but one by one, they have been filled in. There are still

12. Bjorken and Drell, *Relativistic Quantum Mechanics*, 285.

13. Weinberg, *The Quantum Theory of Fields*, 1:259–91.

a few annoying problems with the model, and work is still in progress—at times to refine the model, and at other times to replace it with something radically different. This section describes the standard model.

There are two basic kinds of particles: fermions and bosons. Fermions—named for Enrico Fermi—have spin equal to half of an odd integer times Planck's constant. They obey Fermi-Dirac statistics in which the exclusion principle of Wolfgang Pauli rules; this says that no two identical fermions can occupy the same quantum state at the same time. The situation is analogous to numbered seats at a theater, each of which can be occupied by only one person at a time. Fermions are the building blocks of matter.

Bosons—named for Satyendra Nath Bose—have spin equal to an integer times Planck's constant. They obey Bose–Einstein statistics; any number of them may occupy a quantum state at the same time.

Fermions are conserved. In other words, you cannot make a single fermion out of nothing, even if you have enough energy. Bosons, by contrast, are not conserved. You can create one or annihilate it. This property makes bosons the ideal entity to mediate interactions between and among other particles. A boson serves as the quantum of an interaction field that is the force holding fermions together to form matter.

Fermions come in two main types: quarks and leptons. Quarks can participate in the strong nuclear interaction; leptons cannot. Bosons come in various types, associated with the kinds of interactions that they mediate. Tables 1, 2, and 3 enumerate the species.

Table 1: Quarks

Name	Electric Charge	Spin	Generation	Symbol
Up	2/3 e	1/2	1	u
Down	-1/3 e	1/2	1	d
Charm	2/3 e	1/2	2	c
Strange	-1/3 e	1/2	2	s
Top	2/3 e	1/2	3	t
Bottom	-1/3 e	1/2	3	b

Table 2: Leptons

Name	Electric charge	Spin	Generation	Symbol
Electron	-e	1/2	1	e
electron neutrino	0	1/2	1	ν (e)
Muon	-e	1/2	2	μ
muon neutrino	0	1/2	2	ν (μ)
Tau	-e	1/2	3	τ
tau neutrino	0	1/2	3	ν (τ)

Table 3: Bosons

Interaction	Boson	How many?	Spin
Strong	Gluon	8	1
Electromagnetic	Photon	1	1
Weak	weak boson	3	1

All of the fermions obey the Dirac equation, and therefore each one has a corresponding antiparticle with opposite algebraic sign for the electric charge. The symbol for the antiparticle has an overbar.

The standard model has been successful in many ways. It can readily account for the classification of existing matter. For example, a proton is formed from three quarks, u-u-d; a neutron is formed from u-d-d. The mesons are formed from quark-antiquark pairs. The model accounts for all the readily observed particles, and where it predicts absences, experiment bears that out. Quantitative calculations of interactions mediated by the various bosons typically agree with experimental results.

Yet the standard model is not a theory of everything. A number of puzzles remain to be explained:

1. It does not fit well with gravity.

2. It does not enable a calculation of the masses of the various particles. The experimental values must be inserted by hand into the calculations.

3. Neutrinos have been observed to oscillate from one generation to another. This fact implies that at least some of them have nonzero mass; that is not congenial to the model.

4. Dark energy and dark matter are not a good fit to the model.

5. The apparent asymmetry between matter and antimatter on a cosmological scale is not predicted by the model.

Work remains to be done in interactions at the most fundamental level.

Conclusion

Interactions are absolutely essential to physics. This fact is not controversial among those who have made a career of physics, but it is less familiar to the general public, even if they once studied physics at school.

Reasons for neglect of interactions are many. Symmetry and conservation laws tend to obscure interactions. Taking interactions into account inevitably makes problems more difficult and less suitable for introductory treatments.

One of the most important philosophical questions of physics is whether determinism is required. Newton's physics, especially as developed by Pierre Simon de Laplace, answers in the affirmative. Quantum mechanics responds in the negative for small-scale (atomic scale) objects. But on the average, determinism can take over. These statements are valid whether or not interactions are present, and they tend to distract discussions away from the importance of interactions.

This chapter has been mainly limited to interactions of one body with its environment. The next chapter considers the more complicated—but highly interesting—situations where two or more bodies interact.

Appendix A

Energy Analysis of Mechanical Systems

The method of Lagrange requires multiple steps to analyze a given system:

1. Construct the total kinetic energy of the system, T.

2. Construct the total potential energy of the system, V. The potential energy of each part of the system is the energy that it has by virtue of where it is located. V thus contains the information about the

interactions of the parts of the system between and among one another, as well as their interactions with entities outside the system.

3. Form the Lagrangian function: $L = T - V$.

4. As the system evolves in time, add up the Lagrangian at every instant
   in time; this is called the "action."

5. Use the calculus of variations, developed by Leonhard Euler (1707–
   1783), to find the conditions that cause the action to be minimized
   (or sometimes maximized). These conditions appear as a set of equations called the Euler-Lagrange equations. For simple systems, they
   are identical to Newton's laws.

An additional development was provided in 1834 by William Rowan
Hamilton, who used a function different from the Lagrangian. He used H
$= T + V$, where T and V are the kinetic and potential energy. The sum of T
and V is known as the Hamiltonian. This time the formalism leads to twice
as many equations as Lagrange obtained, but the outcome is the same. Both
the Hamiltonian and the Lagrangian methods are consistent with Newton's
laws; both allow for interactions to appear in the theory in a completely
natural way. Each has certain advantages.

Appendix B

Details of Quantum Mechanics

In 1925, Werner Heisenberg in Germany introduced a new theoretical
structure called *matrix mechanics* to describe phenomena—including interactions—on the atomic scale. A matrix is an array of numbers that are
positioned to obey certain algebraic rules, called *matrix algebra*. Heisenberg
wanted to establish a theory based on observable quantities only, and each
such physical entity is represented by a matrix.

Also in 1925, Paul Dirac in England developed a parallel system using
vectors in *Hilbert space*. A vector space is a Hilbert space if the vectors can
form a scalar product, i.e., two vectors multiply to form a single number.

The following year, Erwin Schrödinger in Austria announced a dif-
ferent-looking quantum theory based on continuous functions that obey a
atrial differential equation (the Schrödinger equation). These functions are
called wave functions because they act like waves: they describe a disturbance that propagates in time and space.

It soon became evident that these three structures are compatible and
not contradictory. The situation is somewhat analogous to the two kinds of

calculus from Newton and Leibniz, except that for quantum theory it took much less time to prove the equivalence of the variant formalisms.

References

Bjorken, James D., and Sidney Drell. 1964. *Relativistic Quantum Mechanics.* International Series in Pure and Applied Physics. New York, McGraw-Hill.

Brown, Laurie M., ed. 2005. *Feynman's Thesis: A New Approach to Quantum Theory.* Singapore: World Scientific.

Bunge, Mario. (1928) 1979. *Causality and Modern Science.* 3rd ed. New York: Dover.

Dirac, Paul Adrian Maurice. "The Quantum Theory of the Electron." *Proceedings of the Royal Society of London* A117,1–610. London, 1928.

Dugas, René. *A History of Mechanics.* 1988. Translated by J. R. Maddox. New York: Dover, 1988.

Dyson, Freeman J. *Birds and Frogs: Selected Papers, 1990–2014.* Singapore: World Scientific.

Heisenberg, Werner. 1925. "Über quantentheoretische Umdeutung kinematischer und mechanischer Begiehung." *Zeitschrift für Physik* 33:879–83.

Huang, Kerson. 2007. *Fundamental Forces of Nature: The Story of Gauge Fields.* Singapore: World Scientific.

Maxwell, James Clerk. 1954. *Electricity and Magnetism.* 3rd ed. 2 vols. in 1. New York: Dover. This is a facsimile of the work originally published in 1873.

Neuenschwander, Dwight E. 2011. *Emmy Noether's Wonderful Theorem.* Baltimore: Johns Hopkins University Press.

Newton, Isaac. (1726) 2010. *Mathematical Principles of Natural Philosophy.* 3rd ed. Ocean Shores, WA: Watchmaker.

Polkinghorne, John, ed. 2010. *The Trinity and an Entangled World: Relationality in Physical Science and Theology.* Grand Rapids: Eerdmans.

Schwarz, Hans. 2014. *Vying for Truth—Theology and the Natural Sciences, from the Seventeenth Century to the Present.* V & R Academic. Göttingen: Vanderhoeck & Ruprecht.

Schweber, Silvan S. 1944. *QED and the Men Who Made It: Dyson, Feynman, Schwinger, and Tomonager.* Princeton Series in Physics. Princeton: Princeton University Press. Page 191 expresses Yukawa's meson exchange as an analog of photon exchange in QED.

Society for Gentlemen in Scotland. 1771. *Encyclopaedia Britannica; or A Dictionary of the Arts and Sciences.* 3 vols. Edinburgh: Printed for A. Bell & C. Macfarquhar.

Welker, Michael. 1999. *Creation and Reality.* Translated by John F. Hoffmeyer. Minneapolis: Fortress.

Weinberg, Steven. 1995. *The Quantum Theory of Fields.* Vol. 1, *Foundations.* 3 vols. Cambridge: Cambridge University Press.

White, Michael. 1997. *Isaac Newton: The Last Sorcerer.* Reading, MA: Perseus. See esp. 205ff.

Yukawa, Hideki. 1935. "On the Interaction of Elementary Particles." *Progress in Physics,* 48–57. (Tokyo) *Mathematics Society of Japan, 1748.*

2

Interaction with Two or More Particles

Chemistry, Chaos, Complexity, and Emergence

John R. Albright

THE PRECEDING CHAPTER HAS mostly been concerned with the interaction of a single particle with its environment. Here we consider more complicated systems in which there are many particles and many interactions. These systems cover a large range, including processes fairly familiar to us such as the exchange of heat energy, melting and evaporation, and the formation of molecules and compounds. They also include more exotic processes such as quantum interaction, entanglement, chaos, complexity, and emergence. All depend upon interaction.

Thermal Interactions

Thermal properties of a system are defined to be those properties for which temperature is a relevant concept. Warming something requires energy; cooling withdraws energy. For simplicity, we will consider temperature to be the average energy of all the particles in a system (even though the individual particles may vary in energy). Therefore, it is clear enough why a system with only one particle is not an interesting thermal system. A macroscopic system, made of really large numbers of molecules, is much more likely to be interesting.

Personal experience enables one to realize that interaction can be part of thermal science. A hot stove can cook your food or, if you are careless, give you a nasty burn. But there could be no thermal system without interactions among the molecules.

Imagine a lot of molecules—small objects moving around—with no interactions among them. If there were such a substance, it would be called an ideal gas. Such a material does not exist, but some gasses behave in approximately that way. Oxygen, nitrogen, helium, and argon, for example, are nearly ideal. It has been known since the late seventeenth century that the volume of such gasses is very nearly proportional to the temperature (in degrees above absolute zero) and inversely proportional to the pressure. The warmer they are, the more they expand (unless they are confined to a container, which exerts pressure against the expanding gas). If you decrease the temperature, they become less active and take up less space. However, if the molecules get closer together, they do interact more. If the process is continued far enough, the molecules form clusters, and condensation begins.

Change of Phase

If a gas (not ideal) is cooled enough, it will condense into a liquid. Cool it some more, and the liquid will freeze into a solid. We have all encountered this sort of thing with water, condensed from vapor (or maybe steam) and frozen into ice. We were taught at an early age that there are three phases of matter: solid, liquid, and gas. That statement is still true but sadly incomplete. There are more phases than three.

If you heat any material to a high enough temperature, the molecules break apart and the electrons start to depart from the atoms. The electrons have a negative electric charge, and the remainder of the atom has a positive charge. The resulting material is called a plasma. (The name is unrelated to blood plasma.)

We have all seen examples of plasma. The most spectacular is the sun, which is a gigantic hot sphere, made of hydrogen and some helium where the electrons have been mostly stripped off the atoms. Other examples are flames (some but not all electrons removed) and lightning bolts. Plasmas are not easily described just because the electrical charges are somewhat random and may either attract each other (opposite charges) or repel (same charges). These electrical interactions are strong and numerous enough to make calculation difficult.

Another complication that increases the number of states of matter is that solids can have more than one way to arrange their molecules. This is true for most materials, including ice. Under various conditions of temperature and pressure, ice takes on a great variety of crystalline forms, most of which you seldom see because they occur only at rather high pressures.

But snowflakes abound, and seen under a microscope, each has a different crystalline arrangement.

Other materials have more than one solid phase, more easily seen. Sulfur has two crystalline forms that look quite different. It is a customary lab experiment in chemistry to demonstrate this fact. Another substance with multiple solid forms is carbon. Diamonds are crystals of pure carbon; graphite, used in pencil leads, is also pure carbon, arranged in flat hexagons instead of the three-dimensional pyramidal structure of diamond. What a contrast due to crystalline form!

All of these phases of matter involve intermolecular interactions. The easiest way to convince yourself of this is by recognizing that it takes energy to melt ice or to boil water. The term latent heat refers to the amount of energy involved in effecting a change of phase.

Also, a change of pressure can modify the temperature at which the phase can change. Ice skating is facilitated by the pressure exerted by the skate blade on the ice, causing a slight melting of the solid into a bit of liquid. At high altitude, water boils at a lower temperature than at sea level, so the potatoes in the pot can boil for a long time and still not be tender. The cure is to use a pressure cooker, so that the water will boil at a higher temperature; or maybe you should just bake the potatoes.

Yet another way to modify the temperature of a phase change is to introduce a chemical to interact with the molecules. This is why municipalities spread salt on roadways in times of snow and ice. The salt lowers the melting temperature of ice and allows it to run off to the side. Chefs know that salt raises the boiling temperature of water, allowing food to cook more quickly and thoroughly.

In all these examples, the key to deeper understanding is to recognize the role played by the interactions of molecules in different circumstances. Gas molecules interact least of all. Liquids interact more, but not enough to allow them to keep their shape. Solids have the strongest interaction, which accounts for strength and rigidity.

Trading Places and Entanglement

In classical physics, an atom that is part of a molecule stays loyal to that molecule. This is called reductionistic physics. It is useful for many kinds of calculations.

In a newer set of understandings called quantum physics, this is not necessarily so. We begin by imagining a collection of many (two or more) electrons. These objects are all identical. As usual, the word identical has a very specific meaning in science. Each electron has the same value for certain physical properties: same mass, same electrical charge, same spin (although not all spins have to point the same way). Interesting things happen, though, if they change places. This produces an outcome called exchange symmetry, which we will discuss in this section. A value called the Hamiltonian (T+V) must remain unchanged (T means kinetic energy and V means potential energy).

We can illustrate the classical physics understanding with a game of pool, otherwise known as billiards. Consider a pool table with plastic balls, as alike as the manufacturer can produce. They have numbers painted on them, from one to fifteen. When the pool balls are scattered about on the table, suppose you take the number three ball and trade its position with that of the number eleven ball. The energy of the system does not change, so you might call the two balls identical. But the rules of the game you are playing might assign different meanings to the two balls. So the exchange leaves the system physically unchanged, but perhaps notionally or symbolically changed.

In fact, if you assigned the rules of quantum physics to the game of pool, the situation would be totally different. The motto becomes, "There ain't no paint!" Of course, it is impossible to paint numbers (or anything else) onto electrons or other quantum particles. In quantum physics, particles can include not only electrons but also protons, neutrons, photons (which have no mass) and even entire atoms. But the particles can be interchanged with other particles of the same type as themselves.

If two identical quantum particles are exchanged, the Hamiltonian stays the same, but the wave function of the system may or may not change. If the two exchanged particles are bosons (particles having integer spins such as 0, 1, 2, 3), the wave function will remain the same. Examples of bosons are photons, alpha particles, and carbon atoms. The result will be different if the two exchanged particles are fermions, whose spin is equal to one half of an odd integer, such as $\frac{1}{2}$, $\frac{3}{2}$, $\frac{5}{2}$). For fermions, such as electrons, protons, or neutrons, the wave function will have the opposite algebraic sign as a result of the exchange.

The question of exchange symmetry (bosons) or anti-symmetry (fermions) may seem abstract, but it is crucial to the establishment of interactions among particles. Atoms as we know them could not exist if their electrons did not exhibit anti-symmetry under exchange. Without atoms, of course, nothing larger could exist.

Another quantum property that particles have is entanglement. Two or more particles can have a sort of correlation, often called coherence. This property is analogous to what you can have with a good marching unit where every person in it moves the left foot at the same time, and then the right foot, all together. This process is facilitated if someone beats a drum so that all the marchers hear the same beat. Then the motion of the feet is coherent.

Suppose now that a second marching unit is a distance away, out of earshot of each other's drums. Then you have no reason to expect the two units to be in step with each other. The two are incoherent. If they get closer, they may actually establish coherence.

At the level of light waves, we mostly have little experience with coherent photons of light. Photons from one side of the sun (or a lamp or a flame, etc.) are uncorrelated with those that come from the other side. We live in a world where most light is incoherent. However, light from a laser is coherent. This is why there are strange bright and dark regions in the light patterns formed by a laser.

If two particles with spin are kept close together such that they interact, and if they are then separated very gently, their spins will remain coherent, or correlated. Such a pair of particles is said to be in an entangled state.[1]

Next, suppose that two particles in an entangled state are kept apart for a time. The entanglement persists, and a measurement on one of the two particles determines the outcome of a measurement of the other one. The entangled property can actually be used to construct a device called a quantum computer, which has significant advantages for certain types of calculations, especially finding prime factors of large numbers. Such a use may seem impractical, but it is of value in cryptography (the science of writing codes that are hard to break). This is one reason why research in quantum computing attracts so much attention.

So why can't we buy a quantum computer off the shelf at an office supply business? The answer lies in the fragility of entangled states. To preserve the entanglement for a long time, one needs to prevent other external particles from interacting with the entangled ones, thereby breaking the coherence. In the laboratory, the phenomenon of entanglement has been observed experimentally over impressive time and distance intervals by Aspect et al.[2] To prevent interactions from destroying the entanglement, they had to use quite good vacuum systems.

---

1. Vedral, *Introduction to Quantum Information Science*, 81ff; Wegter-McNelly, *The Entangled God*.

2. Aspect et al., "Experimental Tests of Realistic Local Theories."

Quantum View of Simple Atoms

The simplest possible atom is hydrogen, consisting of a proton (positive electric charge) and an electron (negative). The two charges are equal in magnitude and opposite in sign, so the two particles attract each other with the inverse-square law of electromagnetism (as explained in Chapter 1).

In the old quantum theory of Niels Bohr the system was regarded as analogous to the earth-sun system in astronomy, with the electron playing the part of the earth, in orbit about the proton in the role of the sun. Bohr had to make two additional assumptions: (1) contrary to the predictions of Maxwell's equations, the electron does not spiral inward to merge with the proton; and (2) the angular momentum (mass times velocity times distance away from the proton) of the electron can take on only integer values (0, 1, 2, 3, etc.). These two assumptions were completely ad hoc, not motivated by anything other than the working of this model of the hydrogen atom.

The Bohr model for hydrogen was successful on many counts. It got correct values for the energies of the various excited states of the hydrogen atom, and hence for the wavelengths of light emitted from excited hydrogen atoms. The model was easy to understand and use. Its intrinsic beauty and simplicity were reason enough for earning the Nobel Prize for Bohr in 1922.

The drawbacks to Bohr's model were serious enough to convince the physics community of the need for something better. In addition to the ad hoc nature of two assumptions mentioned above, there were other problems. Attempts to refine the Bohr model by adding special relativity led to a theory that was difficult, not beautiful, and in disagreement with experiment. When the Bohr model was used to explain the structure of the helium atom (two positives in the nucleus, two electrons in orbit), the results bore no relation to reality. For lithium (element number three) and beyond, the situation got progressively worse.

The discovery of quantum mechanics in 1925 and 1926 by Werner Heisenberg, Paul Dirac, and Erwin Schrödinger marked the end of most of these difficulties. The new quantum theory described a hydrogen atom in which the electron was a wave that did not collapse into the nucleus; no special assumption was needed. The angular momentum of the electron came out correctly. Within a few years it was shown that special relativity is consistent with the new quantum mechanics.

As we shall see, the description of atoms heavier than hydrogen goes well in the new theory. An additional benefit concerns the transition of an atomic electron from one state to another. In Bohr's theory there was no way to account for differing probabilities for the transition. In the new quantum theory there is a natural way to calculate these probabilities, and those calculations agree with experimental observations. This advance in atomic insight came about with the new technique of quantum mechanics applied to the same electrical interaction between proton and electron that was used in the Bohr model, but with greatly improved results.

The next upward step in complexity—and difficulty—is to describe the helium atom. The difficulty is that there are three interactions to consider: each of the two electrons is attracted to the nucleus, and the two electrons have a mutual repulsion. As mentioned above, classical physics could not solve the problem exactly, and the approximate solution bore little resemblance to reality.

Quantum mechanics is likewise unable to provide an exact solution to the helium atom, but approximations enable calculations of energy levels which agree well with the observed wavelengths of light emitted by excited helium atoms.

Pauli's Exclusion Principle

The exclusion principle of Wolfgang Pauli states that in an atom no two electrons can have all their quantum numbers with the same values. That is, no electron can occupy exactly the same position as another electron as both orbit around the nucleus.

This principle seems somewhat abstract but not complex. Yet without it, chemistry could not exist as we know it. To make Pauli's principle less abstract, we can liken the quantum state of an atom to seats in a theater, with the electrons in the role of patrons. The rule is only one patron per seat. The best seats fill first, and people who come later are excluded from those seats already occupied.

This situation actually arises in the case of helium, where there is a lowest-energy state (the ground state) and an electron in it excludes the other electron. But there is a loophole: each electron has two possible states for its spin, so effectively one can have two electrons (but no more) in each quantum state of the atom. One might say that they continually swap seats in the crowded theater.

When we look at the lithium atom, there are three electrons, and only two of them can occupy the ground state—the inner energy shell. The third therefore occupies a position farther from the nucleus (on the average), and it is likely to join the next higher energy level. This level has enough positions to accommodate eight more electrons, if necessary. The inner energy shell of an atom can accommodate one or two electrons, and therefore, only hydrogen and helium can work with only one shell. Atoms with a second energy shell have room for eight more electrons; the elements that work with two shells are lithium, beryllium, boron, carbon, nitrogen, oxygen, fluorine, and neon. The element neon has ten electrons, and they complete the second energy shell. Any additional electrons require that a third shell be constructed.

Atoms with a closed shell are interesting because they are almost entirely excluded from interacting with atoms—either their own kind or any other species. They are called noble gases (sometimes rare gases), and include neon, helium, argon, krypton, xenon, and radon. Their inability to interact with each other explains why they are gases at room temperature. They would need more interaction if they were to aggregate into a liquid.

Elements with a closed shell of electrons plus one more are called alkali metals. They are chemically very reactive. All of them in the pure metallic state burn spontaneously in air. They easily lose their excluded electron and acquire a positive charge. Elements of this kind include lithium, sodium, potassium, cesium, and others. They are said to have a valence of +1 because that is the electric charge of the ion after the single-valence electron is lost. They are also called monovalent elements.

If an atom has two electrons outside a closed shell it is called divalent, because if it loses both of its excluded electrons it forms an ion with a positive charge of +2. Such elements are called alkaline earths. They are quite reactive, but less so than the alkali metals. Members of this group include beryllium, magnesium, calcium, and others.

Another group of atoms has one electron short of a closed shell. These have a valence of 1. They tend to pick up an electron that they need to complete the shell. They are strongly reactive. They are called halogens and are typified by fluorine, chlorine, bromine, and iodine.

How Atomic Interactions Form Molecules: Chemical Bonding

Atoms have a number of ways to form clusters, called molecules. The process, called chemical bonding, always involves an attractive interaction, which always rests upon a saving of energy. The molecule has less energy than its parts would have if they were separated. There are a number of ways in which bonding can take place. The most important are ionic bonding, covalent bonding, metallic bonding, and hydrogen bonding.

Ionic bonding is probably the easiest kind to understand. In this process, an atom gives up an electron to another atom, and this process gives one atom a positive charge and the other a negative charge. These two interact by electrical attraction and form a molecule. The prototypical example is a sodium atom that gives up its single valence electron, which is taken up by a chlorine atom. Then we have a sodium ion (charge equals +1) and a chlorine ion (charge equals 1), forming sodium chloride, common salt. If a macroscopic quantity is present, the ions spontaneously align themselves with the ionic charges, alternating in a cubic lattice. Examination of common table salt with a magnifying glass will reveal the cubic structure. The ionic bond is not especially strong. Evidence for this fact can be obtained at home. Salt crystals are easily crushed. They also dissolve readily in water with the crystals breaking up into a random assortment of sodium ions and chlorine ions.

Ionic bonding occurs in all sorts of materials. Take calcium chloride, for example. The divalent calcium atom loses both of its valence electrons, one to each of two chlorine atoms, forming calcium chloride ($CaCl_2$). This material is often used to melt snow and ice in winter in cold climates.

Covalent bonding is a different way that atoms interact; it is very common and very important. In this case, the nuclei of adjacent atoms repel each other, since both have a positive charge. Each proton is attracted to the electrons in its own atom, since both have a negative charge. However, the proton is attracted to other electrons besides its own—it cannot really tell the difference between one and the other, because "there is no paint." A simple example of covalent bonding is presented in the hydrogen molecule. $H2$. Two atoms of hydrogen that are near each other have four possible interactions of their components, taken two at a time. Each proton is attracted to its own electrons and to the electrons of the other atom; the two protons repel each other, and so do the two electrons. Quantum mechanics allows—in fact, requires—that the electrons be shared between the two protons. This sort of shared relationship defines covalent bonding.

The net result is that the ensemble of four particles is stable, although not very stable. Hydrogen molecules in air will burn explosively, as happened with the explosion of the enormous dirigible Hindenburg over New Jersey in the 1930s.

A more complex molecule with covalent bonding is methane, CH_4. Carbon has two electrons in the lowest energy shell; they do not interact chemically because they are bound to the nucleus. However, in the next energy shell there are four more electrons (valence electrons); this shell is ready to be attracted to more electrons, because it could really accommodate eight. Now suppose a carbon atom encounters four hydrogen atoms, each with one electron, and the five atoms bond together. In this process, the hydrogen retains its identity, and its own electrons; yet at the same time, its electrons fill the four empty spaces in the energy shell of the carbon. This cooperative process is called covalent bonding. In the case of methane, the electrons arrange themselves in the shape of a tetrahedron—a pyramid with triangular base and three triangular sides, and the carbon nucleus at the center. The result is a stable configuration.

The methane molecule is the principal constituent of natural gas, as used for cooking and heating. It burns readily in the presence of air. The tetrahedron breaks up as the carbon and hydrogen it contained combine separately with oxygen to form carbon dioxide and water.

The most important thing about carbon and its covalent bonding is the ability of carbon atoms to bond with each other. They do this in an impressively large number of ways; carbon chemistry is also called organic chemistry because it was once believed that living beings are the sole source of such materials. However, a good deal of carbon chemistry is actually not biochemistry.

Perhaps the most beautiful example of carbon-carbon bonding is not biochemical; it is diamond—a crystal that is pellucid and harder than any other material. To form it, each carbon atom bonds covalently with its nearest neighbors in a tetrahedral structure.

Its qualities are a tribute to the strength of the interaction that forms the covalent bond. It is also related to the fact that light travels rather slowly inside a diamond; the light is internally reflected multiple times and comes flashing out of the crystal at unexpected angles. The beauty of this effect is one reason for the value that is attached to diamonds.

Covalent carbon-carbon bonding does not always produce beauty, but it is the basis of many other materials that are very familiar. Ethanol, C_2H_5OH, has two carbon atoms bonded together in this way. Gasoline (mostly C_8H_{18}) has a chain of carbon atoms linked together with covalent bonds.

And substances that are actually organic are also in this group. Much of the food that we eat is composed of similar chains of carbon atoms with other things attached: all the major food groups—carbohydrates (sugar, starch, etc.), proteins, and lipids (oils and fats)—are examples. It should thus be apparent that living organisms are held together by covalent bonds.

Metallic bonding is almost like covalent bonding run amok. Instead of two nearby atoms sharing a pair of electrons, a metal such as copper has a lattice of copper ions with all the valence electrons shared among all the atoms.

The metallic ions are positively charged, and the electrons are of course negative. The electrostatic attractive force between these two types of objects is the interaction that holds the metal together. The strength of this interaction varies a great deal from one metal to another. Metals known in distant antiquity, such as silver, gold, copper, and lead, are relatively soft.

Other metals came to be valued later for their hardness; they include iron, tungsten, and titanium. It was discovered that admixtures often make the metal harder; adding carbon to iron makes steel; mixing copper and tin makes bronze; combining copper and zinc makes brass. In each case, the alloy is harder and stronger than either of its components.

The valence electrons in a metal are not tied to any particular ion. They can move around in the metal with very little impediment, a fact that leads to some of the important properties of metals. The ease of motion of electrons is the reason that metals are good conductors of electricity. A small voltage (electric interaction) causes the valence electrons to flow copiously. Similar effects are present for heat; if you warm up a part of a piece of metal, the heat quickly flows into the rest of it.

The loose electrons also account for the opacity of metals. Light (made of electric and magnetic fields) shining on to a piece of metal interacts with the electrons and causes them to move with rapid oscillation. The light cannot get very far into the metal; it is either absorbed or reflected very near to the surface.

Hydrogen bonding is probably less familiar than other types, but it is of great importance. This type of bond interacts to hold two molecules together, or often to hold two parts of a large molecule to each other.

The ubiquitous example of hydrogen bonding is the case of water, H_2O). The two hydrogen atoms are held to the oxygen atom by covalent bonds; the electrons from the hydrogens tend to be more closely associated with the oxygen atom, giving it a tendency toward a negative electric charge. The two hydrogen atoms have a corresponding tendency toward positive charges. So a hydrogen atom from one molecule is attracted toward the oxygen atom of a nearby molecule. The consequences are numerous and weighty.

- Clusters of water molecules form.
- The boiling point of water is increased.
- Water tends to wet many materials with which it comes in contact by forming hydrogen bonds with the surface.
- In a small tube, it forms a meniscus, a curved upper surface.
- Water percolates through soil.
- Water rises upward in the small tubules of plants.
- Trees can grow to great heights and still receive water from below.

An additional example of hydrogen bonding of great importance is the DNA molecule, essential for the reproduction of life forms. The molecule is like a twisted ladder with two uprights and many rungs. The upright sections are held together by the interaction of covalent bonds, sturdy and not easily broken. The rungs of the ladder are made of the materials that embody the genetic code. Each rung is covalently bonded at the ends to the uprights. The rung has two parts that are held together in the middle by a hydrogen bond, which is much weaker than a covalent bond.

In cell reproduction, the DNA molecule comes apart like a zipper through the breaking of the hydrogen bonds, but not the covalent ones. Each upright has the entire genetic code and thus can and does reconstitute the original in the new cell that is being formed; now there are two DNA molecules.

How Interaction May Lead to Unpredictable Variety

We have seen how chemistry, including biochemistry, is a consequence of interactions. The basis of it all is electromagnetic, with the details worked by quantum mechanics into the incredibly varied panoply of elements and compounds that make up our world. Simple ingredients—commonplace atoms and their components—are transformed by interaction into an incredibly varied set of outcomes. Now we will examine some of the conditions that help to produce a multitude of physical realities and lead to further interactions that together make up our world: linearity, nonlinearity, chaos, and complexity.

Importance of Being Nonlinear

The basic principles that have guided physics for several centuries—Newton's laws, Maxwell's equations, and quantum mechanics—are at root linear. They are so dominant in physics education that little effort is spent on nonlinear science. There are several reasons for this, but first we need to say what we mean by linear and nonlinear.

> There are precise mathematical definitions
> of linearity, but they are of limited use.

In a nonmathematical description, it may be best to consider a system that responds to a stimulus. If you double the stimulus to a linear system, you double the response. Triple the stimulus, you get three times the response, and so on. A good example of linearity is Ohm's law for ordinary resistance in an electrical circuit; the current is directly proportional to the applied voltage, which leads one to conclude that the resistance remains the same.

So why has nonlinearity suffered so much neglect?

- Basic physics is linear; see above.
- There are a great many ways to be nonlinear, but only one way to be linear.
- Linear systems are easier to analyze.
- Nonlinear systems are often so difficult to analyze that to describe them adequately one needs a computer.

Since the late twentieth century, decent computers have become widely available, so why are we still neglecting nonlinear systems? General properties of such systems provide some answers. Besides the difficulties already mentioned, nonlinear systems tend to offer surprises. Just when you think you understand such a system, it performs in a way that was qualitatively unexpected. Consequently, nonlinear systems often show a resistance to deterministic analysis.

Just for this reason, nonlinear systems are an attraction to the inquiring mind; they deserve attention. The rest of this chapter deals with important examples, distinguished by their need for interactions.

Two interesting examples that we reluctantly refrain from discussing in detail are general relativity and solitons. It is not necessary to discuss Albert Einstein's special theory of relativity here because it is essentially linear, an integral part of understandings of electromagnetism begun by James Clerk Maxwell in the nineteenth century.

The 1915 general theory of relativity, however, is nonlinear; it gives rise to such phenomena as black holes, wormholes, space-time warps, and the Big Bang. Its essential nonlinearity makes it notoriously difficult to merge with quantum mechanics; at this writing, that task has not been done.

Solitons are nonlinear waves that have unexpected properties. They can appear in surface waves on water. Take a cookie sheet with modest sides, fill it three-fourths full of water, and then try to carry it across the kitchen. The organized wave that spills over the edge is a soliton. Organized waves can also go coursing down our waterways, causing problems for shipping.

Chaos

The subject of chaos is quite old. In the first chapter of Genesis in the Hebrew Bible, the earth just after creation is described as "tohu wa-bohu," an obscure term translated by the scholars of the King James Bible as "without form and void." The inference is that our world was chaotic, but that God arranged for some order to appear.

In conventional thought we have envisioned our world as a nonchaotic system that evolves in time. We have believed that the overall system is more important than small differences in starting point. If such evolution proceeds as expected, it will develop in a predictable, deterministic fashion. If the starting point is modified very slightly, the system will also evolve. A stable system will behave such that, after a time, the precise starting point will be irrelevant.

Currently, however, we are developing some different ideas. We are studying chaotic systems, such as those involved in the development of our Earth. For a chaotic system, we now believe, the two starting points—only microscopically different—will lead to future results that bear no resemblance to one another. Although a chaotic system is ostensibly deterministic, its extreme sensitivity to initial conditions renders it indeterministic for all practical purposes.

We consider several examples of chaotic systems. A class of examples is afforded by mathematical studies of population dynamics. Suppose an isolated population of animals reproduces in proportion to the number of individuals present. If that were the only determining factor, the population would simply grow exponentially, but that is not what takes place. Other considerations may act to reduce the population, such as limited food supply, or limited space for breeding. Note that these limits have two properties: (1) they introduce nonlinearity into the system, and (2) they involve interactions, either with other members of the population or with the environment. The outcome can lead to interesting and non-intuitive results, for which the population level is unpredictable, even though the principles by which the population operates are deterministic. The situation is described clearly by Russell, Murphy, and Peacocke (1996).

A second example of a chaotic system is the set of fifteen pool balls racked in a close-packed triangular array. The cue ball is launched toward the array, and what happens next is unpredictable, even though a binary collision of two such balls is governed by deterministic laws (Newton's). If you try to use a computer to predict what will happen when you break the triangular array of balls at pool, you find out that a small change in the angle or the speed of the cue ball has an inordinate influence on the subsequent behavior of each of the other balls. This is typical of chaotic systems. Logical rules seemingly prevail, but sensitivity to tiny variables makes prediction impossible.

Many other examples could be used to illustrate the principle. We limit ourselves to one more: the atmosphere of planet Earth. The time-development of the atmosphere proceeds not only in the three dimensions of latitude, longitude, and elevation, but must also include such variables as temperature, pressure, and humidity. The basic principles are known and can be written down as a set of partial differential equations (the Navier-Stokes equations). Great effort has been put into reducing these equations to computer code for some of the largest and fastest computers available. The sad fact faced by meteorologists is that, even after considerable simplification, the equations are still nonlinear, and sensitive to even tiny changes in the initial conditions. Again, this is the hallmark of chaos.

The sensitivity of the atmosphere is sometimes called the "Chinese butterfly effect." The wings of a butterfly in Beijing can agitate the air ever so slightly and still cause a tornado on the central plains of North America. Chaos in the atmosphere is the reason that weather forecasters do not make predictions more than a week in advance.

A few concluding comments should be made. From what has been said, it might seem that chaos is bad. Occasionally someone will make the claim that chaos, entropy, and indeterminism are (jointly or severally) the essence of evil. Such an attitude is falsified by a few counterexamples.

In medicine, for example, processes in the human body that are too regular are signs of trouble. The electroencephalogram of a normal brain shows brain waves that are somewhat regular, but in which there is a touch of chaos. Completely regular waves are a characteristic of grand mal epilepsy. A similar statement can be made about the electrocardiogram of a human heart. The normal heartbeat has a small component of chaotic vibration. Fibrillation, by contrast, shows great regularity, but it increases the risk of heart failure and stroke, and so devices called defibrillators are used to disturb it a bit.

An intriguing question: Is there such a thing as quantum chaos? To understand why this question is subtle, we need to consider that a classical system can be described by the notion of a point whose instantaneous location is given by the position and momentum of the object under study. The point follows a trajectory as it moves in time. In quantum mechanics, the uncertainty principle insists that neither point nor trajectory can exist with any clarity. Instead of a point, one speaks of a region. Instead of a curved trajectory, there is a fuzzy path. So in a sense, all quantum systems appear chaotic, but not in the sense defined earlier.

To summarize, the classical examples of chaos that we mentioned share the property that it is the interactions of the parts that make the system chaotic. A classical object with no interactions obeys Newton's first law and remains at rest or moves at a constant speed in a straight line. The addition of interaction adds new dimensions and makes life more interesting.

Complexity

The concept of complexity is not easy to define. A good definition should be useful, widely acceptable, and unambiguous. No such candidate has appeared, despite extensive and careful thought.[3]

One partial definition is often called algorithmic complexity. An algorithm is a procedure for calculating something. A system that can be simulated in a computer is more complex if it requires a longer computer program in order to achieve the simulation. There are problems with this way of assigning complexity to a system.

- Consider the Mandelbrot set, the apple-shaped figure that, when you examine it closely, shows many small replicas of itself on the perimeter. Each replica has even smaller replicas attached to it, ad infinitum. Such a construct is called a fractal. People seeing such an object often say it is the most complex thing they ever saw. Yet the program to generate this fractal in a computer has only a few instructions. But to examine the shape to a fine scale, this program will need to run for a long time. In the language of computer algorithms, this one is not complex but very deep.

- In biology, the attractive way to assign an algorithm's complexity is by the length of the genome. This descriptor loses some of its attraction if you realize that a frog has a longer genome than that of a human. The frog genome has to control the animal's development from egg to tadpole to mature frog, with separate genetic instructions for various temperature ranges of the water in which the development occurs. Most people would agree that humans are more complex than frogs. So a different descriptor is needed.

Not every system can be reduced to a computer code. In particular, a biological organism consists of more than its genes. No computer can simulate the entirety of even a very simple organism. If it is alive, that organism is in continual interaction with its unpredictable environment.

3. Mitchell, *Complexity*, 94–111.

The second descriptor relies on the number of interconnections among the parts of a system. Such a criterion is intuitively appealing. A detail is that the numbers get quite large, so it is often more convenient to use the logarithm (the number of digits) of the number of connections. Since a connection generally implies some sort of interaction, this idea of complexity is congenial to the attitude of this book. The ultimate example of a really complex system is the human brain, which contains about ten billion neurons. Each neuron is able to connect to many others, so the total number of connections is impressively large. The human brain represents the most complex entity—for its size—that is known.

Neurons are not physically connected to one another. Rather, signals are carried from one to another through a process involving chemicals called neurotransmitters. There is a degree of randomness in determining which neurons will transmit and receive information to or from one another at any given time. In addition, connections can loop back into an earlier neuron in a chain. Such conditions introduce nonlinearity to the working of the neurons. The system becomes increasingly complex—a process known as complexification.

A religious consequence of these ideas is suggested by the notion that perhaps complexification is an ethical good. A healthy living brain is engaged in positive complexification. The theological question is: Where does God fit into this picture? The ready answer is that God is maximally complex, perhaps infinitely so. The Biblical teaching that humans are cre-ated in the image of God *(ad imaginem Dei)* may reflect the complexity of the human brain.

At any rate, the process of biological evolution represents a long and interesting history of complexification, as was taught by Pierre Teilhard de Chardin[4] and recounted by William C. Burger.[5] An interesting view of how this happens is expressed by Stuart Kauffman,[6] who maintains that the boundary region between order and chaos is where complexity and the capacity for evolution mostly appear. There needs to be a balance between the stability of order and the flexibility of chaos. Once again, interactions are crucial. Without them, complexity cannot exist. With them, life evolves to an amazing diversity. The appearance of unprecedented phenomena is known as emergence.

---

4. Teilhard de Chardin, *The Phenomenon of Man.*
5. Burger, *Complexity.*
6. Kaufman, *At Home in the Universe,* 86; Kaufman, *The Origins of Order,* 218.

Emergence

An emergent phenomenon is one that appears at a higher level of organization and that cannot be predicted on the basis of lower levels. But how do we make a ranking of levels of organization in natural phenomena and human culture? It is difficult to think of emergence in the absence of some kind of hierarchical structure. We can begin with a listing of broad areas of intellectual activity:

11. Religion

10. Philosophy

9. Literature

8. History

7. Sociology

6. Psychology

5. Neuroscience

4. Biology

3. Biochemistry

2. Chemistry

1. Physics

These disciplines are listed crudely in order of complexity (which in the preceding section we have noted is difficult to define), with physics—the study of the least complex systems—numbered 1, and with increasing complexity as the numbers increase. The list will be less than satisfactory for some (where is astronomy? or anthropology?), but it will suffice for the purpose at hand: to agree on a meaning for emergence. For a more elaborate list, one can refer to Peacocke.[7]

Granted the provisional hierarchy in hand, we can return to our description of emergence (not a rigorous definition): An emergent phenomenon is one that appears at a higher level of organization and that cannot be predicted on the basis of the lower levels.

Key concepts here are hierarchy and unpredictability. It is important to distinguish this attitude from reductionism, in which all the phenomena at a level can (in principle) be predicted from complete knowledge and understanding of the next lower level.

7. Peacocke, *Theology for a Scientific Age*, 217.

Reductionism has often been reviled in recent years, rightly so. Yet the habit of thinking that holism is good, and reductionism is evil, is historically short sighted. Ever since the seventeenth century, reductionism has served science very well, making possible all sorts of technological advances. But too many vainglorious statements have appeared, especially in the twentieth century, claiming that we now had enough data to enable the calculation of everything we might wish to know. A little more humility is in order. Emergence is real, and it defies the rule of reductionism, no matter how useful the latter can sometimes be; see Morowitz 2002.

It is instructive to consider a few examples of emergent phenomena. Earlier in this chapter there was mention of chemical bonding of various types. They are all illustrations of how molecules emerge from atoms in ways that would be hard to predict *a priori.*

The DNA molecule and its functions in genetics provide another example. It is crucial to life as an emergent phenomenon coming out of biochemistry.

Assemblies of neurons in a brain give rise to consciousness in ways that are emergent and have been singularly resistant to reductionist explanations. Psychology emerges from neuroscience.

Study of an individual animal gives no real clue as to what will happen when numbers of individuals form a social group.

Sociobiology and sociology are not predictable from biology and psychology. There are common elements in these examples.

- They involve adjacent levels in the hierarchy.
- They all arise from collective behavior.
- They lead to increased complexity.
- They are inconceivable without interactions.

The last of these is one reason why this book came into existence. The world around us is fascinating mostly because of the unpredictability of the emergent phenomena that appear all around us and continue to amaze us with unexpected beauty.

The basic nature of interaction in the character and very existence of our world is worth deep consideration. Interaction is not a thing, but a process. How basic is this fact to our understanding of reality?

References

Aspect, Alain et al. 1984. "Experimental Tests of Realistic Local Theories via Bell's Theorem." *Physical Review Letters* 47/7, pp. 460–63.

Burger, William C. 2016. *Complexity: The Evolution of Earth's Biodiversity and the Future of Humanity.* Amherst, NY: Prometheus.

Clayton, Philip, and Paul Davies, eds. 2006. *The Re-Emergence of Emergence: The Emergentist Hypothesis from Science to Religion.* Oxford: Oxford University Press.

Kauffman, Stuart A. 1995. *At Home in the Universe: The Search for Laws of Self-Organization and Complexity.* New York: Oxford University Press.

———. 1993. *The Origins of Order: Self-Organization and Selection in Evolution.* New York: Oxford University Press.

Mitchell, Melanie. 2009. *Complexity: A Guided Tour.* Oxford: Oxford University Press. (See chapter 7 for definitions of complexity.)

Morowitz, Harold J. 2002. *The Emergence of Everything: How the World Became Complex.* Oxford: Oxford University Press.

Peacocke, Arthur. 1993. *Theology for a Scientific Age: Being and Becoming—Natural, Divine, and Human.* Theology and the Sciences. Minneapolis: Fortress.

Russell, Robert John et al., eds. 1996. *Chaos and Complexity: Scientific Perspectives on Divine Action.* Scientific Perspectives on Divine Action 2. Notre Dame: University of Notre Dame Press.

Teilhard de Chardin, Pierre. 1955. *Le Phénomene Humain.* Paris: Seuil. English, *The Phenomenon of Man.* Translated by Bernard Wall. New York: Harper & Row, 1959.

Vedral, Vlatko. 2006. *Introduction to Quantum Information Science.* Oxford Graduate Texts. Oxford: Oxford University Press. (pp. 81–129 are on quantum entanglement.)

Wegter-McNelly, Kirk. 2011. *The Entangled God: Divine Relationality and Quantum Physics.* Routledge Studies in Religion 15. New York: Routledge.

3

The Interactive Cosmos

Grace A. Wolf-Chase

Introduction

I N WHAT HAS BECOME an oft-repeated line from the 2015 movie, *The Martian*, Matt Damon's character, Mark Watney, exclaims, "I'm going to have to science the (expletive) out of this!" This one sentence communicates the theme of the movie perfectly; science is an incredibly useful tool for solving practical problems. Using the word as a verb shifts the emphasis from science as a collection of facts to science as a process that deepens our understanding of how things work. Of course, modern science is much more than practical problem solving. Many questions that were once relegated solely to the realm of philosophy are now approachable through scientific methods. Although there are numerous examples of this across the sciences, there are two branches of study in astronomy[1] that illustrate this well: the exploration of the beginning and evolution of the Universe[2] (*cosmology*) and the quest to understand the origins, evolution, distribution, and future of life in the Universe (*astrobiology*). A comprehensive review of these fields is well beyond the scope of this chapter. Rather, we will explore some of what these studies reveal about the inter-connectedness of the material Universe and how the word "interaction" characterizes both the

1. Here I use "astronomy" as an umbrella term for the sciences that explore the Universe beyond Earth's atmosphere, including, but not limited to, planetary science, astrophysics, astrochemistry, astrobiology, and cosmology.

2. Note "Universe" is usually taken to refer to all of material reality. The Universe may itself be part of a larger "Multiverse"; however, this chapter will explore our current state of knowledge of the observable Universe. We use the words "Universe" and "Cosmos" interchangeably.

evolution of the physical Universe and the way in which advances are made in astronomy. Our exploration will begin where science begins, using a skill every person has used since early childhood—classification.

Classification: The Beginning of Science

At the 2006 General Assembly of the International Astronomical Union[3] (IAU), IAU members settled on a definition of the word "planet."[4] It may come as a surprise to many that prior to this decision, astronomers had no set of uniform criteria for establishing the status of planethood. The question, "What is a planet?" has been answered in many different ways historically. When Pluto was re-classified from "planet" to a category of objects known as "dwarf planet" based on the criteria outlined in the IAU definition, public reaction to this decision surprised many in the scientific community. Numerous people were angry that Pluto had been "demoted" or "killed," and some even saw this as a step backward to the eight recognized planets prior to Pluto's discovery by Clyde Tombaugh in 1930, reported by *Science News* that year.[5]

The fact is, classification is not the end point of science, but the beginning, and the categories to which we assign things are always open to modification based on new information. The primary purpose of classification in science is to explore the relationships between things, not to provide a definitive answer to the question, what is this? Classification by sorting things into different categories based on their similarities and differences is, in fact, one of the first activities in which we engage as children entering school, and one of the first things we learn, is that there are many ways to classify, depending upon the properties we consider to be most important. An amusing example of this occurs in the Disney movie *Wall-E*, where an endearing robot must decide where to store a "spork." Does it go with the spoons or the forks? In the end, Wall-E apparently decides it is neither, since he places the item in question between the spoon and fork containers.

Astronomers can sympathize with Wall-E's dilemma; what we continue to learn about nature indicates that we live in a "non-binary" Universe, where objects such as stars and planets appear to fall along a continuum. A case in point: *brown dwarfs* have been referred to as "failed stars"; they are not massive or hot enough to sustain the fusion reactions that power most stars, but there is evidence that they may form like stars,

3. http://www.iau.org/

4. https://www.iau.org/static/resolutions/Resolution_GA26–5–6.pdf/.

5. *Science News*, "A New Planet beyond Neptune," x–xiv.

when a *nebula* collapses through gravity. In contrast, planets form in *protoplanetary disks* surrounding stars.

Analogously, Pluto meets two of the IAU criteria listed for planethood status: (1) it orbits the Sun; and (2) it has sufficient mass for its self-gravity to pull it into a (nearly) round shape. There is even evidence that this remote world undergoes active geologic resurfacing, as images from the *New Horizons* mission[6] indicate. However, Pluto is also one of an increasing number of known icy worlds that orbit the Sun beyond the orbit of the planet Neptune, in a region known as the *Kuiper Belt*. It fails to meet the third IAU criterion for planethood; namely, it has not cleared the neighborhood around its orbit. There is still much disagreement in the scientific community regarding how Pluto should be classified, but this debate is useful because it is informed by what we continue to learn about Pluto's relationship to other worlds in our *Solar System*,[7] and this relationship in turn informs our understanding of how our Solar System came to be.

A Plurality of Worlds

Over the course of the twentieth century, we learned that our Solar System is part of an unimaginably large Universe. Our Sun is one of approximately 400 billion stars in the *Milky Way Galaxy*, which in turn is one among hundreds of billions of galaxies in the *observable* Universe.[8] Over the past twenty years, we've discovered many planets that orbit other stars. In fact, well over 3,000 of these *exoplanets*[9] have been discovered at an exponentially increasing rate, using several different methods of detection.[10] The statistics of these discoveries, together with what we have learned about how stars and planets form, suggest that one or more planets may accompany essentially all stars. In other words, planets may outnumber the roughly ten million quadrillion stars in the observable Universe.

Planetary systems are extremely diverse. A few examples of this diversity are systems with giant planets that orbit their stars in a few days; planets that orbit in systems containing two, three, or more stars orbiting

---

6. https://www.nasa.gov/mission_pages/newhorizons/main/index.html/.

7. The Sun and all of the smaller celestial bodies that travel around it.

8. We don't know the true size of the Universe; it may be infinite.

9. Exoplanets are planets that do not orbit our Sun. In most cases, they orbit other stars, but there may be "free-floating" exoplanets as well. Throughout this chapter, I will simply refer to them as "planets" (or more generally as "worlds"), even though the IAU definition specifies that a planet must orbit our Sun.

10. A good reference for information about research teams can be found on The Extrasolar Planets Encyclopaedia website: http://exoplanet.eu/research/.

each other; and planets with masses between those of the *terrestrial planets* and *gas giants* in our Solar System, some of which may even be "water worlds."[11] The diversity of these planets rivals that envisioned by some of the most creative science fiction writers. The new discoveries are coming at such a rapid pace that NASA has provided an application to enable anyone to explore the ever-increasing database of these worlds,[12] a growing number of which lie in the *habitable zones* of their stars. The habitable zone amounts to a torus around the star within which a planet might sustain liquid water, essential for life as we know it on Earth, on its surface.[13] Closer to the star, water would boil away, and further from the star, it would freeze. The closest potentially habitable world outside of our Solar System orbits the nearest star to our Sun, Proxima Centauri.[14]

How many worlds may actually be inhabited by either simple life or life that can, like human beings, reflect on its own existence, remains an open question, but the raw ingredients needed for life are common in the Universe. Note there is a large leap from "simple" life, such as microbes, to life capable of self-reflection! Many surveys, employing diverse methods, are searching for *biosigns* in planetary atmospheres that would indicate some type of life. In February 2017, a NASA press release announced the discovery of seven Earth-sized worlds orbiting a dim, relatively nearby, star known as TRAPPIST 1.[15] Three of these seven worlds lie in the star's habitable zone and will be excellent targets for the *James Webb Space Telescope* (JWST), scheduled for launch in 2018.[16] From its orbit around the Sun, the JWST will study the atmospheres of these worlds for possible indications of life. In addition to surveys for biosigns in planetary atmospheres, complementary surveys search for signs of technology that might be created by advanced civilizations (see, e.g., the webpage of the Center for SETI Research[17]).

11. Kaltenegger et al., "Water Planets in the Habitable Zone."

12. https://eyes.nasa.gov/eyes-on-exoplanets.html/.

13. The Planetary Habitability Laboratory at the University of Puerto Rico at Arecibo maintains a list of these planets at http://phl.upr.edu/.

14. Anglada-Escudé et al., *A Terrestrial Planet Candidate*.

15. https://www.nasa.gov/press-release/nasa-telescope-reveals-largest-batch-of-earth-size-habitable-zone-planets-around/.

16. https://exoplanets.nasa.gov/news/1422/probing-seven-promising-worlds-with-nasas-james-webb-space-telescope/.

17. http://www.seti.org/centerforseti/.

Interactions Characterize Cosmic Evolution

Understanding the origin and evolution of the Universe and its diverse contents is a major goal of contemporary astronomy. Cosmology reconstructs the past history of the Universe, providing a way of understanding what we see today and predicting how the Universe will continue to evolve. This includes projecting what the ultimate fate of everything might be, although extrapolating into the far future comes with some big caveats! The past is accessible to us because information cannot travel faster than the speed of light, roughly six trillion miles per year, and because we live in an expanding Universe with a finite beginning, approximately 13.8 billion years ago. The implications of this are truly profound; we never see the Universe as it is today. Rather, we have a fossil record of its past encoded in light from distant objects. This fossil record allows us to explore how the Universe and its contents have changed over time.

The Interaction of Light and Matter

The application of *spectroscopy* to astronomy gave rise to astrophysics, enabling astronomers to study the compositions of celestial objects. Spectroscopy is a technique whereby light is spread out by wavelength using a spectroscope (an instrument such as a prism or diffraction grating). Father Angelo Secchi, a nineteenth-century Jesuit scientist, was the first person to use spectroscopy to classify stars according to their spectral type.[18] Secchi recognized that the patterns of dark lines in the spectra of different types of stars were related to the stars' compositions, earning him the double-entendre title, the "Father of Astrophysics."

Quantum mechanics, developed in the twentieth century, provided the theoretical foundation for understanding how light interacts with atoms and molecules to produce the distinct patterns of lines that enable determining the composition of remote objects. For astronomers, these patterns serve as "celestial barcodes." In the early twentieth century, Cecilia Payne-Gaposchkin's Ph.D. dissertation extended earlier work to relate stellar spectra to both composition and temperature. She showed that stars are primarily composed of hydrogen and helium. Payne received the first Ph.D. in astronomy from Radcliffe College, since Harvard didn't grant doctoral degrees to women at the time. Astronomers Otto Struve and Velta Zebergs

18. https://www.britannica.com/biography/Pietro-Angelo-Secchi/.

later referred to her dissertation as "undoubtedly the most brilliant Ph.D. thesis ever written in astronomy."[19]

Spectroscopy is also a useful tool to study the dynamics of celestial bodies. Light from moving sources is shifted in wavelength due to the *Doppler Effect*, similar to sound waves from a source (such as a train whistle) that are higher or lower in pitch, depending upon whether the source is approaching or receding. Beginning in 1919, Edwin Hubble and Milton Humason,[20] a janitor at the Mount Wilson Observatory in California who worked his way up to become Edwin Hubble's assistant, began studying distant galaxies. In 1929, Hubble published their results, showing that the distance of a galaxy is proportional to how fast it's moving away from us.[21] This result can be best explained if the Universe is expanding.

Interestingly, Father Georges Lemaître published a solution to Einstein's equations of General Relativity for the case of an expanding Universe in a rather obscure Belgian journal two years before Hubble's publication,[22] but in a translation of Lemaître's paper that appeared in 1931,[23] the equations that described the expansion now known as *Hubble's Law* were omitted. Lemaître himself did this because he felt his own galaxy distance estimates weren't strong enough to validate his discovery. Lemaître went on to propose that the logical consequences of an expanding Universe implied the Universe must have originated at a finite point in time,[24] earning him the title (another double entendre), "The Father of the Big Bang."

The Interaction of Gravitational Fields and Matter

It is a common misconception that the Big Bang took place at some point in "empty space," and the increasing separation of galaxies is akin to "shrapnel" flying away from the source of an explosion, but this would not be a

---

19. https://www.britannica.com/biography/Cecilia-Payne-Gaposchkin/.

20. In Humason's obituary, the Swiss astronomer Fritz Zwicky wrote, "Humason was the ideal of a scientist who knows that society has made it possible for him to pursue in peace the quests that interest him most, and that for this privilege he must in turn serve and repay society. He thus became one of the all-too-small group of scientists who considers it their highest duty to bridge the ever-widening gap between science and the general public. For this many men in all walks of life will remember him as their friend."

21. Hubble, "A Relation between Distance and Radial Velocity."

22. Lemaître, "Un Univers homogène de masse constante."

23. Lemaître, "Expansion of the Universe, A Homogeneous Universe"; Lemaître, "Expansion of the Universe, The Expanding Universe."

24. See https://commons.wikimedia.org/wiki/File:Universe_expansion.png/ for a good illustration of this.

good analogy. Although Isaac Newton envisioned space as something like an empty stage—a passive "thing" that provided an absolute frame of reference, Einstein showed that space and time are inseparable and not absolute. This *space-time* might be better visualized as a dynamic fabric rather than a passive stage. It originated at the Big Bang and space-time itself is what is expanding. One way to think about this is to visualize the surface of an expanding balloon dotted with tiny stickers. In this two-dimensional analogy, you can think of the surface of the balloon as representing three-dimensional space. The diameter of the balloon increases with time, while the separation between all the stickers increases.

Albert Einstein's 1915 General Theory of Relativity was one of the most important developments in twentieth–century physics. It explained gravity is terms of the curvature of space-time. Space-time responds to the presence of matter by stretching, bending, twisting, and rippling. This response, in turn, affects the way matter moves. The eminent Princeton physicist, John Archibald Wheeler, expressed this well: "Spacetime tells matter how to move; matter tells spacetime how to curve."[25] The curvature of spacetime can be visualized as a *gravitational field*. Until 2015, all of the predictions of General Relativity had been experimentally verified except one, *gravitational waves*. Einstein himself believed this prediction would not be verifiable because of the technological requirements to observe the effect of these miniscule ripples in the fabric of spacetime. One hundred years after the General Theory of Relativity was published, the Laser Interferometer Gravitational-Wave Observatory (LIGO) Scientific Collaboration[26] achieved the seemingly impossible—the detection of a wave that stretched space by one part in one million quadrillion, making the entire Earth expand and contract by about the width of an atomic nucleus.[27]

The Interaction of Magnetic Fields and Matter

Many processes in contemporary physics are understood as the interactions between particles and fields (cf. John Albright's Chapter One, above, "Interactions in Physics.")A particularly illustrative example of this in astrophysics arises from considering magnetic fields. In stars (for example, the Sun), magnetic fields are generated from the motions of charged particles. The matter in stars is hot enough to be in the form of *plasma*, where negatively

25. Wheeler, *Black Holes and Quantum Foam*, 235.

26. See http://www.ligo.org/ for illustrations and videos of gravitational fields and gravitational waves.

27. Abbott et al., "Observation of Gravitational Waves."

charged electrons and positively charged atomic nuclei are not bound to each other. The motions of these charged particles create magnetic fields, which in turn affect how the charged particles move. One cannot be considered without the other. The Sun's magnetic field is extremely complex and ever changing. It is the source of explosions of charged particles on the Sun that cause *space weather*, which can produce beautiful aurorae on Earth as well as occasional disruption of satellite communications and radiation potentially harmful to astronauts. The Sun's magnetic field also deflects many energetic *cosmic rays* that originate outside our Solar System, providing a layer of protection against potentially damaging mutations to DNA.

Observations of very young stars indicate that they exhibit particularly strong magnetic activity, producing *superflares* up to ten times a day. Flares of this magnitude occur on the present day Sun only once about every 100 years. Billions of years ago, particularly strong solar magnetic activity may have played a key role in driving the chemistry necessary for the development of life on the young Earth.[28]

Navigating Nature and Nurture in Cosmic Evolution

Many terms from biology, such as "nature" and "nurture," have been applied with increasing frequency to the physical Universe. Stars are "born" in *dark nebulae* through the complex interplay between gravitational attraction of the gas and dust within these nebulae and agents such as turbulence, magnetic fields, radiation and thermal pressure that resist the compression. Competition between these processes, which play out over an enormous range of scales in both time and space, determines both where stars form and how much matter they accumulate; that is, how massive they become. Star formation is highly stochastic in nature and cannot be predicted precisely. For example, very massive stars play a dominant role in determining the future evolution of their natal cloud and subsequent star formation. On the one hand, radiation and *stellar winds* from these stars can disperse the natal cloud material, but they can also compress it to form new stars. Most frequently, stars are born in clusters with many "siblings."

The Orion Nebula is a familiar star-forming region to many observers, both professional and amateur. The constellation of Orion is prominent on clear winter nights in the northern hemisphere, and the nebula can be seen as a faint cloudy patch even with binoculars, if the sky is sufficiently dark. Luminous, massive stars that are intrinsically ten thousand times brighter than our Sun light up the gas in the nebula, but these stars are part of a

28. Airapetian, et al., "Prebiotic Chemistry and Atmospheric Warming."

cluster containing hundreds of dimmer stars, including stars like our Sun. The Hubble Space Telescope first exposed curious dark objects you can see in silhouette against the bright nebular background.[29] Many subsequent observations of these and similar features in other star-forming nebulae have provided robust evidence that these are nascent planetary systems. Five billion years ago, our own Solar System is thought to have formed in a similar environment, bathed by the radiation, winds, and eventually explosion of one or more massive star(s). In particular, the presence of decay products of the short-lived[30] *radioisotope* ^{60}Fe in meteorites provides strong evidence of the explosion of a massive star (known as a *supernova*) in the vicinity of our Solar System while it was forming.[31] A *supernova* is the only known mechanism for producing ^{60}Fe.

Interactions Characterize Scientific Progress

On the cosmic timescale, we are an extremely young species, and our science is younger still. First popularized by Carl Sagan in his 1980 television series *Cosmos: A Personal Journey,* the *Cosmic Calendar* is a helpful way to visualize the immense age of our Universe. If we compress the 13.8 billion-year history of the Universe onto the scale of one calendar year on the Earth, 500 years equals roughly one second. On this scale, the Universe is born at the start of January first; galaxies containing billions or trillions of stars take shape over the next several months; our Sun and the worlds that orbit it form in the Milky Way Galaxy in early September; single-celled life appears later in September and multi-celled life arises in December; anatomically modern humans appear only 6 minutes before midnight on December thirty-first; writing is invented about fifteen seconds before midnight; modern science develops during the last second before midnight; and humans use science to write the history of the Universe itself in the last tenth of a second.

The youth of our science is both humbling and awe-inspiring. How is it that humanity is amassing knowledge at an exponentially growing rate? Science is a collaborative effort and scientific progress is achieved through the interaction of many individuals. Unfortunately, science education at the precollege level can inadvertently paint a misleading picture of the scientific process when the focus is restricted to the contributions of a few individuals

29. See https://apod.nasa.gov/apod/ap091222.html/ to view images of these "protoplanetary disks" in the Orion Nebula.

30. Note that in this case "short-lived" means 1.5 million years, short on the timescale of planet formation.

31. Hester, et al., "The Cradle of the Solar System."

considered to be central to the development of key scientific theories. For example, one often hears phrases such as "Darwin could have been mistaken" among the general public, neglecting the fact that predictions of the theory of evolution have been developed, tested, and refined by thousands of scientists since *On the Origin of Species* was published in 1859. The same holds true of pivotal developments in astronomy and our understanding of the origin and evolution of the Universe.

The Interaction between Observation, Technology, and Theory

Human beings have been able to reconstruct the overall history of the Universe through the close interaction between observations, technology, and the development of theoretical models. Recent technologies have extended human senses in ways that couldn't be envisioned generations ago, enabling us to probe scales from sub-atomic levels to the largest structures in the observable Universe.

As new technologies are developed that make it possible to study hitherto unobservable aspects of the cosmos, we first try to describe or explain those observations in terms of what we know. We do this by constructing mathematical models whose ingredients are the laws of physics and chemistry that we think are important to what we observe. Astronomy is often theory-driven, meaning many astronomical phenomena have been predicted to occur based on known physical laws before they have actually been observed; however, this isn't always the case, and invariably, reality is more complicated than our models.

The development of our understanding of the formation of our Solar System (and other planetary systems) provides an excellent example of the interaction between observations, technology, and theory. In the eighteenth century, the philosopher Immanuel Kant and the mathematical physicist Pierre Laplace independently proposed the *Nebular Hypothesis* as a possible explanation of how our Solar System formed.[32] Based primarily on Newton's Universal Law of Gravitation (cf. John Albright's Chapter One in this volume, "Interactions in Physics") and the observation that the planets lie more or less in a plane and orbit the Sun in the same direction, they proposed that the Solar System formed from a huge spinning nebula that flattened out as it was pulled together by gravity. In this model, the Sun formed at the center, where most of the matter was concentrated and spinning the slowest, and the planets formed in an extended disk of material around the Sun.

32. Kant, *Allgemeine Naturgeschichte und Theorie*; Laplace, *Exposition du systeme du monde*.

The Nebular Hypothesis remained just that—an interesting hypothesis—for 200 years, since there was no way to test this idea in the eighteenth century. Today however, with high-resolution imaging techniques and instruments that can probe the cold, invisible, birthing places of stars, we have been able to re-construct the important stages that take place in the formation of planetary systems through large statistical studies of star-forming regions. As envisioned by Kant and Laplace, gravity is indeed an important ingredient, but it is not the only ingredient, as noted earlier.

If a theoretical model does a good job of reproducing what we see, it gives us a measure of confidence that we are on the right track in understanding the important processes that are involved. On the other hand, if our model doesn't give us a good description of what's going on, we know we're missing something. Perhaps we neglected to include some known physics that is more important to what we observe than we'd thought. In the case of star and planet formation, magnetic fields, radiation and winds from young stars, and turbulence all play essential roles in addition to gravity.

Many of the most exciting discoveries occur when we can't model a set of observations in terms of familiar physical laws and we realize we need to include something currently unknown. *Dark matter* and *dark energy* are examples of twentieth-century discoveries that came about as we were able to observe their influence on matter and spacetime; in other words, by how they interact with known things. Both play important roles in the development of the large-scale structure of the Universe.[33]

A review of the long history of evidence pointing to the existence of dark matter, which goes back to a 1933 paper published by the Swiss astronomer Fritz Zwicky,[34] is beyond the scope of this chapter. It is sufficient to note that dark matter is detected through its gravity. Unlike ordinary matter, it doesn't absorb, emit, or reflect light of any kind. Two of the ways its presence is inferred include the motions of stars and nebulae orbiting the centers of galaxies and from the way light from distant galaxies is bent as it passes through clusters of foreground galaxies, a phenomenon known as *gravitational lensing*, which was predicted by Einstein.

Vera Rubin, the second female astronomer to be elected to the National Academy of Sciences, was instrumental in the discovery of dark matter through her studies of the rotation curves of galaxies.[35] As Rubin studied the orbits of stars about the center of the Andromeda galaxy, the closest *spiral*

33. See Gates, *Einstein's Telescope*, for an accessible treatment of dark matter and dark energy.

34. Zwicky, "Die rotverschiebung," 110–27.

35. Rubin and Ford, "Rotation of the Andromeda Nebula."

galaxy to our own Milky Way, she discovered that stars far from the center of the galaxy orbited faster than could be reckoned by the gravity from the amount of visible matter. She concluded there must be large amounts of unseen matter. Rubin found similar results for sixty galaxies, enabling her to conclude that galaxies typically contain about ten times more "dark" mass than visible matter in the form of stars and nebulae.

We know relatively little about the nature of dark matter, but we know even less about the nature of dark energy. It was discovered in 1998 by two teams of astronomers, who measured light from a particular type of exploding star known as *Type IA supernova*.[36] This type of supernova is extremely useful in determining distances to remote galaxies, because it brightens and fades in a predictable way that can be used to determine its intrinsic brightness. Once the intrinsic brightness of a Type IA supernova is determined, its apparent brightness can be used to calculate its distance, making it an extremely useful *standard candle*.[37] The supernova studies revealed something remarkable. For a long time, cosmologists envisioned two possible scenarios: either gravity would eventually reverse the expansion of the Universe or the Universe would continue to expand forever. In either case, the expansion of the Universe should be slowing down in time due to the gravitational attraction of matter. The supernovae measurements indicated that the expansion of the Universe is actually speeding up over time, pointing to something countering the large-scale effects of gravity. In 2011, Saul Perlmutter, Brian P. Schmidt, and Adam G. Reiss were awarded the Nobel Prize in Physics for "the discovery of the accelerating expansion of the Universe through observations of distant supernovae."

Even though we currently know little of the nature of dark matter and dark energy, their inferred presence explains some previously puzzling aspects of the Universe extremely well.[38] You might say they are "known unknowns." It was only after the effects of dark matter and dark energy became measurable through technology-enabled observations that their presence was noticed, which begs the question, what "unknown unknowns" might we be missing? This is a question we can only address when the unknown is made manifest by interacting with something known, or when the unknown is predicted by theory and subsequently detected.

36. Riess et al., "Observational Evidence," 1009–38; Perlmutter et al., "Measurements of Ω and Λ from 42 High-Redshift Supernovae," 565–86.

37. Astronomers use a hierarchy of methods, applicable over different scales, to calculate cosmic distances. Standard candles are objects whose brightness can be calibrated on an absolute scale.

38. The Wilkinson Microwave Anisotropy Probe (WMAP) website provides accessible resources on this topic: http://map.gsfc.nasa.gov/.

Big Science Requires Big Collaborations

Science is a community endeavor. The rapid pace of discovery depends upon many collaborative interactions. In astronomy, the last few decades have witnessed a trend to ever-larger collaborations as the sheer volume of data from large surveys and the complexities of working with these data mandate specialized skills in many different areas. (Note that many of the recent references cited in this chapter contain large numbers of coauthors.) Of course, there are still important scientific questions that can be addressed by small teams or even individual scientists, but these questions tend to occupy narrow and very specific niches. In contrast, many of the big existential scientific questions demand interdisciplinary teams with complementary, as well as overlapping, skills and expertise.

This demand has become so great that it is rapidly becoming impractical, and often impossible, for even large teams of researchers to mine the wealth of information in databases across many fields of study—not just in the sciences, but in the humanities as well. Although computers can be programmed to extract certain types of information from large databases, there are many tasks better suited for human eyes (or ears). People not only excel at pattern recognition, they possess another feature that computers lack—the ability to make new discoveries by spotting unexpected curiosities. Because of this, the last decade has witnessed a rise in the development of projects that crowdsource people from around the world and from all walks of life to enable research that would otherwise be impossible. These *citizen scientists* become collaborators with the professional teams and play a vital role in advancing research across many fields of study.

Zooniverse[39] is the world's largest and most popular platform for people-powered research. Since *Galaxy Zoo* was first launched in 2007,[40] Zooniverse has expanded to a wide-ranging and ever-expanding suite of academic research projects across many disciplines—the arts, biology, climate studies, history, language, literature, medicine, nature, physics, social science, and space science. To date, these projects have resulted in well over 100 research publications.[41] Using Zooniverse discussion boards, citizen scientists interact with each other and with the research teams. Citizen science enables everyone to participate in the process of research and discovery—no specialized background, training, or expertise is needed, and the level of contribution is entirely up to the time, interest, and convenience of the participant. Specific

---

39. https://www.zooniverse.org/

40. Raddick et al., "Galaxy Zoo," 892.

41. https://www.zooniverse.org/about/publications.

tasks performed by citizen scientists are project-dependent, but many of the projects use similar web tools. Volunteers might be asked to make measurements of objects in beautiful astronomical images, identify elusive animals caught by automated cameras placed in remote areas, or mine information from digitized historical records or diaries.

In addition to performing tasks requested by the research teams, citizen scientists have made important serendipitous discoveries, resulting in acknowledgments and occasionally even coauthorship with researchers, on academic publications. For example, in the *Milky Way Project,* which involves identifying star-forming regions in our galaxy,[42] citizen scientists discovered a previously unrecognized class of very young objects that are helping members of the science team understand the earliest stages in the formation of star clusters.[43] Many media venues picked up on this discovery, which also resulted in the first space science article published in an academic journal aimed at children.[44] Similarly, in the project *Planethunters,* citizen scientists discovered the first planet orbiting in a system containing four stars.[45] In addition to being a coauthor on this paper, citizen scientist Kian Jek was awarded the prestigious Chambliss Amateur Achievement Award from the American Astronomical Society in 2012 for being instrumental in the discovery of several planets that had been missed by previous efforts.[46]

Forging New Collaborations between Human Beings and Machines

Humans and machines both have limitations that affect their abilities to peruse and classify vast quantities of data, motivating the exploration of potential synergies between professional scientists, citizen scientists, and machines. While professional scientists have the expertise in their fields to perform tasks that require specialized knowledge, they are limited in their numbers and available time. On the other hand, citizen scientists outnumber professionals by tens or hundreds of thousands. They are equally capable of general pattern recognition, but lack the specialized expertise. Citizen scientists are also well placed to make serendipitous discoveries of unusual or uncommon objects. Expert and non-expert human classifications are now

42. Simpson et al., "The Milky Way Project First Data Release," 2442–60.

43. Wolf-Chase and Kerton, "Yellowballs."

44. Ibid.

45. Schwamb et al. "Planet Hunters," 122–47.

46. https://aas.org/grants-and-prizes/chambliss-amateur-achievement-award

being used to train computers to become better at recognizing patterns.[47] Once trained, machine-learning algorithms can conduct comprehensive searches of vast quantities of data for cases where exhaustive human searches are not feasible, flagging interesting objects for follow–up study.

This interaction between humans and machines is critical in light of future astronomical surveys, such as the *Large Synoptic Survey Telescope* (LSST),[48] which will result in petabytes (1 PB = 1 quadrillion bytes) of data. To say it will be challenging to fully mine the information in the acquired observations would be a gross understatement! The LSST will conduct a ten-year survey, repeatedly mapping the entire visible sky over the course of a few nights from its location in Chile. The images will be analyzed immediately to identify temporal changes in diverse objects such as supernova explosions and asteroids that might impact the Earth. Over the survey lifetime, LSST will map tens of billions of stars and galaxies, enabling unprecedented explorations of the structure of the Milky Way, the properties of dark matter and dark energy, and of course, many anticipated serendipitous discoveries not yet imagined.

Visualization: The Interaction of Science and Art

Although the word "visualization" carries multiple meanings, I use it here to refer to any technique for creating images, diagrams, animations, or interactives in ways that help human beings represent and understand the meaning of data. Of course, humans have used art to represent concrete and abstract ideas since the dawn of human civilization, but representing information acquired with technology that extends human senses in innumerable ways presents increasingly complex challenges. Technology enables us to "sense" invisible light, magnetic fields, and gravitational waves, to name just a few examples. It also allows us to explore spatial and temporal scales over many orders of magnitude that are completely inaccessible to everyday human experience. Astronomy is hardly the only science to face increasing challenges in visualizing information in a meaningful way. For example, Vesna and Gimzewski[49] write, "In both the philosophical and visual sense, 'seeing is believing' does not apply to nanotechnology, for there is nothing even remotely visible to create proof of existence." In representing realms inaccessible to human senses, the boundaries between art and science necessarily begin to blur.

47. Beaumont, et al., "The Milky Way Project," 3–20.

48. https://www.lsst.org/.

49. Vesna and Gimzewski, "The Nanoneme Syndrome," 7–24.

Data Visualization is a field of modern academic study that can be applied to diverse careers. In the Space Visualization Lab (SVL) at the Adler Planetarium in Chicago,[50] scientists, technology experts, artists, and educators work together to create new ways for people to explore the Universe virtually, through interactive and immersive experiences. These experiences utilize various degrees of human body affordances to support cognition of space-related data and physical forces at work.[51] Visitors to the SVL can rotate and zoom through 3D simulations of assorted astrophysical phenomena; use their arm motions to pan and zoom across space using World Wide Telescope[52] (WWT) software; and use a Gravitational Simulator that tracks the motions of their bodies to create "stars" that orbit each other, form, or escape from, groups, depending upon their velocities.

The Electronic Visualization Laboratory (EVL) at the University of Illinois at Chicago has sponsored systematic collaborations between artists and scientists for decades.[53] At the EVL, artists learn about technology that enables them to create in new ways and scientists learn how to communicate better visually. Sandin et al.[54] note, "in long-term collaboration the various professional collaborators must reap benefits as measured within their own disciplines, in addition to the benefits of learning how other people do things and how to share knowledge across disciplines." Indeed, this point could be applied equally well to academic dialog between scientists and theologians!

Academics, as well as many other professionals, are typically overextended in their time commitments, and the activities in which they engage depend heavily upon the institutions that employ them. It would be a mistake to conclude that lack of participation in a given activity must imply lack of interest. For example, the amount of public outreach in which scientists engage depends strongly upon the value that their institutions place on outreach when scientists come under review for tenure or undergo similar processes of evaluation. What incentives might be developed both to encourage and enable collaborations between scientists and theologians as humanity faces the escalating complexities of the twenty-first century?

50. http://www.adlerplanetarium.org/whats-here/dont-miss/space-visualization -lab/.

51. Aguilaria-Rodriguez, "To Embody the N-Body," 537–46.

52. The World Wide Telescope was developed by Jonathan Fay at Microsoft Research. It is a useful tool for both professionals and the general public, enabling them to explore the cosmos on their own, or take "tours" developed by specialists on selected topics.

53. Sandin et al., "The Artist and the Scientific Research Environment," 219–21.

54. Ibid.

Conclusion: Change and Interaction as "Cosmic Constants"

The quote, "The only constant is change" has been attributed to Heraclitus of Ephesus, although many others have expressed similar sentiments down through the ages. Understandably, ancient peoples thought that change applied to conditions on the Earth, but that the heavens were immutable; however, we now understand that the Cosmos itself is a product of change that comes about through the interaction of its parts. Atoms assemble into molecules. Galaxies and clusters of galaxies form and evolve under the influences of gravity, dark matter, and dark energy. Stars and planetary systems form as a result of a delicate dance of cosmic processes. Life that continuously interacts with its environment has developed on at least one planet, and possibly a countless number of others. Just as interaction characterizes the nature of the Universe, it characterizes how we humans come to an understanding of that nature. This should not come as a surprise to us—after all, we ourselves are a part of (not apart from) the Universe. In human beings at least, we see the Universe becoming aware of itself. If you multiply the neural connections in a single human brain by the number of humans on Earth, you get a number that exceeds the number of stars in the observable Universe. It remains to be seen whether humanity will apply this enormous potential toward preserving and protecting the delicate web of interacting relationships that sustains life on Earth.

Nothing remains the same from one moment to the next, you can't step into the same river twice. Life—evolution—the whole universe of space/time, matter/energy—existence itself—is essentially change.

—Ursula K. Le Guin, *The Lathe of Heaven*

References

Abbott. B. P. et al. (LIGO Scientific Collaboration and Virgo Collaboration-1,013 coauthors). 2016. "Observation of Gravitational Waves from a Binary Black Hole Merger." *Physical Review Letters* 116:061102.

Aguilera-Rodríguez, J. 2013. "To Embody the N-Body: Spatial Perception Utilized in Large-Scale Visualizations." In *Universal Access in Human-Computer Interaction:*

User and Context Diversity, edited by C. Stephanidis and M. Antona, 537–46. Lecture Notes in Computer Science 8010. Berlin: Springer.

Airapetian, V. S., et al. 2016. "Prebiotic Chemistry and Atmospheric Warming of Early Earth by an Active Young Sun." *Nature Geoscience* 9, pp. 452–55.

Anglada-Escudé, G., et al. (+28 coauthors). 2016. "A Terrestrial Planet Candidate in a Temperate Orbit around Proxima Centauri." *Nature* 536/437–40.

Beaumont, C., et al. 2014. "The Milky Way Project: Leveraging Citizen Science and Machine Learning to Detect Interstellar Bubbles." *Astrophysical Journal Supplement* 214.

Darwin, Charles. 1859. *On the Origin of Species by Means of Natural Selection, or the Preservation of Favoured Races in the Struggle for Life*. London: Murray.

Gates, Evalyn. 2009. *Einstein's Telescope: The Hunt for Dark Matter and Dark Energy in the Universe*. New York: Norton.

Hester, J. J., et al. 2004. "The Cradle of the Solar System." *Science* 304/1116–17 .

Hubble, E. 1929. "A Relation between Distance and Radial Velocity among Extra-Galactic Nebulae." *Proceedings of the National Academy of Sciences of the United States of America* 15/3, pp. 168–73.

Kaltenegger, L., et al. 2013. "Water Planets in the Habitable Zone: Atmospheric Chemistry, Observable Features, and the Case of Kepler-62e and Kepler-62f." *Astrophysical Journal Letters* 775/2, pp. L47-L51.

Kant, Immanuel. 1755. *Allgemeine Naturgeschichte und Theorie des Himmels* (Universal Natural History and Theory of the Heavens).

Kerton, C. R., et al. 2015. "The Milky Way Project: What Are Yellowballs?" *Astrophysical Journal* 799, pp. 153–61.

Laplace, Pierre-Simon. 1796. *Exposition du systeme du monde* (*The System of the World*).

Le Guin, Ursula K. 2003. *The Lathe of Heaven*. New York: Perennial Classics.

Lemaître, G., 1931a. "Expansion of the Universe, A Homogeneous Universe of Constant Mass and Increasing Radius Accounting for the Radial Velocity of Extra-Galactic Nebulae." *Monthly Notices of the Royal Astronomical Society* 91, pp. 483–90.

———. 1931b. "Expansion of the Universe, The Expanding Universe." *Monthly Notices of the Royal Astronomical Society* 91, pp. 490–501.

———. 1927. "Un Univers homogène de masse constante et de rayon croissant rendant compte de la vitesse radiale des nébuleuses extra-galactiques." *Annales de la Société Scientifique de Bruxelles* A47, pp. 49–59.

Perlmutter, S., et al. (+32 coauthors). 1999. "Measurements of Ω and Λ from 42 High-Redshift Supernovae." *Astrophysical Journal* 517, pp. 565–86.

Raddick, J., Lintott, C. J., Schawinski, K. et al. (+10 coauthors), 2007, "Galaxy Zoo: An Experiment in Public Science Participation," *Bulletin of the American Astronomical Society* 39.

Riess, A. G., Filippenko, A. V., Challis, P. et al. (+17 coauthors). 1998."Observational Evidence from Supernovae for an Accelerating Universe and a Cosmological Constant." *Astronomical Journal* 116.

Rubin, V. C., and W. K. Ford Jr. 1970. "Rotation of the Andromeda Nebula from a Spectroscopic Survey of Emission Regions." *Astrophysical Journal* 159.

Sandin, D. J., DeFanti, T., Kauffman, L., & Spielmann, Y., 2006. "The Artist and the Scientific Research Environment." *Leonardo* 39, pp. 219-21.

Schwamb, M. E., Orosz, J. A., Carter, J. A., et al. (+17 coauthors), 2013. "Planet Hunters: A Transiting Circumbinary Planet in a Quadruple Star System." *Astrophysical Journal* 768.

Science News. 1930. "A New Planet beyond Neptune." *Science* 71, Issue 1838: x–xiv. doi: 10.1126/science.71.1838.0x/.

Simpson, R. J., Povich, M. S., Kendrew, S., et al. (+9 coauthors), 2012. "The Milky Way Project First Data Release: A Bubblier Galactic Disc." *Monthly Notices of the Royal Astronomical Society* 424.

Vesna, V., and J. K. Gimzewski. 2003. "The Nanoneme Syndrome: Blurring of Fact and Fiction in the Construction of a New Science." *Technoetic Arts: A Journal of Speculative Research* 1:1.

Wheeler, John Archibald, with Kenneth Ford. 1998. *Geons, Black Holes, and Quantum Foam*. New York: Norton.

Wolf-Chase, G., and C. Kerton. 2015. "What Do 'Yellowballs' Have to Do with the Birth of New Stars?" *Frontiers for Young Minds* 3:16 (2015): doi:10.3389/frym.2015.00016.

Zwicky, F. 1933. "Die Rotverschiebung von extragalaktischen Nebeln," *Heletica Physica Acta* 6

Part 2

Interaction in
Biological and Social Sciences

4

Ut Unum Sint

Endosymbiosis as a Major Force in Biological Evolution

Martinez Hewlett

A s fascinating a subject as it might be, this is not a chapter about the biological imperatives pushing us towards ecumenism.[1] Rather, I have usurped the title of Saint John Paul II's encyclical to highlight the unique and seminal endosymbiotic events that have led, over the course of our evolutionary history, to what and who we are.

When we examine the record of the set of contingent processes that represent the trajectory of life on our planet we do so through the powerful lens of the neo-Darwinian model. Certainly the general features of the model, descent with modification from a common ancestor over a geologically significant time frame, are well supported by the data. As only one of many examples, the shared molecular mechanisms by which genetic information is processed in the biosphere is strong evidence for this statement.

An important aspect of this model is the concept of variation and adaptation. The nature of genetic mutations is such that small, often single base, changes in the sequence of the DNA molecule occur essentially at random. These changes can then lead to organismic features on which selective pressures may act over time, leading, in turn, to the greater representation

---

1. The first part of the chapter title, *"Ut Unum Sint,"* is, of course, taken from the name of the encyclical by Saint John Paul II, dealing with ecumenism. The English translation of the phrase is "that they may be one," taken from the Gospel of John (John 17:21).

of said features in the population. That these changes occur at random over deep time has led to the concept that evolution takes place gradually.

Gradualism is defended as the principal, if not the only, mechanism at work in biological evolution, especially by those who espouse an ontologically reductive approach to the science. Indeed, when Gould and Eldredge proposed punctuated equilibrium as an explanation for periods of apparent stasis followed by evidence of rapid change in the fossil record it was met with great skepticism by critics such as Dawkins, argued in some cases with dogmatic fervor.[2]

However, the process of slow, random changes in the genetic sequence of an organism represents only one of several forces that contribute to the evolution of the species. A more dramatic set of events is encompassed by the term symbiogenesis.

My purpose in this chapter is to examine the evidence for symbiogenesis and the serial endosymbiotic theory (SET). I will then discuss the impact that this has had on the Darwinian model. I will finally come to a discussion of the philosophical implications we might draw from this major force in biological evolution.

Symbiosis

Ecosystems are literally communities of organisms living together in various relationships, both independent and dependent. The term "symbiosis," most likely coined in 1879 by Anton de Bary, has been widely interpreted and misinterpreted for much of its history.[3] Current consensus focuses on the intimate, dependent interactions between organisms, termed mutualism, commensalism, and parasitism. Each of these can take place when two organisms interact externally (ectosymbiosis) or when one of the organisms is internal to the other (endosymbiosis).

Mutualism is a relationship where each partner benefits from the interaction. A classic example is the mutualistic interaction between cows and the bacterial species in their rumen that allows the animal to utilize otherwise indigestible cellulose as a source of energy. Commensalism occurs when one partner benefits with no impact on the other, such as the scavenger remoras that feed on the leftover bits from a shark's meal. Parasitism results in the benefit of one partner to the detriment of the other.

---

2. The war of ideas between Stephen Jay Gould and Richard Dawkins was waged both through their own prolific publications but as well in the pages of the *New York Review of Books*.

3. Martin and Schwab, *Current Usage of Symbiosis*.

Parasitic interactions are typical of infectious disease organisms and their human hosts.

The physical relationship between the two partners is critical to the complete definition. For example, while scavenger remoras are an example of ectosymbiotic commensalism, viruses as agents of infectious disease are, in contrast, endosymbiotic parasites.

These interactions have played out over the course of evolutionary history. Of importance for this discussion is the role that endosymbiosis has played to shape the rise of the eukaryotic world, of which we are a part.

The World of Cells

While much of the biosphere is rich with complicated detail, there are some simple axioms that can be stated. One of these is reflected in the division of all living cells into one of two types: prokaryotic and eukaryotic.[4] The division is primarily structural and is based upon the observed intracellular components of the two types.

All cells are surrounded by a limiting lipid bilayer called the plasma membrane. Prokaryotes are cells that contain no internal structures surrounded by such membranes. Specifically, they do not have a defined membrane-enclosed nucleus. Eukaryotes, by contrast, have a prominent, membrane-enclosed nucleus, as well as other internal structures that are surrounded by lipid bilayer membranes.

At the cellular level, we are eukaryotes, as are all animals, plants, fungi, and single-celled creatures such as paramecia and amoeba. Bacteria are prokaryotes: both the eubacteria with which many are familiar, as well as the less well known archaebacteria.[5] The defining microscopic structural features mentioned above as well as numerous molecular details serve to differentiate the two forms of life. Nevertheless, the overarching paradigm of neo-Darwinism is borne out by the commonality of processes by which all cells operate. Descent from a common ancestor is evident in the ways in which we all replicate our DNA, form our proteins, and process our energy.

4. The names derive from Greek. *Prokaryote* from πρόκαρυόν, meaning "pre-kernel" and *eukaryote* from εὔκάρυον, meaning "true kernel."

5. To be more precise, the biological world falls into three domains, two of which are prokaryotic (Archaea and Bacteria) and one which is the eukaryotic (Eukarya). The Eukarya encompasses the three Kingdoms—Fungi, Plantae, and Animalia—along with the single-celled organisms loosely referred to as Protists.

How, then, did this divergence between the two cell types arise? What led to the formation of the structural features that make a eukaryote so distinctly different from a prokaryote?

The fossil record provides us with some intriguing evidence in this regard. It is estimated from the microfossil record that the earliest eukaryotic cells can be found about 1.1 billion years ago.[6] Subsequent to this, both the fossil record as well as phylogenomic analysis argues for a sudden radiation of eukaryotic forms, referred to by some as the "eukaryotic big bang."[7]

The rise of eukaryotes appears to be the result of a unique event in the history of life on our planet. Because of both the suddenness of appearance and rapid proliferation of these cell types it would seem that gradualism in the classical Darwinian sense is not the only force at work here. One solution to this problem has come to be called the serial endosymbiotic theory.

Endosymbiosis

The concept that a symbiotic relationship can exist with one organism dwelling completely inside another has a relatively long history in biology. At the beginning of the twentieth century the Russian biologist Konstantin Mereschowsky proposed the theory of symbiogenesis for the origins of intracellular organelles such as chloroplasts.[8] His theory, although popular with certain European workers, was dismissed and ignored until the 1960s.

By this time, it was recognized, from both microscopic as well as biochemical analyses, that both mitochondria and chloroplasts contained their own DNA. These data were part of what led Lynn Margulis to publish what is now considered the seminal contribution to the start of the new consideration of endosymbiosis as a major force in evolutionary theory.[9]

At the heart of what is now called the serial endosymbiotic theory (SET) is the idea that the rise of eukaryotic cells was the result of some proto-eukaryotic ancestor cell—whose exact identity remains in dispute—engulfing

6. Berney and Pawlowski, *A Molecular Time-Scale.*

7. Koonin, *The Biological Big Bang Model.*

8. He was inspired by his work on lichens, which are symbiotic assemblages of fungi and algae. His work was published in German [Mereschkowsky, (1910). "Theorie der zwei Plasmaarten als Grundlage der Symbiogenesis, einer neuen Lehre von der Entstehung der Organismen." *Biol Centralbl* 30:353–67], with the bold subtitle of "a new study on the origin of organisms."

9. Sagan, "On the Origin of Mitosing Cells." The article was published in the *Journal of Theoretical Biology* and credited to Lynn Sagan, now known as Lynn Margulis. She had been married to astronomer Carl Sagan and was still using this name although their relationship had already ended in 1964.

an oxygen-utilizing cell (most likely an alpha-proteobacter) by a phagocytic mechanism to produce a symbiont. The resulting organism had the ability to exploit ecological niches that were not available to either of the two alone. The sudden rapid (in geological terms) appearance of eukaryotic forms throughout the microfossil record is explained by this event.

Two features of the eukaryotic cell are supported by SET. First, organelles such as the mitochondrion and the chloroplast have their own genetic information in the form of small, circular DNA molecules that have a great deal in common with their proposed bacterial ancestors. Second, these organelles have a double membrane system: an inner membrane that would have enclosed the engulfed cell, and an outer membrane that would have been acquired during the process of phagocytic inclusion.

Not all properties of eukaryotes are easily subsumed by SET. For instance, the extensive endomembrane system of the cells does not appear to be the result of a phagocytic event. In fact, the topology of this system is such that the interior of the endomembrane, such as the endoplasmic reticulum and the Golgi, is contiguous with the exterior of the cell. In an unpublished model, Christopher Langton and I have explained this using parallel endosymbiosis (PET), in which a collaborative colony of cells eventually fuses into a single organism.[10] In this model the space that was exterior to each of the collaborating cells defines the interior of the matrix that becomes the endomembrane system.

Whether the event in question is serial, with one cell engulfing another, or parallel, with the fusion of cooperative cells, it is clear that the data support the models of endosymbiosis as a major force to be incorporated into the Darwinian view of how cellular structures came to be. How, then, can this be incorporated into the current paradigm and included along with gradualism as an explanatory device?

The Impact of Endosymbiosis on Philosophy of Biology

The merger of the Darwinian model, Mendelian genetics, and the understanding of the nature of mutational change into what was called "the modern synthesis" helped to set in place the overarching paradigm by which modern biology continues to operate.[11] The hallmark of gradualism . . . small,

10. Christopher Langton and Martinez Hewlett, unpublished manuscript.

11. Julian Huxley, grandson of Thomas Huxley, the nineteenth-century champion of Charles Darwin, coined this phrase as the title of his 1942 book, *Evolution, The Modern Synthesis*.

mutational changes . . . has become embodied as the principal and, in the estimation of some, the only source of evolutionary innovation.[12]

If selection is based upon variation of characteristics in the individual organism, and if those variations are due to gradual mutational changes, then philosophically gradualism makes perfect sense. This position is also consistent with ontological reductionism or materialism.[13] As a result of this alignment between method and interpretation the reductive approach had become enshrined within the enterprise of twentieth-century biology.

The impact of the Human Genome Project on biology has been tremendous. Not the least of the outcomes has been a sea change in the philosophical perspective through which living systems are viewed. Trying to interpret the immense data sets provided by complete expression-tagged sequencing of genomes using the linear, reductionist tools available proved to be impossible. Instead it required the conceptual framework of systems biology to effectively model the properties of cells, organisms, and ecosystems.

One of the basic methodological tools of systems biology is to construct a network of interactions between all possible encoded products of a particular genome.[14] Such networks are called "scale-free" or "small-world," and have very interesting features.[15] For instance, scale-free networks display emergent properties.

12. See, for example, Richard Dawkins's classic work, *The Selfish Gene*.

13. The molecular sciences in biology (e.g., biochemistry and molecular biology) employ methodological reductionism as an experimental approach. This is not a philosophical position, but rather a practical decision regarding how the molecules that compose living systems can be investigated. If one concludes that the only valid knowledge is obtained by this method (epistemological reductionism) or that the true nature of reality is understood as the sum of the material components that make up everything (ontological reductionism), then one is taking particular philosophical positions.

14. This seemingly daunting task is made possible by both molecular biology as well as engineering. An example is the field of interactomics. The molecular tools involve techniques such as the yeast two-hybrid system, which allows an experimenter access to information about the possible interactions between two proteins. This is coupled with high throughput analysis in which microarrays of such interactions are automatically quantified and the data sets used to generate network maps of protein-protein interactions.

15. A scale-free network is one that has nodes which are highly connected compared to other nodes. Random networks do not have this property. The term "small-world" applied to such networks stems from the work of Stanley Milgram in which he tracked the chains of human acquaintances [Milgram, Stanley (May 1967). "The Small World Problem." *Psychology Today*]. He showed that any one person is linked by approximately six steps to any other person, the so-called six degrees of separation. Although the original work used regular mail and involved two cities in the United States, the experiment was repeated by Duncan Watts and Steven Strogatz, using multiple

Bypassing for now the concepts of weak versus strong emergentism, we can define emergent properties as features of a system that are more than the sum of the individual parts.[16] The term *holistic* is often applied to such features, defined as a philosophical term, and not necessarily synonymous with the way the word is used in other contexts.

To the committed reductionist, the emergent properties of a network are simply epiphenomena that can be explained completely by the properties of the component parts. However, this idea does not stand up to either experimental or philosophical examination. For instance, the property of "wetness" of water cannot be explained by the chemistry of the water molecule itself, but only with reference to a system of interacting water molecules. Similarly, a philosophically satisfying case for the observed features of the living world cannot be made using just a basic understanding of the chemistry of the components from which life is formed.

Endosymbiosis and the Darwinian Model

At the heart of Darwin's bold theory is the concept of descent with modification driven by the force of natural selection. To be clear, Darwin had no real idea how this might operate, given that he had no understanding of inheritance or the nature of what came to be called the gene. Indeed, with the then prevailing model that traits were "blended" from one generation to the next, an important scientific critic of "Origin of Species" argued that the idea could not work, since any advantageous adaptations would be lost when the parental traits were merged in the offspring.[17]

With the advent of the neo-Darwinian paradigm the mechanistic details were made much more specific. Variation is the result of mutational changes, often single base events in the genetic code. Selective pressure takes place as the result of these changes as they are expressed at the organismal level. These events take place over geological time and therefore the

countries and e-mail to get the same result [Watts and Storgatz. 2003. "An Experimental Study of Search in Global Social Networks." *Science* 301/5634, pp. 827–29.]

16. Weak emergence argues that the observed features of the system are the result of interactions of the individual parts, even though the features cannot be predicted a priori. Strong emergence, on the other hand, argues that the features are not only greater than the sum of the parts but also exert a downward causality on the system.

17. Fleeming Jenkin (1833–1885) was a professor of engineering at the University of Edinburgh. He published a review of *Origin of Species* in the *North British Review*, (1867) 277–318.

pace of evolutionary change is gradual, leading to the arguments put forth by Richard Dawkins and Daniel Dennett.[18]

The first modern challenge of any sort to gradualism was punctuated equilibrium, the model put forward by Niles Eldredge and Stephen Jay Gould.[19] At its heart, the model attempts to account for observations of sudden gaps in the fossil record. Their interpretation was that evolution progressed through periods of relative stasis, followed by comparatively rapid speciation. "Rapid" in this sense must be understood in geological time frames and is not to be confused with saltations (see below). The changes themselves take place by small, incremental adaptations. Rather than being an actual challenge, punctuated equilibrium is really just another form of gradualism.

Endosymbiosis presents a very different problem for the standard model. The change represented by the serial endosymbiotic acquisition of an entire cell is in no way a small, gradual shift in the genetic code of the organism. Rather the resulting hybrid cell has features encoded by two different genomes. What are the neo-Darwinian selection criteria for this entity?

Clearly, the standard model of the evolutionary trajectory of a single organism is described by the gradual accumulation of small mutational changes in the genome (microevolution) leading over long periods of time to sufficient genetic differences to warrant speciation (macroevolution). But what about the "sudden" acquisition of an entirely new, genetically defined entity?

Natural selection, the causal force of the neo-Darwinian model, operates by providing a filter through which variations that have increased reproductive survival potential pass. In the gradualist view, each small mutational change is preserved in subsequent generations due to its ability to allow passage through this filter. A gene-centric view of this process argues that it is the replication potential of the DNA that dictates the adaptive advantage of the cell that contains the alteration. Thus, the "selfish gene" replicator model of Dawkins.

Imagine now a cell that has resulted from the endosymbiotic merger of two cells, with their distinct and already evolving genomes. Upon what aspect of this cell would natural selection act so that its reproductive advantage would be passed on to subsequent generations? The gradualist and gene-centric approach does not provide a satisfying explanatory answer.

18. Dawkins's *The Selfish Gene* makes this case specifically. Dennett assumes the gradualist position in his arguments in *Darwin's Dangerous Idea*.

19. Eldredge and Gould, "Punctuated Equilibria," 82–115.

For instance, endosymbiosis is functionally equivalent to lateral or horizontal gene transfer (HGT) by which, in this case, an entire genome is acquired by another cell. HGT in all of its forms presents problems for the gradualist model in that the evolutionary history of the new genome is now merged with that of the host cell. What does this actually mean at the gene level for the causal force of natural selection?

Perhaps a better approach has been suggested by Maureen O'Malley (2015) who posits that rather than trying to let the gene-centric approach explain the observation of endosymbiosis, it might be more fruitful to see if endosymbiosis can indeed provide some new insights into the processes of evolution itself. To this end, she suggests that we consider the actual metabolic properties of the newly formed cell as the feature upon which the causal force can act. For the endosymbiont that would be considered the last eukaryotic common ancestor (LECA), we should think about the acquisition of what would become that cell energy generation system . . . the mitochondrion.

The membrane-based production of ATP that is a common feature of all eukaryotes was the ultimate result of the serial endosymbiotic capture of an proteobacter by the cell that would become the LECA. The network of metabolic reactions of the now merged cell would be altered dramatically by this event.

Metabolic pathways in all cells exist in a network of interactions that are characterized as scale-free rather than random.[20] Such networks have interesting properties that make them more robust than random networks. These properties are said to be emergent, that is, not derivable from the sum of the parts making up the network. The idea that emergent properties have real meaning is something that was not considered in the reductionist paradigm that characterized biology during much of the previous century.[21] Scale-free networks make up much of the living world, from the sub-cellular to the ecosystem levels. This view of biology is characterized as holistic rather than reductionistic.

In fact, it has been suggested that, in the case of the LECA, natural selection might operate at the level of this emergent property of energy metabolism, rather than at the level of genetic variations in either of the

20. A random interaction network has nodes that are equally likely to be connected to any other node. This generates a Gaussian or normal distribution of nodal connections. A scale-free network, however, has a small number of nodes that have a high probability of being connected to other nodes. This generates instead a power law distribution of nodal connections. For a good general understanding of network theory, see Watts, *Six Degrees*.

21. See my discussion of the history of this: Hewlett, "True to Life?," 158–72.

two genomes of the symbionts.[22] That is to say, the holistic property of LECA that allowed it to have a selective advantage in its environment would have been its ability to generate energy using the combined metabolic reactions of the two merged cells.

Philosophical and Theological Implications

Whether it is called "naturalism" or "physicalism" or "materialism," the philosophical stance of biology throughout much of the latter half of the twentieth century was clearly what is termed ontological reductionism. This is the position that all of reality consists of the material pieces of which it is made, and nothing more.[23] This view is coupled with scientism, a belief in the ultimate ability of the scientific enterprise to successfully explain everything in these precise materialistic terms.

For the reductionist biologist, the crowning achievement was the Human Genome Project and the mapping of all of the genes that define us as human beings.[24] To expedite the work it was decided to identify those regions of the genome containing the information for protein products, leaving the rest alone for the time being.[25] These expressed sequences, it was reasoned, would constitute the information required to specify the human person. The guess was that the sequencing data would reveal about 100,000 human genes. When all was said and done there are only on the order of 20,000 human genes. Even worse news for the reductionist viewpoint, this is about the same number as the fruit fly or the round worm. On top of this, the dizzying size of the database proved to be daunting to any kind of analytical approach . . . that is, until the entry of network science which utterly changed and challenged the field of genomics.

22. O'Malley, "Endosymbiosis and Its Implications for Evolutionary Theory."

23. Carl Sagan famously began his Cosmos television series with the statement, "The Cosmos is all that is or was or ever will be." Richard Dawkins, in his book *The Selfish Gene*, takes this one step further, writing, "The universe we observe has precisely the properties we should expect if there is, at bottom, no design, no purpose, no evil, no good, nothing but blind, pitiless indifference."

24. Walter Gilbert, one of the developers of the methodology that led to sequencing the human genome, wrote, "The information carried on the DNA, that genetic information passed down from our parents, is the most fundamental property of the body, so much so, in fact, that one will be able to pull a CD out of one's pocket and say, 'Here is a human being; it's me!'" See Gilbert, "A Vision of the Grail."

25. Expressed (specifically transcribed) sequences are at most 10 percent of the human genome. The rest of the sequences represent noncoding DNA, sometimes called junk DNA.

This presents a serious threat to the philosophical position of reductionism. Given that the message of the human genome was to be "we now know everything about what it means to be human," the lack of a clear superiority in the number of genes must mean that there is something more. And, of course, the finding that all of these human genes operate in a vast, scale-free network does, in fact, provide a solution to this dilemma. It's just that the solution means a 180-degree reversal of viewpoint. We are not simply the sum of our parts. Rather, we have emergent properties that make us so much more than the sum of our parts.

Emergent properties exhibit downward causation. Reductionism allows only for bottom-up causation, since everything at a higher level is completely explained by the properties of the lower level components of the system. For living systems, this is a particularly important aspect of the scale-free system nature. Tabaczek[26] highlights this with specific reference to symbiotic relationships:

> As an example we may think of symbiosis in biological systems. As an emergent phenomenon it is not merely based on the properties of two different organisms. Its nature changes microstructure and physiology of each one of them, oftentimes making their existence possible in an environment which otherwise will be unfavorable."

Emergent properties can be either weak or strong. Weak emergence is the case when the property of the higher level arises unexpectedly from the lower level but is, in fact, predictable from the properties of the lower level, even if techniques to effect this prediction are not presently available. On the other hand, strong emergence is the case when the property of the higher level is, in principle, not deducible from the properties of the lower level. Chalmers[27] defines these terms and makes the case that, in his opinion, the only real example of strong emergence is the phenomenon of consciousness. He further argues that strong emergence has radical consequences, since it invalidates the reductionist materialist argument concerning the nature of reality.

I will not argue whether the scale-free system properties of the LECA represent weak or strong emergence. Rather, I contend that even if it is considered to be the weak version of emergence, it would still demand that the philosophy of biology turn at least to a version of nonreductive physicalism.[28] Further, that position would only hold until the full scope

26. Tabaczek, *The Metaphysics of Downward Causation.*

27. Chalmers, *The Character of Consciousness*, 105.

28. This philosophical position has been championed by Nancey Murphy; see

of human biology, including the mind/body problem, is considered. At that point, as per Chalmers, only strong emergence can provide a robust explanatory framework.

One way of encountering the philosophical implications of emergence is to recover the long-ignored Aristotelian concept of causes. With the advent of the modern scientific enterprise, the original four causes (material, formal, efficient, and final) had been pared down to only two: material and efficient.[29] Emergence, especially in the strong version, could be described as the formal cause of the thing. That is, that set of properties which makes the thing (the eukaryotic cell, for instance) to be the thing it is.

It is for this reason that Tabaczek[30] argues for Aristotelian formal cause being used to describe downward causation as a way of understanding how emergent properties bring about the nature of a complex system such as the living cell. The more difficult case, however, is human consciousness. The very nature of our internal, subjective experience, Chalmers argues, is insubstantial. The "hard problem" of consciousness is really only solvable by accepting the nonphysical nature of experience.[31]

Of course, this is not a simple solution. The causal joint between the laws of physics that govern the behavior of human cells and the immaterial nature of subjective experience has not been established. How can the downward causation of conscious thought as an emergent property affect the physical nervous system that acts in response to that thought? Nonetheless, if the philosophy of biology that engages this discussion now allows for a holistic rather than reductionistic explanatory model, we can entertain hope that there may somehow be a fruitful answer to this question.

Where might this lead? The subjective inner experience of consciousness is exactly the place that constitutes the world of the mystics in all of the spiritual traditions. It is the creative space of artists and poets. It is the locus of the prayer lives of the faithful seeking some connection with the ineffable. And it is the basis for the theologian wishing to follow the path laid out by Saint Anselm . . . faith-seeking understanding.

Murphy, ""Nonreductive Physicalism," in Brown et al., *Whatever Happened to the Soul?*, 127–48.

29. Francis Bacon rejected the notion of the four Aristotelian causes. As a result, for modern science, the Aristotelian material cause that described both the potential of something coming to be as well as the material out of which it is made became only the physical matter of the thing. The efficient cause, according to both Bacon and David Hume, could only be considered as a temporal relationship between two events.

30. Tabaczek, *The Metaphysics of Downward Causation.*

31. Chalmers, *The Character of Consciousness.*

References

Berney, Cédric, and Pawlowski, Jan. 2006. "A Molecular Time-Scale for Eukaryote Evolution Recalibrated with the Continuous Microfossil Record." *Proceedings of the Royal Society B*, 273, pp. 1867–72.

Brown, W. S., et al., eds. 1998. *Whatever Happened to the Soul? Scientific and Theological Portraits of Human Nature*. Theology and the Sciences. Minneapolis: Fortress.

Chalmers, David. 2010. *The Character of Consciousness*. Philosophy of Mind Series. New York: Oxford University Press.

————. 2006. "Strong and Weak Emergence." In *The Re-emergence of Emergence: The Emergentist Hypothesis from Science to Religion*, edited by Philip Clayton and Paul Davies, 244–56. Oxford: Oxford University Press.

Dawkins, Richard. *The Selfish Gene: 40th Anniversary Edition*. New York: Oxford University Press, 2016.

Dennett, D. C. *Darwin's Dangerous Idea: Evolution and the Meanings of Life*. New York: Simon & Schuster, 1995.

Eldredge, N., and S. J. Gould. 1972. "Punctuated Equilibria: An Alternative to Phyletic Gradualism." In *Models in Paleobiology*, edited by T. J. M. Schopf, 82–115. San Francisco: Freeman Cooper.

Gilbert, Walter. 1992. "A Vision of the Grail." In *The Code of Codes: Scientific and Social Issues in the Human Genome Project*, edited by Daniel J. Kevles and Leroy Hood, 83–97. Cambridge: Harvard University Press

Hewlett, Martinez. "True to Life? Biological Models of Origin and Evolution." In *Evolution and Emergence: Systems, Organisms, Persons*, edited by Nancey Murphy and William R. Stoeger, 158–72. Oxford: Oxford University Press, 2007.

Huxley, Julian. *Evolution: The Modern Synthesis*. London: Allen & Unwin, 1942.

Jenkin, Fleeming, 1867. Review of *The Origin of Species*, in *The North British Review*, June, 46, pp. 277–318.

Koonin, Eugene. 2007. "The Biological Big Bang Model for the Major Transitions in Evolution." *Biology Direct* 2, 21.

Martin, Bradford D., and Ernest Schwab. 2011. "Current Usage of Symbiosis and Associated Terminology." *International Journal of Biology* 5/1, pp. 32–45.

Mereschkowsky, C. 1910. "Theorie der zwei Plasmaarten als Grundlage der Symbiogenesis, einer neuen Lehre von der Ent-stehung der Organismen." *Biologisches Centralblatt* 30/353–67.

Murphy, Nancey, and William Stoeger. 2007. *Evolution and Emergence: Systems, Organisms, Persons*. Oxford University Press.

O'Malley, Maureen. 2015. "Endosymbiosis and Its Implications for Evolutionary Theory." *Proceedings of the National Academy of Sciences, USA*, 112, pp. 10270–77.

Sagan, Lynn. 1967. "On the Origin of Mitosing Cells." *Journal of Theoretical Biology* 14/3, pp. 225–74.

Tabaczek, Mariusz, 2013. "The Metaphysics of Downward Causation: Rediscovering the Formal Cause." *Zygon* 48, pp. 380–404.

Watts, Duncan. 2003. *Six Degrees: The Science of a Connected Age*. New York: Norton.

5

Honoring the Earth, Honoring God

Paul G. Heltne

THE EARTH HAS BEEN around for 4.6 billion years. Mammals appeared around 250 million years ago; human ancestors first developed only about two million years ago. Modern humans appeared only about 200 thousand years ago during the third of the four most recent Ice Ages. In other words humans have existed in the slightest sliver of time of Earth's existence. About 150 years ago my ancestors from Norway made their way to Iowa and settled in the northern tier of counties, on land that had rich deep soil, left behind as the last glaciers melted. I worked that soil with my father and grandfather and eventually was able to engage with other ecosystems in southern Africa, and Central and South America. Those experiences revealed how tenuous the soil ecosystem can be in many places in the world, and they deepened my love for the bounty of Iowa farmland.

I engage in this manner because I think personal experiences can help us learn to walk softly on the Earth, and honor this astonishing ecosystem in which we now live. Aldo Leopold condensed the idea of caring for the Earth in his dictum, "A thing is right when it tends to preserve the integrity, stability, and beauty of the biotic community. It is wrong when it tends otherwise."[1] Many of our modern practices are, indeed, less than wise and, given our enormous population of *Homo sapiens*, we are often destructive and dangerous.

Leopold was committed to maintaining biotic communities rich in species because the near-term and long-term well-being of a community depends on a complex set of interactions that are the foundation of ecological well-being. Put another way, we may treasure a beautiful stand of trees

1. Leopold, *A Sand County Almanac*, 189.

which by their age and height evoke our thoughts of human and planetary history. But the larger astonishment comes when we recognize that the trees made themselves from carbon dioxide in the air and large amounts of water they drew from the soil. When we investigate the story of our trees below ground, it becomes even more amazing because a tree depends on millions of filamentous hairs on the tree's roots to draw in the water needed for photosynthesis. This is the way that photosynthesis works in all green terrestrial plants. Enormous amounts of energy from sunlight drive this fundamental process of energy capture and nutrient synthesis.

Photosynthesis is a process in green plants that provides the energy for the giant sequoia trees, and eventually for all living organisms, including microscopic bacteria. We revere the trees and other beautiful creatures, but we should also know enough about bacteria to revere their activities, as well. For these small creatures set the stage for the rest of life and continue to do so, providing essential elements to all creatures. They are unseen but their numbers are staggering. James B. Nardi is a biologist at the University of Illinois and the Illinois Natural History Survey. He estimates that in a square meter of soil extending down from the Earth's surface, there are 10,000,000,000,000 (ten million million) bacteria and actinomycetes, ten billion protozoa (single-cell creatures with nuclei), and five million nematodes (tiny worm-like creatures) plus 100,000 mites, 50,000 springtails, 10,000 rotifers and tardigrades, 5,000 insects and spiders, 3,000 earthworms and potworms, 100 snails and slugs and 1 vertebrate.[2] His research shows that these microscopic creatures alone "easily outnumber, and often outweigh, all the other categories of larger soil creatures" summed together. We must honor these invisible creatures as they prepared the Earth for our larger kinds of life and continue to do so, though, indeed, some of them can become harmful when out of balance.

Thus, we recognize that soil is a community of these species and many more. It is a home for living beings which act individually, jointly as a species, or together with other species, as a community. The interactions are the work of the bacteria, fungi, blue-green algae and some actinomycetes. Actinomycetes have the ability to convert nitrogen gas (which most creatures cannot use as an element directly) into ammonia or nitrates which other species use directly or by consuming the converter species.

Algae and fungi can engage in partnerships which we know as the lichens. The algal partner synthesizes sugar using the energy of sunlight, CO_2, and water. The fungal partner provides water and the elements which

2. Nardi, *Life in the Soil*, 27.

it slowly breaks down from the rocks on which the fungi may already have lived for hundreds or thousands of years.

Mosses also photosynthesize sugars and have a long history of providing shelter and food for waves of bacteria, fungi, tardigrades, and other tiny organisms. These creatures form a community that replaces itself barring major catastrophes (glaciation, sea level rise, destructive farming including erosion, pesticides and herbicides, drainage, and loss of natural creatures).

These ancient/modern creatures may spend their entire lives underground in the conditions left behind by the last glaciation ten thousand years ago. When the ice withdrew, the soil has maintained a constant temperature of about 65 degrees Fahrenheit through most of its depth, a water vapor pressure very close to saturated atmosphere, and a multitude of interactions between the animate and inanimate world. Given these conditions, the soil community and its dependent organisms fare very well in the absence of catastrophe. Even in stressful times, many of the species may go into stasis and become active again when the soil conditions support resumption of activity.

The normal life of a soil community includes significant above-ground partnerships. Above-ground creatures move soil around, eat fruits, leaves, and other creatures, defecate, disperse seeds, reproduce themselves, and die and decay or are eaten. Some of the above-ground creatures defend favored plants from other creatures, so, for instance, ants and bees and butterflies enjoy the nectar of flowers and decaying fruit, and the first two can fend off other browsers. In any case, plant materials and animal feces are quite rapidly pulled into burrows by earthworms and other smaller creatures of the soil, the particles now being small enough for them to consume. In a healthy soil community one often sees well-worked materials pushed up onto lawns or gardens by earthworms.

Earthworms are particularly impressive members of the soil ecosystem. They create passageways in the soil which provide for aeration and movement of creatures, water and food. Earthworms consume plant materials such as fallen leaves which they have dragged into their burrows; they leave fecal material behind which becomes food for other soil creatures including micro-organisms, and at the same time create fertilizer for plants, closing wondrous loops of shared or recycled resources.

Every plant in the soil community is an active participant. Those that photosynthesize make their own sugar in their own leaves, supplying all of the new metabolic energy for other parts of the ecosystem. This photosynthetic sugar provides the energy for most of the rest of the living world that cannot photosynthesize. And when the plant or part of a plant dies, that material is quickly picked up by earthworms and insects and other creatures of the soil that mostly drag the material back into the soil where it is consumed or stored for later consumption. Some of these materials have been buried deeply by glacial debris or mud accumulated at the bottom of lakes or oceans, and they eventually may give rise to coal, oil, or natural gas. There are also unusual creatures such as those microbes found living in steaming hot springs, which may be the descendants of the earliest creatures of all.

The creatures of healthy soil work and rework every last bit of food, which is consumed, transmitted into other creatures, or stored in humus. Humus is the residue of the metabolism of above ground energy capture and the cycles of digestion above-ground and within the soil. Humus is highly effective at holding the critical minerals and water close to the root hairs of the above-ground plants. It is this recycling and reuse that keeps the ever scarce minerals in the soil community rather than being flushed downstream.

So, when we see a redwood, or an elm, or a rose or a potato or an earthworm, it is important to remember at the same time that the whole soil community, and its interactions, are of fundamental importance to our human existence. We honor the soil ecosystem by being mindful that we are a part of it and utterly dependent upon it for food, for oxygen, and for ecological stability and adjustments.

Since there are now so many people on our planet and so many activities oriented to support human life and activities, it is imperative that we understand and, more specifically, honor the larger ecological system. We humans are completely dependent on the ecosystem but tend to disrupt the only home we have as well as significant parts of the rest of the ecosystem. A little investigation reveals that, though the astonishing soil ecological system is wide-spread over the land of the globe, but the soil community engages in fine adjustments to local conditions. Nevertheless it is susceptible to disruption, degradation, and total destruction. However, by understanding the communal aspect of our biosphere, as experienced in our daily living (and in exotic places), we can preserve this wondrous support system. Our main adversaries are ignorance and greed. Given our vast human population, it is urgent to recognize that we can be important protectors of our ecosystem, even though we humans are currently the most disastrous destroyers of species and communities on the globe. Rather let us repeatedly educate ourselves in new ways to honor the well-being of soil and all its constituents.

In 2015 the United Nations observed the International Year of Soils, the first event of its kind.[3] The stark background to the event is that at least 33 percent of the soils around the world are in "a state of degradation,"

3. Wall and Six, "Give Soils Their Due," 695.

according to the Food and Agricultural Organization. The UN organization also acknowledged that there is "increasing pressure" on soils as well as the ripple effects of that pressure which reach into every corner of our planet. The celebration of the International Year of Soils seeks to make sure that everyone knows that as the human population grows, the soil on which animals and plants depend is degrading or in danger of being lost entirely.

The Fragility of the Soil Ecosystem

Soils are not static, they can build or rebuild, but only at the pace of less than an inch of soil every thousand years, or less than a foot every thousand years.[4] But if soil husbandry is not carefully practiced, that foot of soil may be carried away in a heavy rainstorm if there are no plant roots anchoring the soil or plant material covering the soil. Some farming traditions protect the soil, but some modern practices are destructive, and seem to have forgotten the nature of the soil ecosystem. The result: Soil doesn't fail us. Rather, our civilizations have failed because we assumed that the soils would always be there no matter what stresses or demands we made of this foundational wealth. We continue to see ourselves as owners rather than humble, thoughtful caretakers.

What is it that we are caretakers of? The soil ecosystem, as we have glimpsed it, is extraordinarily complex. Fortunately it takes care of itself, absent catastrophe, and provided we do not excessively stress that system. The composter or compost pile is home to a variety of insects and bacteria which slowly break down the vegetative refuse, such as lawn clippings and table scraps (provided there are no pesticides or herbicides or huge amounts of scraps). But given the enormous pressure we put on our ecosystem in our times we need to look further.

We know that humans have put excessive pressure on the soil for thousands of years. The Old Testament is full of references to times of plenty and times of famine. I believe that a close reading of the Bible suggests that God's chosen people and their neighbors were not particularly good stewards of the land. Of course, natural climate cycles were little understood, in part because people did not live long enough to detect changes extending beyond several decades. Climate variation was seen as the work of deities who seemed to be dispensers of punishments. But people knew that soil was central to well-being, even if they did not understand how to care for it.

4. Nardi, *Life in the Soil*, 3.

Laments over soil and land come down through the ages providing warning and counsel to our own time. For example, in the fourth century BCE, Plato grieved the loss of soil in his work *Critias*:

> What now remains of the formerly rich land is like a skeleton of a sick man, where all the fat and soft earth have wasted away and only the bare framework remaining. Formerly, many of the mountains were arable. The plains that were full of rich soil are now marshes. Hills that were covered with forests and that produced abundant pasture now produce only food for bees. Once the land was enriched by yearly rains which were not lost, as they are now, by flowing from the bare land into the sea. The soil was deep, it absorbed and kept the water in the loamy soil, and the water that soaked into the hills fed springs and running streams everywhere.[5]

The "fat and soft earth" is what we now call humus.

I have come to think that "soil," as a name, does not do justice to the extraordinary complexity of the soil ecosystem. Often, when we hear the word *ecosystem,* we may think of pristine, nearly inaccessible places, not where we grow our carrots. And we don't think about why carrots can actually grow in that place. Likewise, we think of pristine places like national parks, or places where we don't see any other people around, but hope to see a coyote or a bald eagle or some now rare plant in flower. The facts of our soil ecosystem are really more interesting. There might be wild animals and rare plants and a soil of increasing fertility. But, as suggested above, this can also occur in back yards and fields of corn with the appropriate care, such as crop rotation. Important, also, is the ability to provide food for those far from a field or garden. Gardening and farming require us to learn about particular places, to renew and sustain those places, and thus provide fresh food during the whole growing season and healthful food year around.

In the 1950s the era of the big tractors and big machines took over. Farms and fields grew larger and the number of farmers diminished. Huge swaths of land could be covered in one pass across a field. Legumes and manure, which traditionally enriched soil, were replaced with chemical fertilizers. With all the nitrogen put into the fields, crop rotation was largely abandoned, especially on large acreages. The soil flora and fauna were starved; humus was lost, and the soil became an inanimate mulch to anchor the roots of whatever was planted. Tillage was kept to a minimum because the big tractors could pull the seeding machinery through the soil without further loosening the ground. The production of food became a mechanized

---

5. Plato, *Critias*, 1296–97.

operation on the soil. As a result, the original soil community has been deeply challenged and nearly destroyed. Today, in many places the soil is gray, not black. Plato would have recognized the devastation.

Why, in our day and age, have we allowed such a devastating loss of soil and soil fertility? I believe we have become committed to a sort of arithmetic decisiveness in husbandry which does not allow us to honor complexity and its uncertainties. That commitment has blinded us to the need to understand and honor the more profound complexities of the natural world. This would include the complexity of the soil communities and the ecosystem at large; the partially predictable dynamics of weather and climate; and the activities of our brains. The solution is in understanding and honoring the complexity of natural systems. It is the whole system of the soil which must be nurtured and, thus, preserved and built up. Soil health is lost when whole portions of the soil's complex web of interactions is diminished or destroyed. We are blessed with pathfinders like Nardi. His book *Life in the Soil: A Guide for Naturalists and Gardeners*[6] is accessible to the novice gardener and a joy to all who love and care for the soil. Likewise, we may learn from the research of the Land Institute founded by Wes Jackson. At the Land Institute in Kansas, the researchers have bred corn back into the perennial plant it once was, with deep roots going down as far as twenty feet, not the six-inch roots of the annual corn varieties. Perennial agriculture means less tractor fuel use, less artificial inputs, and less soil erosion, and actual building of the soil. Jackson has discussed this approach to agriculture in his book *Consulting the Genius of the Place.*[7]

In conclusion, our current soil husbandry has led us to toy with the boundaries of catastrophic failure. We need to be reminded how slight changes in global climates have ended or displaced whole empires because soil systems that were already damaged were confronted with other ecological changes which were beyond the response systems available to the people of that time and place.

In a healthy soil ecosystem—a grassland, wetland, or forest—the interactions are so constant and complicated that it would take a very large computer to model the interactions of a part of even a small field. Nevertheless, the natural dynamics of a local part of an ecosystem are going on in ways that produce humus, aerate and hydrate the ecosystem, convert water and carbon dioxide into sugars, produce oxygen and purify water. We might model a soil system but we would not be able to create a soil system without the engagement of many other species. We might promote

6. Nardi, *Life in the Soil.*
7. Jackson, *Consulting the Genius of the Place.*

a specific outcome but could not command its success without drastic (and destructive) oversimplification.

The soil ecosystem reaches from bacteria to redwoods, to the clouds above and to the slowly decomposing rocks deep in the soil. The system has a phenomenal pattern of renewal if all the parts remain in the mix and are not exposed to harsh or thoughtless use. But, as a starting point, all soils need to be protected by a ground cover, because this retains moisture and reduces wind velocity. We also know that soils need to be loose—not compacted—and this work is done by the organisms that live in the soil, not by heavy machinery travel over it. As the various soil creatures move about, feeding on materials or other creatures in the soil, they mix and churn the particles, provide pathways for water, and maintain the diversity of creatures so that all the necessary work of the soil ecosystem is nurtured, and all its organisms remain in balance. But, by and large, whether the soils support large empires or small tribes we tend to take the soil ecosystem too much for granted and care for it poorly. Honoring and promoting the natural complexity of the soil ecosystem may be our highest calling. Let us behave in ways that keep our fields and forests and wetlands teeming with a grand diversity of life.

References

Jackson, Wes. 2010. *Consulting the Genius of the Place: An Ecological Approach to a New Agriculture.* Berkeley: Counterpoint.

Leopold, Aldo. 1949 *A Sand County Almanac, and Sketches Here and There.* New York: Oxford University Press.

Nardi, James. 2007. *Life in the Soil: A Guide for Naturalists and Gardeners.* Chicago: University of Chicago Press.

Plato. *Critias.* In *Complete Works,* edited by John M. Cooper, 1292–306. Indianapolis: Hackett.

Wall, Donna H., and Johan Six. 2015, "Give Soils Their Due." *Science,* 13 February, vol. 347/6223, p. 695.

6

Ecological Interconnections and Interactions

A Tamarin's Architectural Tour of a Brazilian Rainforest

SANDRA A. HAM

SOUTH AMERICAN TROPICAL RAINFORESTS are to the ecologist a chapter out of the history of a primeval time. In Brazil, the forests with their great diversity of flora and fauna date to the last Ice Age, the Pleistocene.[1] The system of organic and inorganic interactions by which all influence and control each other has remained substantially unchanged from a remote geological epoch.

The animals of such lush environments are, as a whole, closely related among themselves and richly interconnected with the plants and the warm, humid climate. The trees make the place home for the inhabitants. Towering to the sky yet blocking the hot sun, the ancient wood creates communities of older, lower levels of life in the midst of the higher, more recent life nesting in its multi-storied structure. The forest forms a little world within itself, a microcosm containing all the elemental forces at work.

Nowhere can one see more clearly an illustration of what Stephen A. Forbes, a nineteenth-century pioneer in the field of ecology, called the "*sensibility* of such an organic complex."[2] Forbes believed that the most basic tenet of the natural order was that whatever affects any species belonging to the ecosystem, also necessarily influences the entire assemblage of

1. Bush and de Oliveira, "The Rise and Fall of the Refugial Hypothesis," 8; Carnaval and Moritz, "Historical Climate Modelling," 1187–201.

2. Forbes, "The Lake as a Microcosm," 256.

inhabitants in some way. The astute observer of nature would realize the impossibility of studying any species adequately in isolation from the other species and physical environment; one must take "a comprehensive survey of the whole as a condition to a satisfactory understanding of any part." If one wishes to become acquainted with a rainforest primate, such as the squirrel-sized, golden-haired lion tamarin of the coastal lowland rainforest in eastern Brazil, for example, our key species of this chapter, one will learn little by a study limited to that species.[3] Golden-haired lion tamarins are small monkeys with bodies covered with short, black fur and long, thin, black and gold tails.[4] Their most distinctive feature is a lion-like mane of bright golden fur encompassing a little black, hairless face like a fiery nimbus surrounding the head of a South American monkey-god. They run on all fours and are adept at climbing and leaping through the rainforest, usually forty to ninety feet above the forest floor. Tamarins are diurnal creatures, active in travel, foraging, play, and socializing from early morning through afternoon before retiring to nooks in trees where they sleep. Typically, tamarins live in social groups of around five adults and juveniles who travel together through the rainforest foraging for food.

Continuing with Forbes, one must also study the species upon which the monkey depends for its existence, and the various conditions upon which these depend. In our example ecosystem, the tamarin cooperates and competes with other species for food within an entire system of conditions affecting their prosperity, including mutualistic behaviors and predation, both by and upon the primate. By the time an ecologist has studied all these conditions sufficiently one will find that one "has run through the whole complicated ecological mechanism of the . . . life of the locality, both animal and vegetable, of which the species [of interest is merely] a single element."

Today we recognize ecology as the science of interaction *par excellence*. Ecology is the branch of biological science concerned with biological communities interacting with their environment. Plants interact with animals and all are interacted upon by fungi, microorganisms, soil, water, and the atmosphere. Another influential ecologist once said that "Among academic subjects, ecology stands out as being one of the few dedicated to holism."[5] It is insufficient to talk about interaction without foregrounding the structural interactions of the system. Populations establish themselves in a web of life that has both architecture and function. Ecology has a set of

3. Dietz, Dietz, and Nagagata, "The Effective Use of Flagship Species, 32–35.
4. Cawthorn Lang, "Primate Factsheets."
5. Odum, "The Emergence of Ecology," 1289.

concepts and a language for understanding structure and the dynamics, the interconnections and interactions.

This chapter describes interconnections and interactions in ecology using as an example one ecosystem, the tropical rainforest that the golden-haired lion tamarin calls home. We will become acquainted with the monkey and the various conditions upon which its existence depends. At the end of this visit to the Atlantic rainforest in southern Bahia, readers will have "run through the whole complicated ecological mechanism of the . . . life of the locality, both animal and vegetable, of which the species [of interest is merely] a single element." Section one describes the geography and landscape of the Atlantic Forest in southern Bahia state, Brazil. Section two describes the architecture and functions of the coastal lowland rainforest ecosystem using the tamarin as our species of interest. In section three, human interconnections and interactions in the Bahian ecosystem are introduced to explore the history, degradation, and conservation efforts of the tamarin's home, concluding our tour.

Atlantic Forest in Bahia, Brazil

Brazil's Atlantic Forest is a biome which for a long time covered around 1.3 million km², stretching along most of the Brazilian coast for 2000 miles from the northeastern-most point on the continent (3° S) southward to the border with Uruguay (30° S) and westward to Paraguay and Argentina, covering approximately 17 percent of Brazilian land area. The tropical and subtropical forests stretch across topographic and climatic conditions, encompassing wet lowlands, coastal mountain regions, and relatively dry interior plateaus. The Atlantic forests are home to more than 20,000 plant species including 8,000 trees. Animal species include 261 mammals, 688 birds, 200 reptiles, 280 amphibians, and many more unknown species.[6] Although only 7 percent of forest remains, it is very rich in biodiversity.

Bahia is a state in northeastern Brazil, located on the Atlantic coast, east of the Amazon at the middle latitudes of the country. It is the fourth most populous state in Brazil, with its capital city São Salvador da Bahia de Todos os Santos, commonly shortened to Salvador. The capital city overlooks the turquoise waters of Todos os Santos, or All Saints' Bay. The history of Salvador is interesting because it is known as the first point in South America that European explorers saw on a voyage in the year 1501 that opened South

6. Metzger, "Conservation Issues in the Brazilian Atlantic Forest," 1138; Mesquita et al., "COOPLANTAR: A Brazilian Initiative," 199.

America to European colonization.[7] Bahia has the most ecologically rich portion of the Atlantic Forest.[8] The coastal lowland rainforest on the eastern slopes of a mountain chain extends between 13° S to 18° S with an average temperature of around 75° F and 78 inches annual rainfall.[9] The coastal area is low to medium elevation (< 3280 feet) approximately 40 miles wide from east to west; beyond it is a transition zone from coastal to mountainous that extends from 40 miles to 90 miles inland but is still considered coastal by many (but not necessarily by the flora and fauna).[10] The entire coastal rainforest area extends approximately 300 miles from the Rio De Contas in the north to the southern border of Bahia. To the west is a mountain range that runs north–south called the Chapada Diamantina, dividing the state into rainforest and tropical arid highlands.

The Atlantic Forest in Bahia has a northern half where the golden-haired lion tamarins (*Leontopithecus chrysomelas*) are endemic, bounded by the Jequintinhonha River that cuts across the middle of the strip of land from the mountains to the ocean.[11] The southern half, with similar rainforest ecology but fewer tamarins, is called the Central Corridor of the Atlantic Forest; it includes the Caraíva River Basin and parts of the Frades and Trancoso River Basins. The rivers flow from the mountainous inland west to the east where they empty into the Atlantic Ocean. The landscape is a patchy matrix of cacao and eucalyptus plantations, cattle pastures on cleared land, old-growth rainforest, and second-growth forest less than 50 years old.[12] Although most of the remnants of old-growth forest are < 100 ha, larger patches of > 1000 ha exist in the cacao-producing region.[13] The region includes two national parks (Pau-Brasil National Park and Monte Pascoal National Park), the Monte Pascoal–Pau Brasil Ecological Corridor for the conservation of forest and biodiversity, and the Una and Serra Grande Biological Reserves.

7. Meyer, "Bahia."

8. Metzger, "Conservation Issues," 199; Thomas et al., "Plant Endemism," 319.

9. Pardini et al., "The Challenge of Maintaining Atlantic Forest Biodiversity," 1179.

10. Cawthorn Lang, "Primate Factsheets."

11. Ibid.

12. Pardini et al., "The Challenge of Maintaining Atlantic Forest Biodiversity,"1179; Mesquita et al., "COOPLANTAR: A Brazilian Initiative," 199–201.

13. Pardini, "The Challenge of Maintaining Atlantic Forest Biodiversity," 1179.

Coastal Lowland Rainforest Ecosystem

The amount and variety of life in the rainforest is dependent upon the hot, humid climate, elevation, and the trees. The rainforest in Bahia is the only region of the Atlantic Forest that does not have a dry season, but receives more than 4 inches of rain per month year-round.[14] Mean annual temperature is 75°F with little seasonal variation. The geography supports an incredible diversity of species of trees that thrive in the heat and humidity at low to moderate elevation. Trees convert water and sunlight into forms that animals are able to digest. The landscape supports the habitats of trees and plants that turn the abundant water into abundant plant material by growing fleshy, sumptuous fruits that are much larger than fruits and nuts that are grown in temperate climates. Orchids among thousands of species of flowers endemic to the area can have abundant, sweet nectar and heavy, intoxicating fragrances of vanilla or floral or spice. The air is continuously heavy with moisture and tropical scents.

The forest architecture is built upon its trees; the ecosystem functions cannot be considered separately from the architecture.[15] Trees can be classified by their height and requirements for sun into categories that grow to 160 feet with canopies soaking in the full sun, smaller trees that need less sun, and still smaller trees of 10–30 feet that need shade and therefore grow in the understory; each kind plays a different role in the forest architecture. One common species, *Inga affinis*, also known as the Ice Cream Bean tree, grows seed pods that contain sweet, juicy, white fruit. The pods, which are yellow before turning green then brown as they mature, can grow from a few inches to up to 3 feet long and two inches in diameter.[16] The tree's seeds resemble lima beans when green and turn white and fat like little scoops of vanilla ice cream. The tamarin, preferring to spend the mornings foraging in the tree canopy for fruit, finds the pulpy fruit quite to its liking. Other mammals and birds also know about the food that can be found in the *Inga affinis*. Prior to setting out its seed pods, the ice cream bean tree flowers with fans of white needle-like petals reminiscent of the crown of a peacock. Insects and hummingbirds find delicious meals in the flowers and in the other animals who visit the flowers.

Since the area is so humid, epiphytes, plants that live not in soil but on other plants, find a home on the *Inga affinis* too. Bromeliads such as the

14. Oliveira-Filho and Fontes, "Patterns of Floristic Differentiation," 795.

15. Pardini et al., "The Challenge of Maintaining Atlantic Forest Biodiversity," 1186–88.

16. Montagnini, Fanzeres, and Da Vinha, "The Potentials of 20 Indigenous Tree Species," 842; Top Tropicals, "Tropical Plant Catalog."

Aechmae multiflora with tough, fibrous, strap-like green leaves and single pink blooms that resemble old-fashioned cut-glass doorknobs covered with rose thorns have aerial roots that take up all the moisture they need from the humid air. (This is just one of dozens of species of bromeliads that live in the Bahia rainforest.) Since they do not need to be rooted in soil, many species of bromeliads live attached to tree trunks, in nooks, and in outstretched woody arms. The effect of hosting bromeliads is truly profound. These plants host microclimates of their own with their own moisture and communities of permanent residents and transient visitors. Moisture collects in the nested layers of leaves and petals of the bromeliads. Permanent residents might include hairy black and brown spotted arboreal spiders who build silk webs as retreats for raising families within the safety of the spiky structures.[17] (Just as the plants grow fat and fleshy, the insects do too.) Ants take up residence in the roots, also benefitting from the plant in several ways by foraging for nectar and insects for food within the plant and finding a hospitable location for nesting.[18] In exchange, ants protect their host plants by competing with other herbivorous insects and parasites.

Transients who visit the bromeliads include the tamarins that, in the afternoons, move from foraging fruits to animal protein by foraging for insects. The primates are predators of fruits, nuts, insects, lizards, frogs, and bird eggs.[19] (Other afternoons they might forage for frogs and lizards on the forest floor among the leaf litter—which provides cover for animals and decomposes to provide nutrients for terrestrial plants rooted in the soil.) Tamarins are expert insect foragers. The black tufted-ear marmoset (*Callithrix kuhli*), another small primate, travels through the forest with the tamarins, partly for safety in numbers from hungry hawks and partly for an easy meal in the bromeliads that the tamarins disturb. But marmosets are not the only animals who know the value of following tamarins while they hunt among the flowers: omnivorous white-fronted nunbirds (*Monasa morphoeus*) and woodcreepers know this too. They fly near the tamarins, patiently waiting their turn at the spoils of the hunt. The entire entourage along with other omnivores control the populations of the insects, frogs, lizards, and other small animals they eat because abundant prey are easier to find and catch than small populations. The spider's brood of 40 offspring in the bromeliad does not remain intact very long with omnivores who hunt cooperatively and may compete with each other for their dinners. Prey

17. Dias and Brescovlt, "Notes on the Behavior of Pachistopelma Fuonigrum Pocock," 13–16.

18. Almeida and Figueiredo, "Ants Visit Nectaries," 552–56.

19. Cawthorn Lang, "Primate Factsheets."

species such as spiders might or might not affect the population sizes of their predators, depending upon factors including the number of different species any omnivore eats. The animals in return for their meals in the trees, pollinate and transport pollen and seeds from the trees and plants, thereby facilitating the reproduction of forest flora.

Here I have given just a small sampling of an assemblage of the ecosystem of the coastal lowland rainforest where the golden-haired lion tamarin is one species woven into the web of life. The tamarin's story cannot be told without also understanding the other species with which it interacts and the conditions for the flourishing of all of them. Yet, the tamarin's story gives sufficient description of the whole that it is possible to imagine additional species in the landscape such as palm heart among hundreds of species of trees that also produce unusual but tasty fruits. The rainforest is also home to dozens to hundreds of species of tree ferns, butterflies, bats, and orchids.[20] Bromeliads are not the only taxonomic group of epiphytes in the forest.[21] Picture an understory with trees heavily populated by not only bromeliads of various sizes and colors but also orchids of all kinds. On other branches are the monstrous, bushy and vining cousins of many common humidity- and shade-loving tropical houseplants including philodendron and anthurium. Lichens, mosses, and ferns also claim their woody turf, sometimes piled on top of each other as orchids might colonize mosses that grow near lichens that are attached to a tree trunk. Thus from the story of one species we get a sense of the whole complicated ecological mechanism of the life of the locality.

Anthropogenic Effects on the Rainforest Ecosystem

So far I have described the mature or old-growth rainforest ecosystem in the coastal lowlands of Bahia as it probably existed for millennia before the European settlers arrived 500 years ago.[22] Humans are a species in the natural ecosystem too. We are part of the architecture and functioning of the rainforest that the golden-haired lion tamarins call home. The Europeans discovered economic opportunity by exploiting the natural resources of the Atlantic Forest, beginning the colonization of Brazil at the coast in Bahia, the beginning of marked anthropogenic pressure on the biome. Over the next 400 years

20. Pardini et al., "The Challenge of Maintaining Atlantic Forest Biodiversity," 1182; Brown and Freitas, "Atlantic Forest Butterflies," 937–38.

21. *Learning about Rainforests*, "Learning about Rainforests: Epiphytes."

22. Bush and de Oliveira, "The Rise and Fall of the Refugial Hypothesis," 787.

land throughout the entire biome was cleared mainly for timber, firewood, charcoal, agriculture, cattle ranching, and the construction of cities. The rate of deforestation peaked in the decades since 1970.[23]

Today only 7 percent of the original extent of the forest remains.[24] Throughout the entire Atlantic Forest area, the mature forest areas exist as patches; 80 percent of the habitat fragments are smaller than 50 hectares, mainly composed of second-growth forest and immersed in land pattern matrices that are urban or agricultural.[25] Since 1990 ecologists brought attention to the alarming rate of deforestation, spawning conservation efforts throughout the biome. Consequently, many of the national parks and conservation areas have been established only recently as part of this movement. Many of the larger patches today exist in conservation areas. Nevertheless there is continued anthropogenic pressure on fragments from hunting, logging, and fire. Within the patches, between 50% and 95% of taxonomic groups (depending on the group) are endemic, meaning that the species are not found outside the local area or region.[26] Habitat fragmentation of forest is problematic because many species of trees, plants, and animals require continuous ranges for all of the species of various taxa, sizes, and positions in the food web to exist and participate in the interactions that support the existence of any patch of forest.[27] Thus, fragmentation increases the likelihood of habitat loss and species extinction.

Most of the deforestation south of the tamarin's range in South Bahia took place between 1945 and 1975.[28] Roads were opened in the region which facilitated large-scale timber extraction. Today the entire coastal lowland has approximately 18 percent of its original forest area. The Uma Biological Reserve is a conservation area of >1000 ha of mature forest remnant that was established for the maintenance of native biodiversity. The rest of the area has primary forest remnants in small patches < 100 ha. Cattle pastures and cultivation of perennial crops including coffee, cacao, and papaya were the primary land use until the mid-1990s. Today the land is comprised of heterogeneous anthropogenic habitats: primarily agricultural with shade-cacao plantations and silviculture on eucalyptus plantations. Veracel, a joint venture between the Swedish-Finnish company StoraEnso and Fibria, and

23. Mesquita et al., "COOPLANTAR: A Brazilian Initiative," 199.

24. Moratello, "Introduction," 787.

25. Mesquita et al., "COOPLANTAR: A Brazilian Initiative," 199; Pardini et al., "The Challenge of Maintaining Atlantic Forest Biodiversity," 1179.

26. Moratello, "Introduction," 787; Costa et al., "Biogeography of South American Forest Mammals," 872–74; Thomas et al., "Plant Endemism in Two Forests, 311.

27. Pardini et al., "The Challenge of Maintaining Atlantic Forest Biodiversity," 1179.

28. Mesquita et al., "COOPLANTAR: A Brazilian Initiative," 199–201.

Brazilian company, grows eucalyptus as raw materials for cellulose products. Eucalyptus and shade-cacao plantations and cattle farming are the predominant land uses.

Humans are inhabitants of the biome, a level of the food web, modifiers of landscapes, and an architect of the ecosystem. Unfortunately, anthropogenic activities in the ecosystem too often result in the breaking of structural and functional ties that existed for millennia. Deforestation and land conversion disrupt the food web by reduction of population sizes (abundance) of plants (e.g., ice cream bean tree, bromeliads) and animals (tamarins, spiders, butterflies, birds) which are necessary for the existence of the system. Redundancies in the food web by omnivory when multiple species have the role of predator or prey in relation to a single other species provide somewhat of a buffer against disturbance. In this way, ecosystems are typically resilient to lesser degrees of disturbance that frequently occur from storms and the natural processes that lead to fire.

Disruption is not limited to the food web but also affects reproduction by decreasing the number of tamarins and individuals in other species who are able to reproduce. When the species of animals that pollenate and disperse seeds are reduced, the reproductive capacity of the trees and plants is also reduced because of the structural and functional interconnections in the ecosystem. When reproduction rates are reduced, predator species can experience food shortages, especially among species which have diets of only a small number of foods. Species can become extinct, reducing the richness of biodiversity. The golden-haired lion tamarin is among many species in the area that are endangered. In 1997, the population size in the wild was estimated at between 6,000 and 15,000 individuals found in over 100 sites within their range. At the same time, about 600 individuals were in captivity around the world.[29]

Ecosystems have thresholds for the amount of stress they can absorb without undergoing a permanent (or, at least, long-term) transformation of architecture and functioning. Ecosystem degradation may be slow and recovery rapid if the stress is removed for degradation up to the threshold. The ability to absorb changes and still persist is called resilience.[30] Another sense of resilience that is used in ecology is the ability of an ecosystem to recover to a predisturbance state after the stressors are removed.[31] In cases of degradation beyond the threshold, ecosystems have three possible fates: quick recovery to an initial state with mildly reduced ecosystem functioning, slow

29. Cawthorn Lang, "Primate Factsheets."

30. Holling, "Resilience and Stability of Ecological Systems," 1–23.

31. Mori, "Resilience in the Studies of Biodiversity–Ecosystem Functioning," 87.

recovery with significantly reduced functioning until nearly all of the stressors are eliminated, and moderately slow recovery to an alternative state of the system in which architecture and function are significantly reduced yet stable. In the Atlantic Forest ecosystem, the most significant stressor was deforestation and land conversion. Secondary forest and agricultural habitats replaced mature forest in fragments. Ecologists have been interested in assessing the extent to which the secondary forest and agricultural habitats support the biodiversity of native flora and fauna, particularly the richness and abundance of tree species.

Forest cover affects patterns of species richness, abundance, and traits related to ecosystem function. Below the threshold tree density, the trees cannot support the population sizes of flora and fauna that are needed to support each other and the trees themselves. Since the trees are of central importance, research has examined the effects of the existence of habitat fragments with different characteristics in the Atlantic Forest on the richness and abundance of trees, assuming that if the trees are absent, the rest of the ecosystem inhabitant populations will be disturbed or unable to survive. For some genera of trees, richness and abundance are proportional to the percentage of forest cover,[32] mature forest remnants are superior to other habitats. However, research has shown that shade-cacao plantations which have smaller cacao trees shaded under larger trees, can support a significant proportion of the biodiversity in the region.[33] Even tamarins are able to live in shade-cacao plantations.[34] Secondary-growth forests are those which grow from natural processes after old-growth forests are cleared. In Bahia, a substantial proportion of habitat patches are secondary-growth forests on land that was cleared in the last century. Recent studies have shown that these habitats, although not as supportive as mature forest remnants, can support more tree species richness than agricultural habitats.[35] Recent studies of the forest remnants continue to show remarkable biodiversity despite the fragmentation and endemic characteristic of many species.[36]

Not all human effects on the Atlantic Forest ecosystem have been destructive. Ecological research about the severe loss of habitat and biodiversity and intensive agriculture have raised awareness of the long-term

32. Piotto et al., "Forest Recovery," 261.

33. Pardini et al., "The Challenge of Maintaining Atlantic Forest Biodiversity," 1182–86.

34. Cawthorn Lang, "Primate Factsheets."

35. Piotto et al., "Forest Recovery," 261.

36. Pardini et al., "The Challenge of Maintaining Atlantic Forest Biodiversity," 1182–86.

effects.[37] The ecosystem actually provides services, include provision of abundant clean water for residential, agricultural, and industrial activities and for hydroelectric power generation. The forest also provides cultural services: recreation destinations in the national parks and conservation areas, and aesthetic and spiritual benefits.[38] The services that are essential for the Brazilian economy and society are at risk. Tourism and industry are two of the top sources of economic activity for the state. Another long-term effect has resulted from the exploitation of former forest areas for agriculture (sugar cane, coffee, cattle). The soil's productivity has been degraded, leaving many rural communities in a state of poverty.

The scenario of long-term effects of deforestation and land conversion indicates an urgent need for conservation and restoration, especially actions that restore forest cover and establish ecological corridors between strategic protected areas and old-growth fragments. Conservation activities also aim to protect ecosystem services while generating work and income for local communities.

In response to the recognition of the need for action, the government established national parks and conservation areas. South Bahia has two national parks (Pau-Brasil National Park and Monte Pascoal National Park), the Monte Pascoal–Pau Brasil Ecological Corridor for the conservation of forest and biodiversity, and the Una and Serra Grande Biological Reserves.[39] The Monte Pascoal National Park was created in 1961, encompassing 14,000 ha with at least 14 bird and 3 primate species that are threatened, including the howler monkey (*Alouatta guariba guariba*).[40] The Pau-Brasil National Park is located in the municipality of Porto Seguro, a major tourist destination. The park was created in 2000 as part of the celebrations of the 500-year anniversary of the first Portuguese landing in Brazil. This park has an area of 11,500 ha and is home to the largest surviving population of brazilwood trees (*Caesalpinia echinata*). In addition to providing habitat for orchids and fruit, brazilwood trees have dense, red-orange wood that yields a red dye and has been the standard wood for bows for stringed musical instruments since the sixteenth century. The Portuguese cut brazilwood trees for trade in Europe, driving the species to near extinction in the nineteenth century, an ecological disturbance from which it has yet to recover.[41]

37. Mesquita et al., "COOPLANTAR: A Brazilian Initiative," 199.
38. Galatowitsch, *Ecological Restoration*, 6.
39. Mesquita et al., "COOPLANTAR: A Brazilian Initiative," 199.
40. Ibid., 201.
41. Global Trees Campaign, "Threatened Trees: Pau Brasil."

The Una Biological Reserve is the only area where the golden-haired lion tamarin is protected and thus also studied in the wild by zoologists.[42] Both the Una and Serra Grande Biological Reserves harbor plant species, providing places for protection of the species and study by ecologists and botanists. Several of the studies used for this chapter to describe the ecosystem were conducted in the biological reserves.

The Monte Pascoal–Paul Brasil Ecological Corridor (MPPBEC) covers an area of approximately 94,000 ha adjacent to the largest concentration of protected areas in the Central Corridor of the Atlantic Forest in southern Bahia.[43] This area is home to four municipalities with combined population 8,800 and several Indian villages with population around 4,000 or more. In 2004, community groups representing the residents, a regional planning and sociodevelopment organization, and a local environmental organization obtained funding from the Critical Ecosystem Partnership Fund for a conservation project. The project's main objective was to start a sustainable process of environmental restoration and conservation in the Caraíva River Basin that involved the participation of local residents and organizations. It was through this project that the MPPBEC was established.

An important component was the planting of trees by local residents who were employed by the program. The tree saplings were grown by local nurseries. The program provided training in forest assessment for planters, so that the diversity of trees in intervention habitats would be restored and maintained without the need for expert consultants for day-to-day activities. Following the training, the Cooperative of Mata Atlântica Reforestation Workers of Far Southern Bahia (COOPLANTAR) was founded, with an initial membership of 45 trained planters from the local population. The program has been successful in planting tree saplings and clearing weeds, and in attracting additional funding and partner organizations that provide technical support in field work and cooperative management techniques. Cooperative members were hired by Veracel to establish and maintain it eucalyptus plantations and to plant native species in its preservation areas. Veracel has a number of environmental obligations to its stockholders, including the restoration of 400 ha of Atlantic Forest per year.

In 2009, COOPLANTAR was recognized as a model for conservation by the formation of specialized and qualified community cooperatives, presenting a viable and sustainable method for landscape-scale forest restoration. The cooperative demonstrated that it is possible for small, not-for-profit

---

42. Cawthorn Lang, "Primate Factsheets."
43. Mesquita et al., "COOPLANTAR: A Brazilian Initiative," 201–4.

community groups to successfully participate in a forest restoration market dominated by larger, established, for-profit companies.

Conclusion

This chapter describes interconnections and interactions in ecology using as an example one ecosystem, the tropical rainforest which the endangered golden-haired Lion Tamarin calls home. Section one described the geography and landscape of the Atlantic Forest in southern Bahia state, Brazil. Section two described the architecture and functions of the coastal lowland rainforest ecosystem using the tamarin as our species of interest. In section three, human interconnections and interactions in the Bahian ecosystem were introduced to explore the history, degradation, and conservation efforts of the tamarin's home, concluding our tour. Now at the end of this visit to the Atlantic rainforest in southern Bahia, readers should have, as Stephen Forbes would say, "run through the whole complicated ecological mechanism of the . . . life of the locality, both animal and vegetable, of which the species [of interest is merely] a single element." This tour of the rainforest as a mini-course in ecology covered most of the major concepts and patterns that are of scientific interest to ecologists.

The golden-haired lion tamarin is endangered because of anthropogenic pressures that have existed on the Atlantic Forest for 500 years, intensifying in the past 70 years. However, humans have also recognized long-term problems associated with deforestation and conversion of land to agriculture. Anthropogenic activities break the interconnections and interactions in the "whole complicated mechanism of life," thereby reducing the ability of the entire ecosystem and each inhabitant species to survive. Ongoing conservation efforts are rebuilding coastal lowland forest habitat even as pressures from hunting and fire continue. Time itself is healing some of the anthropogenic damage in secondary forests, though it will take an unknown duration of at least several more decades before secondary forests could become as viable for supporting native biodiversity as old-growth habitat. Agricultural habitats have more recently been studied to assess their ability to support native biodiversity and were found to support some, but not as well as mature forest. Therefore, the tamarin's future, while still uncertain, might be restoration of the species' habitat and de-listing from the endangered species list.

References

Almeida, A. M., and R. A. Figueiredo. 2003. "Ants Visit Nectaries of Epidendrum Denticulatum (Orchidaceae) in a Brazilian Rain Forest's Ecological Interconnections Forest: Effects on Herbivory and Pollination." *Brazilian Journal of Biology* 63/4.

Brown, Keith S. Jr., and Andri Victor L. Freitas. 2000."Atlantic Forest Butterflies: Indicators for Landscape Conservation." *Biotropica* 32/4, pp. 934–56. doi:10.1646/0006–3606(2000)032[0934:AFBIFL]2.0.CO;2.

Bush, Mark B., and Paulo E. de Oliveira. 2006."The Rise and Fall of the Refugial Hypothesis of Amazonian Speciation: A Paleoecological Perspective." *Biota Neotropica* 6/1. doi:10.1590/S1676–06032006000100002.

Carnaval, Ana Carolina, and Craig Moritz. 2008. "Historical Climate Modelling Predicts Patterns of Current Biodiversity in the Brazilian Atlantic Forest." *Journal of Biogeography* 35/7 (July) pp. 1187–201. doi:10.1111/j.1365-2699.2007.01870.x.

Cawthorn Lang, K. A. 2005."Primate Factsheets: Golden-Headed Lion Tamarin (Leontopithecus Chrysomelas) Taxonomy, Morphology, & Ecology," July 20. http://pin.primate.wisc.edu/factsheets/entry/golden-headed_lion_tamarin.

Costa, Leonora Pires, Yuri L. R. Leite, Gustavo A. B. da Fonseca, and Mônica Tavares da Fonseca. 2000."Biogeography of South American Forest Mammals: Endemism and Diversity in the Atlantic Forest." *Biotropica* 32/4, pp. 872–81. doi:10.1646/0006–3606(2000)032[0872:BOSAFM]2.0.CO;2.

Dias, Sidclay Calaça, and Antonio Domingos Brescovlt. 2003. "Notes on the Behavior of Pachistopelma Fuonigrum Pocock (Araneae, Theraphosidae, Avicularlinae)." *Revista Brasileira de Zoologia* 20/1.

Dietz, J. M., L. A. Dietz, and E. Y. Nagagata. 1994."The Effective Use of Flagship Species for Conservation of Biodiversity: The Example of Lion Tamarins in Brazil." In *Creative Conservation: Interactive Management of Captive and Wild Animals,* edited by Peter J. S. Olney, et al., 32–49. London: Chapman & Hall.

Forbes, Staphen A. 1887. "The Lake as a Microcosm." In *An Anthology of Nineteenth-Century American Science Writing*, edited by C. R. Resetarits. New York: Anthem.

Galatowitsch, Susan M. 2012. *Ecological Restoration*. Sunderland, MA: Sinauer.

Global Trees Campaign. 2017. "Threatened Trees: Pau Brasil." http://globaltrees.org/threatened-trees/trees/pau-brasil/.

Holling, C. S. 1973. "Resilience and Stability of Ecological Systems." *Annual Review of Ecology and Systematics* 4, pp. 1–23

Learning about Rainforests. 2017. "Learning about Rainforests: Epiphytes." http://www.srl.caltech.edu/personnel/krubal/rainforest/Edit560s6/www/plants/epiphytes.html/.

Mesquita, Carlos Alberto B., Christiane G. D. Holvorcem, Claudio Henrique Lyrio, Paulo Dimas de Menezes, José Dilson da Silva Dias, and José Francisco Jr. Azevedo. 2010. "COOPLANTAR: A Brazilian Initiative to Integrate Forest Restoration with Job and Income Generation in Rural Areas." *Ecological Restoration* 28/2, pp. 199–207.

Metzger, Jean Paul. 2009."Conservation Issues in the Brazilian Atlantic Forest." *Biological Conservation* 142/6, pp. 1138–40.

Meyer, Amelia. 2017. "Bahia." www.brazil.org.za. http://www.brazil.org.za/bahia.html/.

Montagnini, Florencia, Anna Fanzeres, and Sergio Guimaraes Da Vinha. 1995."The Potentials of 20 Indigenous Tree Species for Soil Rehabilitation in the Atlantic Forest Region of Bahia, Brazil." *Journal of Applied Ecology* 32/4, pp. 841–56.

Moratello, L. Patricia C. 2000. "Introduction: The Brazilian Atlantic Forest." *Biotropica* 32, no. 4, pp. 786–92. doi:10.1646/0006–3606(2000)032[0786:ITBAF]2.0.CO;2.

Mori, Akira S. 2016. "Resilience in the Studies of Biodiversity–Ecosystem Functioning." *Trends in Ecology & Evolution* 31/2, pp. 87–89.

Odum, E. P. 1977. "The Emergence of Ecology as a New Integrative Discipline." *Science* 195/4284, pp. 1289–93.

Oliveira-Filho, Ary T., and Marco Aurelio L. Fontes. 2000. "Patterns of Floristic Differentiation among Atlantic Forests in Southeastern Brazil and the Influence of Climate." *Biotropica* 32/4. doi:10.1646/0006–3606(2000)032[0793:POFDAA]2 .0.CO;2.

Pardini, Renata, Deborah Faria, Gustavo M. Accacio, Rudi R. Laps, Eduardo Mariano Neto, Mateus L. B. Paciencia, Marianna Dixo, and Julio Baumgarten. 2009."The Challenge of Maintaining Atlantic Forest Biodiversity: A Multi-Taxa Conservation Assessment of Specialist and Generalist Species in an Agro-Forestry Mosaic in Southern Bahia." Special issue, *Conservation Issues in the Brazilian Atlantic Forest*, edited by J. P. Metzger and N. Sodhi, *Biological Conservation* 142/6, pp. 1178–90.

Piotto, Daniel, Florencia Montagnini, Wayt Thomas, Mark Ashton, and Chadwick Oliver. 2009. "Forest Recovery after Swidden Cultivation across a 40-Year Chronosequence in the Atlantic Forest of Southern Bahia, Brazil." *Plant Ecology* 205 (December). doi:10.1007/s11258–009–9615–2.

Silva, Jose Maria C. da. "Bahia Coastal Forests." 2017. World Wildlife Federation. https://www.worldwildlife.org/ecoregions/nt0103/.

Thomas, William Wayt, Andre Mauricio V. de Carvalho, Andre M. Amorim, Judith Garrison, and Alba L. Arbelaez. 1998. "Plant Endemism in Two Forests in Southern Bahia, Brazil." *Biodiversity & Conservation* 7/3, pp. 311–22. doi:10.1023/A:1008825627656.

Top Tropicals, LLC, and TTmagazine.info. 2017. "Tropical Plant Catalog: Inga Edulis, Inga Affinis." https://toptropicals.com/catalog/uid/inga_edulis.html/.

7

Brains, Minds, and Persons

Interaction within—and among—Individuals

Michael Spezio

Introduction

WHAT CAN BE GAINED by an understanding of interaction via decisional-valuational social, cognitive, and affective neuroscience within an interdisciplinary perspective? First, interactionism benefits inquiry via attention to the meanings of the broad term "interaction" across scientific approaches, aiding the science directly, as well as interdisciplinary engagement with science. While science seeks to understand regular and idiosyncratic relations between phenomena, not all relations are interactions. Interactions themselves come in different forms, and without a typology of interaction that is informed by the interactive relationships of interest, category mistakes and confusions will arise. Fields such as ecological science, for example, have their own broad typology of interaction,[1] though this does not suffice for the present inquiry involving networks of the brain, body, mind, person, and pair.

A second benefit of interactionism is advancing understanding of the human and of human brains by providing alternatives to forces of mistaken individualism in describing the human, our brains, our evolutionary history, and our possible futures. Since 2005, emphasis on types of neural networks throughout the brain has supplanted emphasis on types of isolated neurons,

---

1. Mougi and Kondoh, "Diversity of Interaction Types and Ecological Community Stability," 349–51.

giving prominence to neural hodology,[2] a branch of cerebral connectomics.[3] Interactionism suggests that individualism is ultimately opposed to accurate models of individuals—cells, brains, minds, persons—within their embedded networks. Another benefit of interactionism is opposition to rational choice theories in economics, political science, and decision science, which substitute models of individualistic "subjective utility" for nuanced study of real values in the lives of real persons.[4] Individualistic gains and losses favoring conflict, social "expertise," and Machiavellian success dominate these theories and continue to draw attention in the face of widespread evidence of the overwhelming importance of social affiliation.[5] In the area of social neuroeconomics, for example, growing evidence supports the central importance of interaction-dependent social preferences in economic and other valuationally grounded choices.[6]

To be sure, this evidence does not support more sweeping claims about the supposed naturalness of the universality of fairness or other moral or proto-moral dynamics,[7] since most of these grander claims do not adequately address the limitations of group extent and transactional cooperation, especially under threat of antagonistic competition (e.g., conformity; for clarification of these terms, see below). Yet interactionism helps identify the centrality of social affiliation beyond the false leads of individualism and its entailments. One of those false leads is spectatorialism, which abounds in cognitive approaches to the human. According to spectatorial approaches in method and theory, persons, minds, and brains are reduced to entities outside of the systems they are construed to observe, evaluate, perceive, and process. Neuroscience's laser focus on methods that

2. Hodology is the study of paths and connections.

3. Harris and Shepherd, "The Neocortical Circuit," 170–81; Van Essen et al., "The Human Connectome Project," 2222–31; Rubinov and Sporns, "Complex Network Measures of Brain Connectivity," 1059–69; Sporns, "The Human Connectome," 109–25.

4. Taylor, *Rationality and the Ideology of Disconnection*.

5. Dunbar, "The Social Brain," 163–81; Dunbar, "The Social Role of Touch," 260–68; Fuentes, "It's Not All Sex and Violence," 710–18. See also the change in emphasis between the two books titled *Machiavellian Intelligence* and *Machiavellian Intelligence II*, published eight years apart, in 1989 and 1997 respectively. Importantly, human affiliative interactions are evident across species as well as within species, though space limitations prevent inclusion of interspecies affiliative interactions in this study. But see the work of Agustín Fuentes and colleagues, Agustin Fuentes and Linda D. Wolfe, eds., *Primates Face to Face*.

6. Camerer and Fehr, "When Does 'Economic Man' Dominate Social Behavior?," 47–52; Fehr and Camerer, "Social Neuroeconomics," 419–27; Krajbich et al., "Economic Games Quantify Diminished Sense of Guilt in Patients with Damage to the Prefrontal Cortex," 2188–92.

7. For examples of this kind of overreach, see Haidt and Joseph, "Intuitive Ethics."

electrically isolate signals from single neurons in a brain—so-called "single unit recordings"—has resulted in great advances, while simultaneously giving the misleading impression that single neurons hold the properties of the complex networks to which they belong. In each domain, the artificial removal of neurons, brains, minds, persons, and pairs, from the conditions that constitute them—the interaction-dependent groundedness out of which they develop—restricts them to passive receivers/perceivers of flows of information. Even in recent theories of brain function, methodological individualism and spectatorialism reign supreme. These theories include homeostatic, control-theoretic, predictive, and free-energy-minimization models, and they helpfully reduce the passivity of cerebral systems, while not overcoming it. For example, active inference theories of brain function hold that a brain or a specific perceptual system acts individualistically to refine its models of the environment, and it does so by minimizing the discrepancy between prior expected probabilities about sensory signals and actual sensory signals.[8] Theories of active inference make assumptions about which narrow set of sensory signals is critical to a task at hand without specifying how the organism or brain or brain system developed either a focus on the task at hand or the narrow feature sensitivity that prioritizes certain sensory signals over others. Attending to the interactive embeddedness of brains and minds brings the domains of persons and pairs into the effort to understand the origins of feature sensitivities, priors, values, and the choices on which they depend and which ultimately also shape them. Interactionism therefore increases epistemic connections between these domains and ecological validity within them.

Finally, a third benefit of foregrounding interaction as understood by DV SCAN highlights the importance of interactions between domains of phenomena, and between the domains of inquiry into those phenomena. Cerebral systems are not minds, minds are not persons, and persons are constituted by but are not identical to the close pairs and larger groups in which they exist. There is no way to discover emotions or dreams or words among the neurons, glia, cerebral spinal fluid, ions, neuropeptides, blood, oxygen, etc., of a brain, however marvelous that brain is. There is no truth at all to the common quip that "the mind is the brain in action" or that watching cerebral signals qualifies as watching thoughts take shape.[9] Watching brains in action means watching chemical and electrical signals; no one has ever seen

8. Friston, Daunizeau, and Kiebel, "Reinforcement Learning or Active Inference?," e6421; Friston, Mattout, and Kilner, "Action Understanding and Active Inference," 137–60; Friston, "Prediction, Perception and Agency," 248–52; Friston et al., "The Anatomy of Choice," 598.

9. Chodosh, "Mind Aglow."

a feeling only in the flesh. Making interaction thematic, then, highlights the need for so-called "bridge laws" between domains, and the need to push for greater ecological validity within each domain itself. Bridge laws are broadly accepted hermeneutic/interpretive guidelines for navigating questions, evidence, and models between domains.[10] Bridge laws are not scientific laws in any sense, but rather they both facilitate and constrain inquiry into interactive phenomena involving brains, minds, persons, and pairs. The most common way to refer to bridge laws in decisional-valuational social, cognitive, and affective neuroscience is by the term "neural encoding," as in, "The activation in ventromedial prefrontal cortex encodes the expected reward probability of choice A." Neural "codes" are the spatiotemporal patterns of cerebral signals that correspond to specific cognitive subprocesses, often modeled as computations. Not all "codes" are directly related to individual neurons or specifically configured networks. Signals from fMRI, EEG, and MEG are cerebral and depend on signals from specific neural networks, but there is no comprehensive model for this dependence.[11] Bridge laws substitute for the absence of quantitative, exhaustive models of such (inter) dependence. Interaction as a focus of inquiry motivates interdisciplinary work engaging decisional-valuational social, cognitive, and affective neuroscience to keep the interaction of the domains of inquiry in mind, hopefully leading to better models within and between domains.[12]

Interactive approaches to brains, minds, persons, and pairs help to resituate and advance inquiry into the human. Attention to interaction studies highlights the surprising fact that studies of interaction often go without defining it, and that specific types of interaction (e.g., intersubjectivity) often stand in for all possible interaction types of interest. Interaction studies show the interdependence of neurons and smaller neuronal networks across the brain, and that humans are primarily affiliative, often cooperative (if also transactionally so), and that these smaller scale interactions shaped the history of human evolution. Elevating inquiry from isolated processes to the interconnected dynamics involving and perhaps constituting them serves also to highlight the need for interpretation among domains. The bridges provided by bridge laws do not just allow movement, they make possible a fruitful exchange that increases scientific and scholarly understanding. The

10. Nathan and Del Pinal, "Mapping the Mind," 637–57.

11. Srinivasan et al., "Spatial Sampling and Filtering of Eeg," 355–66. For a summary that is still relevant to the discussion, see the generally accessible chapter: Spezio, "The Cognitive Sciences."

12. This chapter and its use of terms like cognition, affect, mind, and value rely on assumptions consistent with bridge laws between philosophy of mind and the psychology and neuroscience of mental processes.

paper frames a typology of interaction before taking up the second emphasis on neural and social connection.

Toward a Typology of Interaction in DV-SCAN

Clarity regarding the meanings of "interaction" can only help motivate interest in and understanding of interaction in decisional-valuational social,
cognitive, and affective neuroscience (DV-SCAN; "dove-scan"[13]). This advance could be especially important with regard to models of how groups,
organisms, and cognitive and cerebral systems assign and prioritize value
(and signals relating to value) under different kinds of interaction. Getting
clear on a typology of interaction also helps to draw attention to category
mistakes both within DV-SCAN and its interdisciplinary engagement. For
example, empathy in the sense described by E. B. Titchener[14] is an epistemic
empathy that requires being right or nearly right about someone's intentions,
especially intentions emerging out of the person's character. However, much
of the neuroscientific literature that claims to study empathy not only sets
this epistemic criterion of empathy aside, but also sets aside all consideration
for shared valuational representation. In the place of shared valuational representation is a focus on the neuroimaging signals that stand in for and are
taken to index the shared value.[15] In doing so, much of the time DV-SCAN
confuses empathy, which requires interaction to have an effect at the level of
valuational representation, with shared circuits, which only requires a statis
tical similarity between neuroimaging patterns. Philosophical and theological scholarship on empathy that draws on the neuroscience of shared circuits
often reproduces this category error. Even work in DV-SCAN that seeks to
address an "interactive brain" fails to distinguish between and capture key
categories of interaction in the domains of brain, mind, person, and pair.[16]
Careful attention to types of interaction under study would avoid or at least
mitigate such problems in DV-SCAN, and hopefully create better chances
for successful interdisciplinary engagement.

A typology of interaction for DV-SCAN and its interdisciplinary engagement requires attention to both arrangement of value (i.e., information,

13. SCAN is a term of art that reflects the combination and, in many cases, interdisciplinary engagement between social, cognitive, and affective neuroscience. Decision neuroscience and neuroeconomics are outgrowths of SCAN that focus strongly on
valuational representations, hence DV-SCAN.

14. Titchener, *Lectures on the Experimental Psychology of the Thought-Processes*,
38.

15. Schleim, "How Empathy Became a Brain Function," 41–62.

16. Di Paolo and De Jaegher, "The Interactive Brain Hypothesis," 163.

affective salience, goal shaping, learning) and categories of measureable effects. For example, two children playing with a ball will view ball and the possession of the ball differently depending on whether the play is antagonistically or cooperatively competitive, or whether the play is a version of joint, recurrent, transactional, or reciprocal, or mutual cooperation (see below for clarification of these terms). In general, war and sport, despite mistakenly being lumped together as similar human interactions, result in different interactive structures of valuation because war is antagonistically competitive while sport is cooperatively so. Which type of competition or cooperation exhibited by the children should be evident in the measurable properties of their behaviors while at play, including language, gestures, and facial expressions. As another example, two brain networks may develop interactions via recurrent or reciprocal activation, recurrent or reciprocal inhibition, or asymmetrical activation and inhibition, and this may depend in large part on the kinds of interactions that occur outside the brain, which are interactions of the organism.

In the current study, interaction will only include phenomena that involve two or more centers or categories of dynamic processes (e.g., group, organism, network, neuron) in which there is 1) a distinct valuational orientation of each toward the other and 2) a change in each that is dependent upon the other.[17] Two persons or networks need not be in direct contact for there to be an interaction event, since a person or network may mediate or modulate the interaction between others. Also, immediate temporal proximity need not be a requirement of interaction. For example, if a person sends a card or an email to another person and there is no reply for a year or more, once the reply occurs, so does interaction. This example also illustrates the possible importance to "interaction" of those absent or apparently absent phenomena that are nonetheless expected or predicted by one or more centers of dynamic processes in an interaction. Cases of only-apparent-absence also make interaction possible. For example, riding on a crowded subway train or driving at high speed on a crowded highway relies on everyone driving by agreed-upon rules, including respecting others' needs for space and privacy. Social contract theory trades on the widespread reciprocal (possibly transactional) cooperative interaction on which such coordinated activity depends. Social trust as required by some

17. Any analysis of interaction depends completely upon how one defines or circumscribes the interacting centers of dynamic processes or systems. The current study lacks space to consider larger-scale centers beyond individual human brains, minds, and persons, though their exclusion here should not imply dismissal of their importance. The focus here on individual systems and persons should not be read as endorsing any form of individualism.

versions of contractarianism is an example of interaction that depends both on extended temporal scales and on the presence of reciprocal other-regard that only appears to be absent until its real absence results in annoyance, difficulty, and even tragedy. In the brain as well, specific networks whose measurable complex patterns of activity seem required for learning can have those patterns fall to undetectable levels, only for them to be "reactivated" during intervening periods of rest or sleep.[18]

Valuational Orientation in Interaction

Valuation is the primary consideration in defining types of interaction, as suggested by the categories from ecological science given in the introduction. In general, types of valuational orientations in different types of interactions are mutually exclusive, though different interaction types can occur in near temporal proximity to one another and valuational orientations may shift dynamically and rapidly in such occurrences. In this framework, value is understood broadly, from basic conative processes to intentional, conscious valuation. So interactions forming small neural networks are valuational in that they have a valence (e.g., activation vs. inhibition). An interaction cannot be both antagonistic and cooperative, or both transactional and mutual.

Antagonistic v. Competitive Interaction

Antagonistic interaction is one in which the values in the interaction are entirely or almost entirely counter to one another, and in which the interactors value their own processes positively and other interactors' processes highly negatively. For example, two neurons that reciprocally inhibit one another engage in antagonistic interaction from the narrow perspective focusing only on the pair. Competitive interaction is one in which the interactors share at least some values (e.g., participating and doing well in the French Open; controlling access to oil), but may or may not value one another. Some versions of competition are antagonistic, some are mixed, and some are cooperative. War can be pure antagonism or antagonistic competition. Cooperative competition sounds strange, but it is characteristic of most contests among consenting adults.

18. Mack and Preston, "Decisions about the Past," 144–57; Schlichting and Preston, "Memory Reactivation during Rest," 15845–50.

Cooperative Interaction

Cooperative interaction can be joint, recurrent, reciprocal, transactional, or mutual. In all but the last case, the process or outcome that is valuationally central is external to the interactors and will influence how each interactor values the others. Joint cooperation—often called "joint action" in the DV-SCAN literature[19]—generally involves cooperation aimed at accomplishing a common value (e.g., goal). Cooperative competition is a form of joint cooperation. Recurrent cooperation involves an exchange of value that may or may not be equal and in which the exchange itself is equally valued by all interactors, but not contingent on any threshold criterion. Transactional cooperation is a contingent exchange of value in which the outcome depends upon all interactors meeting some threshold criterion (e.g., the Ultimatum Task in behavioral economics[20]). Reciprocal cooperation is a form of recurrent or transactional cooperation in which the exchange is equal. Finally, mutual cooperation requires shared valuation among all interactors for all interactors, and can include outcomes that are equally valued by all and external to the immediate interaction.

Types of Changes in Interaction

Interaction depends on changes occurring in the interacting systems, so it is also important to ask what kinds of changes result from interaction. More than one type of change can occur in a given interaction, and only some of them will be directly measurable. As the sociologist William Bruce Cameron noted, "not everything that can be counted counts, and not everything that counts can be counted."[21] Thus, direct measurability is not an index of the importance of a given change of interest, while the absence of direct measurability should motivate a carefully developed operationalization of that change.[22]

19. Sebanz, Bekkering, and Knoblich, "Joint Action," 70–76; Schilbach et al., "Toward a Second-Person Neuroscience," 393–414.

20. Sanfey et al., "The Neural Basis of Economic Decision-Making," 1755–58; Ensminger, "Market Integration and Fairness."

21. Cameron, *Informal Sociology*, 13.

22. In any science, "operationalization" means constructing a way to quantify a phenomenon of interest or its expected effects. Operationalizing an experience of epistemic empathy, for example, might include adding up the self-report ratings on a questionnaire or counting the number of correct evaluations of emotion from a person's tone of voice or facial expression, or counting the number of seconds it takes for someone to respond to another's expression of pain (assuming such a response is a goal state of the person).

Property Effect Interaction

The first type of change, property effect interaction, involves measurable changes in measurable properties of the system. This does not require that there be any awareness of the changes. For example, two members of a cooperative or competitive pair may adopt bodily postures that reciprocally promote continued engagement, without either of them being aware of their postures or their effects. Behavioral, physiological, or cerebral properties could be measured to assess this type of change.[23]

Shared Representation/Value Interaction

A second kind of change results in shared information interaction, meaning indirectly measurable, shared representation, especially of value. For example, one member of a cooperative or competitive pair follows positively valenced cues from the second member of the interaction in positively viewing a third member of a new interaction. Importantly, the shared representation may or may not be itself directly measurable, but at least its behavioral outcome, or its physiological or brain properties will be. Neither member of the original dyad may be aware of the positively valenced cues or the resulting shared representation.

Shared Meaning Interaction and Intersubjectivity

A third kind of change is reflected in intentional interaction and requires awareness and reflection in that it involves shared meaning, understanding, even intersubjectivity, a property often thought to be a hallmark of human social interaction.[24] Shared meaning, understanding, and intersubjectivity rely on shared awareness to at least some degree, and interactional changes in this category overlap with concerns raised by philosophers of theory of mind (ToM), empathy, language, agency, morality, artificial

23. Of course, brain properties are also physiological, but for convenience, physiological properties here mean those that occur in the body but outside the brain. "Brain properties" and "cerebral properties" are awkward phrasings that include neural signals, both chemical and electrical, but also signals from other cells in the brain, such as glia, signals from summed sources (such as those measured in electroencephalography [EEG] and magnetoencephalography [MEG]), and signals from the blood (such as the blood oxygenation level dependent (BOLD) response used in much of functional magnetic resonance imaging [fMRI]).

24. Enfield and Levinson, *Introduction*, 3.

intelligence, and consciousness who emphasize the central importance of conscious awareness.[25]

Necessary Constitutive Interaction

Finally, many interactions actually constitute the very systems that interact and are interactions without which the systems would either fail to form or form very differently. Constitutive interaction challenges individualistic approaches to the study of interaction, and suggests multiple scales of an individual beyond those typically endorsed. For example, while a person's brain is a physically separable object from the person's surrounding context, that brain will form differently depending on its ability to use visual information from its environment in goal-directed behavior.[26] Adults who are congenitally blind showed patterns of BOLD response in canonical "visual" areas of the brain that look very different from BOLD responses in adults who can see. Importantly, resting state connectivity patterns differed between persons who are congenitally blind and persons who can see, even at rest. The patterns differ with eyes closed.[27] This evidence points to constitutive interaction that shapes the brain and, likely, the person as well.

The work of Lev Vygotsky unifies intentional and constitutive interaction in emphasizing that our individual mental processes, minds, and persons depend entirely upon what he calls the interactive "interpsychological," which others have likely drawn on in positing models of "interactive brains"[28] and "participatory sense-making,"[29] and to which my theory of symnesis is indebted.[30] Vygotsky stressed the constitutive priority of the interpersonal for the intrapersonal:

> Every function in the child's cultural development appears twice: first, on the social level, and later, on the individual level; first, between people (interpsychological), and then inside the child (intrapsychological). This applies equally to voluntary attention, to logical memory, and to the formation of concepts.

---

25. See, for example, the influence of Paul Grice in models of human social interaction, in ibid.

26. Wang et al., "How Visual Is the Visual Cortex?," 12545–59.

27. Ibid., 12547.

28. Di Paolo and De Jaegher, "The Interactive Brain Hypothesis," 163.

29. De Jaegher and Di Paolo, Participatory Sense-Making, 485–507.

30. Spezio, Forming Identities in Grace.

All the higher functions originate as actual relations between human individuals.[31]

To summarize, interaction in the current study refers to processes between two or more centers of dynamic systems in which there is a recognizable organization of value and a clear change in one or more of the interactors. Interaction can be antagonistic, competitive, or cooperative. Competition can be either antagonistic or cooperative. Cooperation can be joint, recurrent, transactional, reciprocal (either recurrently or transactionally), or mutual. Each of these types of interaction can result in one or more changes to one or both interactors, including changes to measurable properties, changes to shared value, changes to shared meanings (i.e., intersubjectivity), and necessary constitutive changes, without which the interactors would not exist. Examples of these kinds of interaction occur within the domains of brain, mind, person, and pair. The current study treats broad themes of interaction in the domain of the human brain prior to turning to how DVSCAN uses these themes to inform its analysis of interaction in minds, persons, and pairs.

Interactive Brains

Recent reflection on interaction involving structurally delimited individual brains reveals a reorientation from concern with single nodes to a vigorous inquiry into connections, otherwise categorized as a shift from localist to distributed or population processing. The reorientation away from single node theory does not do away with the importance of recording from single neurons in the brain. Indeed, such recordings, when done in parallel among many neurons in a network, highlight the importance of interactions between interconnected neurons and the necessity of understanding network interactions for understanding the brain and neural coding.[32] Single neuron recordings continue be important, along with measures of neuronal population responses, for discovery in DV-SCAN, but single neuron methodology is itself overturning single node theories of brain and mind function. Single node theories dominated DV-SCAN since at least the time of the cognitive turn and the origins of cognitive science in the late 1950s.[33] Perhaps reaching their apex in the notion of the "grandmother cell," single node theories of neural processing hold that a complex behavior of an organism

---

31. Vygotsky, *Mind in Society*, 57.
32. Cash and Hochberg, *The Emergence of Single Neurons*, 79–91.
33. Miller, *The Cognitive Revolution*, 141–44.

is dependent on a very limited number of single neurons that code for the requisite complexity.[34] Grandmother cells are those cells whose responses are so specific that they appear to react only to one visual or auditory item (e.g., a photo of one's grandmother) and to no others. Single neuron recordings in the human brain can result in patterns of activity that misleadingly resemble those of grandmother cells, yet even the researchers who observe these patterns dismiss such hyper-localist extremes, for good reasons.[35] While localist and even hyper-localist theorists continue to argue for their views, even their models increasingly acknowledge that a single neuron's highly selective response properties emerge from that neuron's place within a complex network. Given that the human neocortex shows evidence of an average 30,000 synapses per neuron, ranging between about 15,000 to over 100,000, and with new methods that make the study of wider networks more feasible, the option to ignore or marginalize network interactions is no longer attractive.[36] Estimates are that each pair of interconnected neurons has four to five synapses, so this means that on average, a single neuron interacts with 3000 to 30000 other neurons via synaptic connections. The recent neuroscientific areas of hodology and connectomics take this intense interactive reality very seriously.

Hodology and Connectomics

One of the outcomes of the growing appreciation for extreme interconnectedness in the brain is new interest in identifying stable types of smaller networks between neurons that occur again and again in forming larger networks across the brain. These networks may help to explain the relatively rapid evolution in nonhuman primate and human brain size, along with the concurrent development of cognitive capacities. The new focus on specific classes of networks, replacing a much more limited focus only on classes of individual cells, includes the importance of identifying individual neuronal cell types capable of forming those classes. Yet the new unit of analysis for the evolution and development of specific higher-level cognitive functions is no longer a given cell type, as in using so-called spindle or Von Economo neurons to explain empathy and other aspects of social cognition,[37] but

---

34. Gross, "Genealogy of the 'Grandmother Cell,'" 512–18; Barlow, *Single Units and Sensation*, 371–94.

35. Quiroga et al., "Sparse but Not 'Grandmother-Cell' Coding," 87–91.

36. DeFelipe, Alonso-Nanclares, and Arellano, "Microstructure of the Neocortex,"299–316.

37. Raghanti et al., "An Analysis of Von Economo Neurons," 2303–4.

rather the types of networks to which these and other cells belong, and the "canonical computations" to which they give rise.[38]

The new emphasis on stable and stably replicable neural networks at small scales, known as neural hodology, has analogues at large scales, as well. Hodology is the study of pathways, and neural hodology orients analysis to the interactive, connecting pathways between neural nodes, and the broader networks that emerge. On larger scales, still within the limits of a single physical brain, hodology is typically taken up into the field of theory and analysis called connectomics.[39] As with smaller scale neural hodology, connectomics is concerned with identifying the evolutionary and developmental significance of relatively stable structural and dynamically functional networks within the brain (i.e., connectomes). Gone are the days when DV–SCAN celebrated pictures of colorful blobs on pictures of grey brains. "Blobology," or focusing on single areas of activation for understanding how the brain works, largely resulted from limitations of neuroimaging methods and computational capabilities. Happily for DV–SCAN and for interdisciplinary engagement of it, focusing on brain blobs is no longer a priority, due to the influence of the Human Connectome Project, along with more sophisticated tools for analyzing and validating functional brain networks on large scales.[40] Unfortunately, much philosophical and theological work that draws on DV–SCAN, most often from books about neuroscience that are not intended for scholarly consumption, continues to miss the current developments outlined here and thus misses out on the fruitful implications of taking interaction seriously in engaging DV–SCAN.

Interactive Minds for Interactively Constituted Persons

There are two primary areas of recent scholarly activity in applying interaction theory within the domain of brain processes to inquiry into the relation between domains of mind and person. Both seek to apply interactionism to expand DV–SCAN beyond individualistic, spectatorial approaches that have thus far been so dominant in cognitive scientific study of the human. First is an emphasis on the situatedness or groundedness

38. Harris and Shepherd, "The Neocortical Circuit," 170–81; Miller, "Canonical Computations of Cerebral Cortex," 75–84.

39. Sporns, 109–25; Van Essen and Ugurbil, "The Future of the Human Connectome," 1–12; Van Essen et al., "The Human Connectome Project," 2222–31; Park and Friston, "Structural and Functional Brain Networks," 1238411–11.

40. Mill et al., "Empirical Validation of Directed Functional Connectivity," 275–87.

of the brain, mind, and person. Second is an emphasis on the importance of relational pairs and their evolutionary and developmental importance, along with attempts to account for recurrent influence between a) the cerebral and cognitive systems serving social interaction and b) the types of social interactions that shape those systems.

Enactivism, Interactionism, and the Extended Mind

External scaffolding,[41] embodied cognition,[42] grounded cognition,[43] enactivism,[44] predictive brain theory,[45] control theory,[46] interactionism and participatory sense-making,[47] and the extended mind (or body[48]) are theories of brain, mind, and person that all point to the brain and mind as basically dependent upon constitutive interactions with their specified contexts. All of them tend to resist varieties of disembodied symbolism when seeking to understand links between brain, mind, and persons. The exact nature of the dependence and which contexts are of central interest serve to differentiate these approaches.

For example, Barsalou clarifies that grounded cognition does not assume that all cognition is dependent on primary sensory processing, and more easily addresses the challenge that abstract concepts and logic pose to situated cognition theories.[49] Grounded cognition and similar theories include a brain's and an organism's situatedness in trying to explain relations between cerebral processes, physiological processes, the organism's behavior, and the surrounding relations and interactions involving the organism. The core claim of grounded cognition theories is that no aspect of cognition or intentional meaning is amodal—free of a body's "mode" of interaction

---

41. Clark, "The Many Faces of Precision," 1–9.

42. Pezzulo et al., "The Mechanics of Embodiment," 5; Pezzulo, "Why Do You Fear the Bogeyman?," 902–11; Anderson, Richardson, and Chemero, "Eroding the Boundaries of Cognition," 717–30; Thompson and Varela, "Radical Embodiment," 418–25.

43. Barsalou, "Grounded Cognition," 617–45.

44. Froese and Di Paolo, "The Enactive Approach," 1–36.

45. Friston and Kiebel, "Cortical Circuits for Perceptual Inference," 1093; Friston, "Prediction, Perception and Agency," 248–52.

46. Eliasmith, "How We Ought to Describe Computation in the Brain," 313–20; Eliasmith et al., "A Large-Scale Model," 1202–5.

47. De Jaegher and Di Paolo, "Participatory Sense-Making," 485–507; Fuchs and De Jaegher, "Enactive Intersubjectivity," 465–86; De Jaegher, "Social Understanding through Direct Perception?," 535–42; De Jaegher, Di Paolo, and Gallagher, "Can Social Interaction Constitute Social Cognition?," 441–47; Di Paolo and De Jaegher, "The Interactive Brain Hypothesis," 163; De Jaegher et al., "Grasping Intersubjectivity," 1–33.

48. Froese and Fuchs, "The Extended Body," 205–35.

49. Barsalou, "Grounded Cognition," 617–45.

with the world—and that all such cognition and intentional meaning require and arise out of "modal simulations, bodily states, and situated action."[50] This is their key positive proposal, and needs to be kept free of some easy confusions, which Barsalou reviewed in 2008.[51] First, grounded cognition includes processes that are genetically and developmentally properties of the cerebral system, the body, and the organism, unlike some theories that seek to reject "interiority" of this sort altogether. Second, grounded cognition includes memory of various kinds, so it is not limited to simplified sensory-motor processes. Third, valuation, often in the form of affective and emotional processing, accompanies cognition and intentional meaning. Indeed, much of the evidence for grounded cognition comes via clear effects of an organism's and an interaction's "task-at-hand," including goal states and pathways between them. Signal transformation and statistically describable representations within the multiple systems of perceptual, conceptual, learning, memory, and even language, are both included in grounded cognition theories. Grounded cognition accentuates the importance of the body and situatedness, both for the brain's systems, and for the action of the mind and organism and person in forming, learning, relaying, and enacting perceptual and conceptual representations. It is important to keep in mind that while grounded cognition critiques the sufficiency of amodal, statistical models of neural and cognitive representations, it embraces statistically representational models as central for understanding interactions between brain, mind, and person. For example, Barsalou notes that many Bayesian approaches to complex concept learning are agnostic about the modal or multimodal nature of their modeled cognitive parameters, but that this need not stand in the way of grounded cognition:

> Bayesian statistics can be viewed as statistical accounts of the multimodal information stored in the dynamic systems that generate simulations and guide situated action. Depending on the particular distribution of multimodal content captured for a category, the Bayesian statistics describing it will vary, as will the simulations and situated actions generated from it.[52]

---

50. Ibid., 617. A "mode" is an embodied system that is somewhat selective for specific sensory signals (e.g., vision, audition, somatosensation), and within modes there are submodal systems with their own sensitivities (e.g., motion and color in vision). Bodily modes and multimodal systems include attention, memory, emotion, and language. "Multimodal" systems both transform and combine transformations from the various modes.

51. Ibid.

52. Ibid., 633.

Statistical representations of conceptual-valuational learning, then, are compatible with and likely advance interactionist views such as grounded cognition.

Some views of enactive or interactive cognition believe that they need to deny any forms of representation whatsoever, shared or otherwise, and/or to deny that they play significant roles in the interaction between brain/mind and context, and between persons. These perspectives believe that representation risks disembodiment and non-interaction with respect to cognition. As others have noted,[53] these extreme, anti-cognitivist views—advanced primarily by Hanne de Jaegher, Thomas Fuchs, and Ezequiel di Paolo[54]—are rife with "rhetorical excess"[55] and often leave behind sound scientific and philosophical criteria in favor of "ideology."[56] Interactionism is not a set of approaches that overturn solid lines of empirical evidence in DV–SCAN simply for the sake of saying something new. Such activity is counterproductive, especially since, as indicated in the previous sections, mainstream DV–SCAN is producing evidence favoring an increased emphasis on interactionist perspectives that include shared representation.[57]

Further, the heavy-handed denial, by di Paolo, Fuchs, de Jaegher and others claiming to advance enactivist and interactionist theory (as opposed to simply advancing anti-representationalism), of all representational processes inside of a physically limited brain, is unhelpful in the extreme. These views champion dynamical systems processes in which the brain, mind, and person are only the time series of their interactions. They rest on a profound misunderstanding of the importance of time and temporal functions in living, thinking, feeling systems. Such systems do not respond instantaneously—on femtosecond or even microsecond scales—to their situatedness. Rather, they require a multitude of integration windows in time—temporal bins of signal processing—to store, transform, and integrate the millions to billions of signals they receive over 2 to 20 milliseconds in time. This occurs before the organism or person can initiate an evaluation or some other response. Any system requiring integration windows for so many signals to transduce, store, transform, and communicate those signals is representing the original signals in some way.

53. Gallotti and Frith, "Response to Di Paolo et al.," 304–5; Eliasmith, "The Complex Systems Approach," 72–77 (discussion 94–102); Gallotti and Frith, "Social Cognition in the We-Mode," 160–65.

54. Fuchs and De Jaegher, "Enactive Intersubjectivity," 465–86; Di Paolo and De Jaegher, "The Interactive Brain Hypothesis," 163.

55. Eliasmith, "The Complex Systems Approach," 72–77 (discussion 94–102; p. 72).

56. Gallotti and Frith, "Response to Di Paolo et al.," 304–5 (p. 305).

57. See especially Botvinick, "Commentary," 78–83.

These internal systems are representations—hardly passive, individualistic, or spectatorial—of the continuous systems that are outside of them. Of course their adaptive function relies on—unsurprisingly—interaction. While it is true that DV–SCAN only rarely addresses the problems of time and temporality in its accounts, as noted by Eliasmith in a recent paper,[58] integration windows and processes occur in models of representation for learning, predictivity, control theory, and valuation.

Extreme views coming from some enactivists and dynamical systems theorists in DV–SCAN are not influential because they lack the evidence-based criteria generally agreed upon for sound science. Unfortunately, the same cannot be said for their influence in philosophy and theology. For example, Wentzel van Huyssteen cites the work of Thomas Fuchs while un-critically accepting Fuchs' view that dynamical systems approaches to social interaction rule out representation altogether. This embrace of Fuchs' theory is seemingly unaware that the theory rejects, with little or no evidence, rigorous research programs yielding insight on empathy, as well as concepts of representation and empathy on which van Huyssteen's and others' theologies depend.[59] More attention to technical accuracy, more engagement of peer-reviewed literature, and more intentional collaboration in interdisciplinary teams are all necessary for philosophy and theology to make better use of DV–SCAN. Were philosophy and theology to take up this challenge, they could advance arguments in ways that could both speak more effectively to scientists and the sciences about how they need to change and to popular audiences about how evidence-based inquiry advances rather than opposes systems of meaning.

Interactionism foregrounds the situatedness of brains, minds, and persons and is evident in Barsalou's grounded cognition, Eliasmith's control theoretic frameworks, Frith's predictive brain theory. Further, interactionism need not be thrown like a wrench into the mix of mainstream DV–SCAN or into the ongoing sound, rigorous, interdisciplinary engagement of DV–SCAN by philosophy and theology. Wide review of the mainstream literature supports the growing importance of interaction and interactionism, beginning in the hodology of small networks, moving to the connectomics of networks over larger scales, and then culminating in considering how brains dynamically rely on organisms and their bodies, and how both rely on specific contexts for their past, present, and future instantiations. The study concludes with a consideration of how these systems facilitate interaction between persons, with special attention to persons in pairs.

58. Eliasmith, "Dynamics, Control, and Cognition," 134–54.
59. Van Huyssteen, "From Empathy to Embodied Faith?" 132–50.

Relational Pairs and the Second Person

Relational pairs arise in and recurrently sustain the structure and dynamics of affiliative groups. Why then place an emphasis on social interaction in pairs rather than on larger groups? The primary answers come from a serious consideration of development and of the practical limitations on our current capabilities in research. The social brain hypothesis proposes that brain size in nonhuman primates and in humans increased over evolutionary history in large part to facilitate affiliative interactions.[60] Larger brains covary with larger group size, and group size covaries, somewhat nonlinearly, with the number and extent of affiliative interactions. Affiliative interactions (e.g., recurrent grooming, mother-infant bonding) largely occur in pairs, and the developmental influence of affiliative and other social interactions on young offspring, especially infants, is almost entirely dependent upon pairwise relationships. Thus, the pair forms a dynamical system of social interaction embedded within a larger connectome that includes the group. Most of the influence of the group in early development—whether through direct interaction or social learning—happens via pairs. The pair is also a scale of social interaction for which current methodologies in DV–SCAN allow robust inquiry. Expanding to larger group sizes is currently beyond most of the capabilities of DV–SCAN that measure and formally model cerebral, physiological, and behavioral responses and their interactions. Doubtless as new technologies develop, it will be possible to study even large groups of pairs. In the meantime, DV–SCAN should proceed with expanding interactionist approaches by focusing on pairs, keeping foremost in mind that this expansion is only a first step in developing fully grounded cognitive theories.

One of the most interesting, promising, and prominent lines of research on social interaction in DV–SCAN is the focus on simulation theory, theory theory, empathy, and theory of mind. After a brief review of some of the lessons and pitfalls from this work, this chapter turns to examine the promise of second-person neuroscience for DV–SCAN.

Empathy and Simulation Theory:
The Misleading Mystique of Mirror Neurons

Empathy and theory of mind are core aspects of interpersonal interactions that are often linked to intersubjectivity. They result in shared representations of value, intention, and meaning, and so are critical to the kinds

60. Dunbar, "The Social Role of Touch," 260–68.

of interactions of interest in nonhuman primate and human evolution and development. Most DVSCAN addresses a kind of empathy emerging from the work of E. B. Titchener, meaning empathy that contributes to knowledge about another person, especially her motivations and character.[61] This kind of empathy, called epistemic empathy, has evolutionary antecedents that are important for developing social brain theory and understanding how brain size, group size, and affiliative and antagonistic interactions relate. Empathic theories of interactional shared representations differ from more symbolic, rule-based accounts because empathy relies on the grounded nature of both the representations and the sharing. So-called "theory theories" of shared representation interaction keep to amodal symbolic systems and to logical inference that is abstracted from any grounded mode. Proto-empathic and empathic theories, by contrast, include affectivity as a constitutive part of information sharing and conceptual understanding between organisms and persons. The controversies surrounding empathy and theory theory are beyond the scope of this paper, but their resolution will have lasting consequences for understanding the origins, scope, and future of human morality.[62]

In the 1990s, before the related sets of questions and methods gave rise to DVSCAN, several researchers announced findings of "mirror neurons" and a "mirror neuron system" in the brains of Rhesus monkeys and humans.[63] It was not long before the researchers responsible for reporting

61. Titchener. But note that some empathy theorists object that epistemic empathy is not the only form of empathy, nor even the most interesting one. Shaun Gallagher, for example, emphasizes empathy as an "an other-directed feeling of concern or interest, distinct from both sympathy and mindreading." See Gallagher, "Comment," 4–65 (65).

62. For a review, see especially Krebs, "Empathy and Altruism," 1134–46; Toi and Batson, "More Evidence That Empathy Is a Source of Altruistic Motivation," 28–92; Batson et al., "Influence of Self-Reported Distress and Empathy," 706–18; Davis, "Measuring Individual Differences in Empathy," 113–26; Batson, Fultz, and Schoenrade, "Distress and Empathy," 19–39; Cialdini et al., "Empathy-Based Helping: Is It Selflessly or Selfishly Motivated?," 749–58; Batson et al., "Immorality from Empathy-Induced Altruism," 1042–54; Batson et al., "Is Empathy-Induced Helping Due to Self-Other Merging?," 495–509; Batson and Moran, "Empathy-Induced Altruism in a Prisoner's Dilemma," 909–24; Halpern and Weinstein, "Rehumanizing the Other," 561–83; Decety and Lamm, "Human Empathy through the Lens of Social Neuroscience," 1146–63; Lamm, Batson, and Decety, "The Neural Substrate of Human Empathy," 42–58; Singer and Lamm, "The Social Neuroscience of Empathy," 81–96; Bloom, "Against Empathy"; Prinz, "Against Empathy"; Singer, "Against Empathy"; Singer and Klimecki, "Empathy and Compassion," R875–R78; Spezio, "Embodied Cognition and Loving Character," 25–40.

63. Fadiga et al., "Motor Facilitation during Action Observation," 2608–11; Jeannerod et al., "Grasping Objects," 314–20; Gallese et al., "Action Recognition in the Premotor Cortex," 593–609; Hari et al., "Activation of Human Primary Motor Cortex"

about these neurons in the monkey and the supposed system to which they belong claimed that the neurons were the substrate for human empathy and intersubjectivity in social interaction.[64] The "mirror neuron" concept came from intracranial, single-unit recordings in the monkey that showed that a small portion of neurons in regions of the brain specified for executing actions also responded to observations of actions. The use of the concept of "mirroring" took shape in the observation that the specialized neurons in these small populations selectively responded to certain actions, but not others (e.g., to grasping food with the hand but not to other simple hand movements), both when a monkey executed the action and when it saw another monkey, or even a person, execute the action. The selectivity of these "visuomotor" neurons—neurons selectively responding when the monkey both sees and does specific actions, but not others—is the foundation of "mirror neuron theory." Statistically shared representations—responses statistically indistinguishable under conditions of seeing an action A and also of doing an action A, but not action B, C, D, etc.—in statistically shared circuits was and is the claim of "mirror neuron theory." If the neurons did not selectively respond to some actions and not others, they could not be a basis for distinguishing between actions or action understanding.

The early work following up on "mirror neuron theory" in the human brain did not attempt to replicate the fine detail of the results seen in the monkey. Technical and ethical challenges to recording from single neurons in human brains prevented such fine detail. Instead, the work in humans relied on neuroimaging systems to measure cerebral signals such as BOLD responses, which depend on the oxygen in the blood and are incapable of resolving statistical similarity or dissimilarity at the level of neurons or small networks. From that early work in humans until today, almost all of the evidence taken to support "mirror neuron theory" in humans relies on methods for measuring or perturbing signals that are incapable of resolving the same kind of statistically shared circuits as seen in the monkey. The neuroimaging and neuroperturbation data in humans is highly replicable, generally showing broad swaths of statistically similar, selective cerebral signals when seeing or hearing and when executing a given action (e.g., grasping a drink, making a facial expression, smelling a pleasant or unpleasant

15061–65; Rizzolatti and Arbib, "Language within Our Grasp," 188–94; Rizzolatti and Fadiga, "Grasping Objects and Grasping Action Meanings," 81–95, discussion 95–103; Craighero et al., "Action for Perception," 1673–92; Rizzolatti et al., "Resonance Behaviors and Mirror Neurons," 85–100; Fadiga et al., "Visuomotor Neurons," 165–77; Gallese, Keysers, and Rizzolatti, "A Unifying View," 396–403.

64. Fadiga et al., "Motor Facilitation during Action Observation," 165–77; Gallese, Keysers, and Rizzolatti, "A Unifying View," 396–403.

aroma).[65] These broad swaths of cerebral signals occur over hundreds of thousands to millions of neurons in the human brain, particularly in supplementary motor cortex (SMA) and pre-SMA, leading one to suspect that if ever there were single neuron studies of "mirroring" in the human brain, they would identify huge numbers of "mirror neurons."

In 2010, a research team led by Mukamel, Fried, and Iacoboni recorded signals from severely epileptic patients undergoing intracranial monitoring, in search of human "mirror neurons."[66] Their findings were surprising. Recordings from nearly 1200 neurons across 7 brain regions in 21 patients—652 neurons in SMA, pre-SMA, and anterior cingulate cortex (ACC)—yielded just 90 neurons that responded in the same way when the person saw and executed the same action but not other actions (e.g., to seeing a smile and giving a smile, but not a frown). Note that neurons that respond in the same way when a person sees another person smile as when that person sees the other person frown cannot in any way be part of a system for understanding the emotions of others. In the SMA and pre-SMA, where the less neurally precise methods of fMRI, EEG, and MEG consistently identify evidence for huge networks of shared circuits, only 23 neurons showed up. That reveals that the evidence of "mirror neurons" in human SMA and pre-SMA relies on identifying just over 1 neuron per participant. This low level is difficult to reconcile with the evidence of shared circuits from cerebral signals measured using fMRI, EEG, and MEG.

Prior to the astounding paucity of "mirror neurons" in the 2010 intracranial recording paper, Greg Hickok and others had already pointed out in 2009 some evidential and theoretical problems with "mirror neuron theory."[67] Hickok expands on this and outlines a number of these problems in his recent book,[68] though the 2009 paper is more rigorously written. These challenges to "mirror neuron theory" include a) a lack of evidence that monkeys require or use responses from "mirror neurons" for social interaction; b) a lack of robust testing of alternative theories for the observed phenomena, especially in humans; c) robust evidence showing that SMA and pre-SMA responses are not required for humans to understand language; and d) robust evidence, again from neuroimaging signals, that action understanding in humans recruits networks that do not show "mirror neuron" properties. These are serious problems for the theory. Taken together with

65. Keysers et al., "A Touching Sight," 335–46; Etzel, Gazzola, and Keysers, "Testing Simulation Theory," e3690.

66. Mukamel et al., "Single-Neuron Responses in Humans," 750–56.

67. Hickok, "Eight Problems for the Mirror Neuron Theory," 1229–43.

68. Hickok, The Myth of Mirror Neurons.

the 2010 intracranial recording paper, there really is no good evidence that "mirroring" or "mirror neurons" lie behind the signals of shared circuits so replicably observed across two decades of careful work in humans. Thus, despite the lure of looking to "mirror neurons" and "mirror neuron theory" to highlight the evolutionary and developmental capacities for embodied social interaction, interaction studies that seek to draw on DV–SCAN should look elsewhere. Evidence of shared circuits is undeniable, at least in terms of larger scale models, but what the networks are sharing, how they are sharing it, and how their activity may contribute to social interaction dependent on empathy is all far from being understood.

Recent work drawing on "mirror neuron theory," both in philosophy and theology, however, has missed these deep problems. For example, Eleanor Stump's 2010 book uncritically lauds "mirror neurons" as "the foundation for the capacity of all fully functional human beings at any age to know the mind of another person,"[69] and she and other philosophers and theologians continue to draw on DVSCAN for support by claiming that the "mirror neuron system" is evidence of human knowledge systems that are grounded in experiential and narrative interaction, as opposed to amodal propositional and symbolic representation.[70] Yet the lines of evidence coming from DV–SCAN show that this line of interdisciplinary engagement is not at all promising, and that rather than a focus on popularized accounts of so-called "mirror neuron systems," interdisciplinary scholars would do better by thoroughly engaging the literature that DV–SCAN itself relies on for its claims and counterclaims. Without such care to the science involved, interactionism in philosophy and theology cannot hope to provide robust and lasting contributions to understanding the basis of the operations under investigation.

The Promise of Second-Person Neuroscience
for Understanding Interactive Persons

One of the most promising areas for interactionist exploration of putative deep interconnections between brain systems and social interaction is that of second person neuroscience.[71] The basis in second-person neuroscience

---

69. Stump, *Wandering in the Darkness*, 68.

70. Ibid., 71.

71. Schilbach et al., "Being with Virtual Others," 718–30; Engemann et al., "Games People Play," 148; Pfeiffer et al., "Towards a Neuroscience of Social Interaction," 22; Schilbach et al., "Toward a Second-Person Neuroscience," 393–414; Schilbach et al., "Authors' Response," 441–62; Pfeiffer et al., "Why We Interact," 124–37.

is a claim that a full understanding of how the interactions within the brain-body-mind system of an individual organism contribute to social interaction requires inquiry that foregrounds individual organisms and persons in pairs. Such a strong claim requires a robust basis and strong evidence. Thus far, the basis of the claim is robust in that it draws strongly on the social brain hypothesis in evolution and on the centrality of pair bonding when offspring are young, a centrality that exists both for humans and nonhuman primates. The evidential claims are thus far mostly missing, but the field itself is only about five years old at the time of this writing. Recent developments in technology will permit robust tests of the claims of second person neuroscience in DV–SCAN, and should yield new discoveries about how brains, bodies, minds, and persons support interactions in pairs, discoveries that would be impossible absent these new methods.

Hyperscanning is one of the most interesting methods making possible investigations within the framework of second-person neuroscience.[72] Hyperscanning is the simultaneous measurement of brain signals from two persons who are interacting with one another.[73] One of the earliest uses of hyperscanning used simultaneous fMRI measures from two persons to show that as they engaged in a task testing the trust between them, the brain signals of one person gave evidence of predicting what the other person was expected to do, akin to a representation of reputation.[74] More recently, hyperscanning methods are in use to identify novel interactive networks within and between brains that may signal shared action and valuational representations, meanings, and intentions. Advanced signal analyses should allow researchers to identify patterns of measurable effects of interaction that index shared representations, and that provide insight into the dynamics of mental coordination at much higher temporal resolution than is possible from behavior or self-report alone.

For interdisciplinary scholars in philosophy and theology, second-person neuroscience deserves attention. Yet caution in terms of the evidence and how it is obtained should remain high, especially when it seems to either easily conform to or surprisingly challenge plausible and attractive claims regarding the human person, human pairs, and human character and moral potential. As always, careful scholarship will be its

72. Montague et al., "Hyperscanning," 1159–64.

73. Krill and Platek, "Working Together May Be Better," e30613; Toppi et al., "Graph Theory in Brain-to-Brain Connectivity," 2211–14; Liu et al., "NIRS-Based Hyperscanning," 82; Nozawa et al., "Interpersonal Frontopolar Neural Synchronization," 484–97; Zhou et al., "Neural Signatures," 731–38; Szymanski et al., "Teams on the Same Wavelength Perform Better," 425–36.

74. King-Casas et al., "Getting to Know You," 78–83.

own reward, and resisting smooth popularizations of the science will be critical for the work ahead.

Acknowledgments

I gratefully acknowledge helpful conversations with Carol Albright, Robert Roberts, Brent Field, Gregory Peterson, Jan Glaescher, Valeria Gazzola, Christian Keysers, Warren Brown, Stephen Pope, Andrea Hollingsworth, Nancey Murphy, Andrew Dreitcer, Ted Peters, and Teresa Sabol Spezio. I am also grateful to the Center of Theological Inquiry for a year-long residential fellowship, and for funding from the Self, Motivation, and Virtue Project, the John Templeton Foundation, the Center for Theology and the Natural Sciences, the Fetzer Institute, and the Mind and Life Institute.

References

Anderson, Michael L., Michael J. Richardson, and Anthony Chemero. 2012. "Eroding the Boundaries of Cognition: Implications of Embodiment 1." *Topics in Cognitive Science* 4/4, pp. 717–30.

Barlow, H.B. 1972. "Single Units and Sensation: A Neuron Doctrine for Perceptual Psychology?" *Perception* 1/4, pp. 371–94.

Barsalou, L. W. 2008. "Grounded Cognition." *Annual Review of Psychology* 59, pp. 617–45.

Batson, C. D., J. Fultz, and P. A. Schoenrade. 1987. "Distress and Empathy: Two Qualitatively Distinct Vicarious Emotions with Different Motivational Consequences." *Journal of Personality* 55/1, pp. 19–39.

Batson, C. D., T. R. Klein, L. Highberger, and L. L. Shaw. 1995. "Immorality from Empathy-Induced Altruism: When Compassion and Justice Conflict." *Journal of Personality and Social Psychology* 68/6, pp. 717–30.

Batson, C. D., and T. Moran. 1999. "Empathy-Induced Altruism in a Prisoner's Dilemma." *European Journal of Social Psychology* 29, pp. 909–24.

Batson, C. D., K. O'Quin, J. Fultz, M. Vanderplas, and A.M. Isen. 1983. "Influence of Self-Reported Distress and Empathy on Egoistic versus Altruistic Motivation to Help." *Journal of Personality and Social Psychology* 45/3, pp. 706–18.

Batson, C. D., K. Sager, E. Garst, M. Kang, K. Rubchinsky, and K. Dawson. 1997. "Is Empathy-Induced Helping Due to Self-Other Merging." *Journal of Personality and Social Psychology* 73/3, pp. 495–509.

Bloom, Paul. "Against Empathy." 2014. *Boston Review* September/October, September 10, 2014. http://www.bostonreview.net/forum/paul-bloom-against-empathy/.

Botvinick, Matthew. 2011. "Commentary: Why I Am Not a Dynamicist." *Topics in Cognitive Science* 4/1, pp. 78–83.

Byrne, Richard W., and Andrew Whiten, eds. 1997. *Machiavellian Intelligence II: Extensions and Evaluations*. Cambridge: Cambridge University Press.

———, eds. 1989. *Machiavellian Intelligence: Social Expertise and the Evolution of Intellect in Monkeys, Apes, and Humans.* Oxford Science Publications. Oxford: Clarendon.

Camerer, C. F., and E. Fehr. 2006. "When Does 'Economic Man' Dominate Social Behavior?" *Science* 311/5757, pp. 47–52.

Cameron, William Bruce. 1963. *Informal Sociology: A Casual Introduction to Sociological Thinking.* Random House Studies in Sociology. New York: Random House.

Cash, S. S., and L. R. Hochberg. 2015. "The Emergence of Single Neurons in Clinical Neurology." *Neuron* 86/1, pp. 79–91.

Chodosh, Sara. 2016. "Mind Aglow: Scientists Watch Thoughts Form in the Brain." *Scientific American*, 24 August. https://www.scientificamerican.com/article/mind-aglow-scientists-watch-thoughts-form-in-the-brain/.

Cialdini, R. B., M. Schaller, D. Houlihan, K. Arps, J. Fultz, and A.L. Beaman. 1987. "Empathy-Based Helping: Is It Selflessly or Selfishly Motivated?" *Journal of Personality and Social Psychology* 52/4, pp. 749–58.

Clark, Andy. 2013. "The Many Faces of Precision: (Replies to Commentaries on 'Whatever Next? Neural Prediction, Situated Agents, and the Future of Cognitive Science')." *Frontiers in Psychology* 4/270, pp. 1–9.

Craighero, L., L. Fadiga, G. Rizzolatti, and C. Umilta. 1999. "Action for Perception: A Motor-Visual Attentional Effect." *Journal of Experimental Psychology: Human Perception and Performance* 25/6, pp. 1673–92.

Davis, M. H. 1983. "Measuring Individual Differences in Empathy: Evidence for a Multidimensional Approach." *Journal of Personality and Social Psychology* 44/1, pp. 113–26.

Decety, J., and C. Lamm. 2006. "Human Empathy through the Lens of Social Neuroscience." *Scientific World Journal* 6, pp. 1146–63.

DeFelipe, Javier, Lidia Alonso-Nanclares, and Jon I. Arellano. 2002. "Microstructure of the Neocortex: Comparative Aspects." *Journal of Neurocytology* 31:299–316.

De Jaegher, Hanne. 2009. "Social Understanding through Direct Perception? Yes, by Interacting." *Consciousness and Cognition* 18/2, pp. 535–42.

De Jaegher, Hanne, and Ezequiel Di Paolo. 2007. "Participatory Sense-Making." *Phenomenology and the Cognitive Sciences* 6/4, pp. 485–507.

De Jaegher, Hanne, Ezequiel A. Di Paolo, and Shaun Gallagher. 2010. "Can Social Interaction Constitute Social Cognition?" *Trends in Cognitive Sciences* 14/10, pp. 441–47.

De Jaegher, Hanne, Barbara Pieper, Daniel Clénin, and Thomas Fuchs. 2016. "Grasping Intersubjectivity: An Invitation to Embody Social Interaction Research." *Phenomenology and the Cognitive Sciences*, 16/3, pp. 491–523.

Di Paolo, Ezequiel A., and Hanne De Jaegher. 2012. "The Interactive Brain Hypothesis." *Front Human Neuroscience* 6, p. 163.

Dunbar, R. I. 2010. "The Social Role of Touch in Humans and Primates: Behavioural Function and Neurobiological Mechanisms." *Neuroscience and Biobehavior Review* 34/2, pp. 260–68.

Dunbar, R. I. M. 2003. "The Social Brain: Mind, Language, and Society in Evolutionary Perspective." *Annual Review of Anthropology* 32, pp. 163–81.

Eliasmith, C. 2012. "The Complex Systems Approach: Rhetoric or Revolution." *Topics in Cognitive Science* 4/1, pp. 72–77; discussion on pp. 94–102.

Eliasmith, Chris. 2008. "Dynamics, Control, and Cognition." In *The Cambridge Handbook of Situated Cognition*, edited by Philip Robbins and Murat Aydede, 134–54. New York: Cambridge University Press.

———. 2010. "How We Ought to Describe Computation in the Brain." *Studies in History and Philosophy of Science* 41/3, pp. 313–20.

Eliasmith, C, T. C. Stewart, X. Choo, T. Bekolay, T. DeWolf, Y. Tang, and D. Rasmussen. 2012. "A Large-Scale Model of the Functioning Brain." *Science* 338/6111, pp. 1202–5.

Enfield, N. J., and Stephen C. Levinson. 2006. "Introduction: Human Sociality as a New Interdisciplinary Field." In *Roots of Human Sociality: Culture, Cognition and Interaction*, edited by N. J. Enfield and Stephen C. Levinson, 1–35. Wenner-Gren Center International Symposium Series. Oxford: Berg.

Engemann, D. A., D. Bzdok, S. B. Eickhoff, K. Vogeley, and L. Schilbach. 2012. "Games People Play: Toward an Enactive View of Cooperation in Social Neuroscience." *Frontiers in Human Neuroscience* 6, p. 148.

Ensminger, Jean. 2004. "Market Integration and Fairness: Evidence from Ultimatum, Dictator, and Public Goods Experiments in East Africa." In *Foundations of Human Sociality: Economic Experiments and Ethnographic Evidence from Fifteen Small-Scale Societies*, edited by J. Henrich, R. Boyd, S. Bowles, C. Camerer, E. Fehr and H. Gintis, 356–81. New York: Oxford University Press.

Etzel, J. A., V. Gazzola, and C. Keysers. 2008. "Testing Simulation Theory with Cross-Modal Multivariate Classification of Fmri Data." *PLoS ONE* 3.11: e3690.

Fadiga, L., L. Fogassi, V. Gallese, and G. Rizzolatti. 2000. "Visuomotor Neurons: Ambiguity of the Discharge or 'Motor' Perception?" *International Journal of Psychophysiology* 35/2–3, pp. 165–77.

Fadiga, L., L. Fogassi, G. Pavesi, and G. Rizzolatti. 1995. "Motor Facilitation During Action Observation: A Magnetic Stimulation Study." *Journal of Neurophysiology* 73/6, pp. 2608–11.

Fehr, E, and C. Camerer. 2007. "Social Neuroeconomics: The Neural Circuitry of Social Preferences." *Trends in Cognitive Sciences* 11/10, pp. 419–27.

Friston, Karl. 2013. "Prediction, Perception and Agency." *International Journal of Psychophysiology* 83/2, pp. 248–52.

Friston, Karl J, Jean Daunizeau, and Stefan J. Kiebel. 2009. "Reinforcement Learning or Active Inference?" *PLoS ONE* 4.7:e6421.

Friston, Karl, and Stefan Kiebel. 2009. "Cortical Circuits for Perceptual Inference." *Neural Networks* 22/8, p. 1093.

Friston, Karl, Jérémie Mattout, and James Kilner. 2011. "Action, Understanding and Active Inference." *Biological Cybernetics* 104/pp. 137–60.

Friston, K., P. Schwartenbeck, T. Fitzgerald, M. Moutoussis, T. Behrens, and R. J. Dolan. 2013."The Anatomy of Choice: Active Inference and Agency." *Frontiers of Human Neuroscience* 7, p. 598.

Froese, Tom, and Thomas Fuchs. 2012. "The Extended Body: A Case Study in the Neurophenomenology of Social Interaction." *Phenomenology and the Cognitive Sciences* 11/2, pp. 205–35.

Froese, Tom, and Ezequiel A. Di Paolo. 2011. "The Enactive Approach." *Pragmatics & Cognition* 19/1, pp. 1–36.

Fuchs, Thomas, and Hanne De Jaegher. 2009. "Enactive Intersubjectivity: Participatory Sense-Making and Mutual Incorporation." *Phenomenology and the Cognitive Sciences* 8/4, pp. 465–86.

Fuentes, Agustin. 2004. "It's Not All Sex and Violence: Integrated Anthropology and the Role of Cooperation and Social Complexity in Human Evolution." *American Anthropologist* 106/4, pp. 710–18.

Fuentes, Agustin, and Linda D. Wolfe, eds. 2002. *Primates Face to Face: Conservation Implications of Human-Nonhuman Primate Interconnections.* Cambridge Studies in Biological and Evolutionary Anthropology 29. New York: Cambridge University Press, 2002.

Gallagher, S. 2012. "Comment: Three Questions for Stueber." *Emotion Review* 4/1, pp. 64–65.

Gallese, V., L. Fadiga, L. Fogassi, and G. Rizzolatti. 1996. "Action Recognition in the Premotor Cortex." *Brain* 119 (Part 2), 593–609.

Gallese, V., C. Keysers, and G. Rizzolatti. 2004. "A Unifying View of the Basis of Social Cognition." *Trends in Cognitive Science* 8/9, pp. 306–403.

Gallotti, Mattia, and Chris D. Frith. 2013. "Response to Di Paolo et al.: How, Exactly, Does It 'Just Happen'? Interaction by Magic." *Trends in Cognitive Sciences* 17/7, pp. 304–5.

———. 2014. "Social Cognition in the We-Mode." *Trends in Cognitive Sciences* 17/4, pp. 160–65

Gross, C. G. 2002. "Genealogy of the 'Grandmother Cell.'" *Neuroscientist* 8/5, pp. 512–18.

Haidt, Jonathan, and Craig Joseph. 2004. "Intuitive Ethics: How Innately Prepared Intuitions Generate Culturally Variable Virtues." *Daedalus* 133/4, pp. 55–66.

Halpern, Jodi, and Harvey M. Weinstein. 2004." Rehumanizing the Other: Empathy and Reconciliation." *Human Rights Quarterly* 26/3, pp. 561–83.

Hari, R., N. Forss, S. Avikainen, E. Kirveskari, S. Salenius, and G. Rizzolatti. 1998. "Activation of Human Primary Motor Cortex During Action Observation: A Neuromagnetic Study." *Proceedings of the National Academy of Sciences U S A* 95/25, pp. 15061–65.

Harris, Kenneth D., and Gordon M. G. Shepherd. 2015. "The Neocortical Circuit: Themes and Variations." *Nature Neuroscience* 18/2, pp. 170–81.

Hickok, G. 2009. "Eight Problems for the Mirror Neuron Theory of Action Understanding in Monkeys and Humans." *Journal of Cognitive Neuroscience* 21/7, pp. 1229–43.

Hickok, Gregory. 2014. *The Myth of Mirror Neurons: The Real Neuroscience of Communication and Cognition.* New York: Norton.

Jeannerod, M., M. A. Arbib, G. Rizzolatti, and H. Sakata. 1995. "Grasping Objects: The Cortical Mechanisms of Visuomotor Transformation." *Trends in Neuroscience* 18/7, pp. 314–20.

Keysers, C., B. Wicker, V. Gazzola, J.L. Anton, L. Fogassi, and V. Gallese. 2004." A Touching Sight: Sii/Pv Activation During the Observation and Experience of Touch." *Neuron* 42/2, pp. 335–46.

King-Casas, Brooks, Damon Tomlin, Cedric Anen, Colin Camerer, Steven R. Quartz, and P. Read Montague. 2005. "Getting to Know You: Reputation and Trust in a Two-Person Economic Exchange." *Science* 308/5718, pp. 78–83.

Krajbich, I., R. Adolphs, D. Tranel, N. L. Denburg, and C. F. Camerer. 2009. "Economic Games Quantify Diminished Sense of Guilt in Patients with Damage to the Prefrontal Cortex." *Journal of Neuroscience* 29/7, pp. 2188–92.

Krebs, D. 1975. "Empathy and Altruism." *Journal of Personality and Social Psychology* 32/6, pp. 1134–46.

Krill, A. L., and S. M. Platek. 2012."Working Together May Be Better: Activation of Reward Centers During a Cooperative Maze Task." *PLoS One* 7/2: e30613.

Lamm, C., C. D. Batson, and J. Decety. 2007. "The Neural Substrate of Human Empathy: Effects of Perspective-Taking and Cognitive Appraisal." *Journal of Cognitive Neuroscience* 19/1, pp. 42–58.

Liu, N., C. Mok, E. E. Witt, A. H. Pradhan, J. E. Chen, and A. L. Reiss. 2016. "Nirs-Based Hyperscanning Reveals Inter-Brain Neural Synchronization during Cooperative Jenga Game with Face-to-Face Communication." *Frontiers of Human Neuroscience* 10, p. 82.

Logothetis, N. K., and B. A. Wandell. 2004. "Interpreting the BOLD Signal." *Annual Review of Physiology* 66, pp. 735–69.

Mack, Michael L., and Alison R. Preston. 2016. "Decisions about the Past Are Guided by Reinstatement of Specific Memories in the Hippocampus and Perirhinal Cortex." *NeuroImage* 127, pp. 144–57.

Mill, Ravi D., Anto Bagic, Andreea Bostan, Walter Schneider, and Michael W. Cole. 2017. "Empirical Validation of Directed Functional Connectivity." *NeuroImage* 146/C, pp. 275–87.

Miller, G. A. 2003. "The Cognitive Revolution: A Historical Perspective." *Trends in Cognitive Sciences* 7/3, pp. 141–44.

Miller, Kenneth D. 2016. "Canonical Computations of Cerebral Cortex." *Current Opinion in Neurobiology* 37, pp. 75–84.

Montague, P. R., G. S. Berns, J. D. Cohen, S. M. McClure, G. Pagnoni, M. Dhamala, M. C. Wiest, *et al.* 2002. "Hyperscanning: Simultaneous Fmri During Linked Social Interactions." *Neuroimage* 16/4, pp. 1159–64.

Mougi, A., and M. Kondoh. 2012. "Diversity of Interaction Types and Ecological Community Stability." *Science* 337/6092, pp. 349–51, 750–56.

Mukamel, R., A. D. Ekstrom, J. Kaplan, M. Iacoboni, and I. Fried. 2010. "Single-Neuron Responses in Humans during Execution and Observation of Actions." *Current Biology* 20/8, pp. 750–56.

Nathan, Marco J., and Guillermo Del Pinal. 2016. "Mapping the Mind: Bridge Laws and the Psycho-Neural Interface." *Synthese* 193/2, pp. 637–57.

Nozawa, T., Y. Sasaki, K. Sakaki, R. Yokoyama, and R. Kawashima. 2016. "Interpersonal Frontopolar Neural Synchronization in Group Communication: An Exploration toward Fnirs Hyperscanning of Natural Interactions." *Neuroimage* 133/1, pp. 484–97.

Park, H. J., and K. Friston. 2013. "Structural and Functional Brain Networks: From Connections to Cognition." *Science* 342/6158, 1238411–11.

Pezzulo, G., L. W. Barsalou, A. Cangelosi, M. H. Fischer, K. McRae, and M. J. Spivey. 2011."The Mechanics of Embodiment: A Dialog on Embodiment and Computational Modeling." *Frontiers of Psychology* 2, pp. 5.

Pezzulo, Giovanni. 2013. "Why Do You Fear the Bogeyman? An Embodied Predictive Coding Model of Perceptual Inference." *Cognitive, Affective, & Behavioral Neuroscience* 14/3, pp. 902–11.

Pfeiffer, U. J., L. Schilbach, B. Timmermans, B. Kuzmanovic, A.L. Georgescu, G. Bente, and K. Vogeley. 2014. "Why We Interact: On the Functional Role of the Striatum in the Subjective Experience of Social Interaction." *Neuroimage* 101, pp. 124–37.

Pfeiffer, U. J., B. Timmermans, K. Vogeley, C. D. Frith, and L. Schilbach. 2013."Towards a Neuroscience of Social Interaction." *Frontiers of Human Neuroscience* 7, pp. 22.

Prinz, Jesse. 2014. "Against Empathy." Forum Response. *Boston Review* September/ October, September 10, 2014. http://bostonreview.net/forum/against-empathy/ jesse-prinz-response-against-empathy-prinz/.

Quiroga, R. Q., G. Kreiman, C. Koch, and I. Fried. 2008. "Sparse but Not 'Grandmother-Cell' Coding in the Medial Temporal Lobe." *Trends in Cognitive Science* 12/3, pp. 87–91.

Raghanti, M. A., L. B. Spurlock, F. R. Treichler, S. E. Weigel, R. Stimmelmayr, C. Butti, J. G. Thewissen, and P. R. Hof. 2015. "An Analysis of Von Economo Neurons in the Cerebral Cortex of Cetaceans, Artiodactyls, and Perissodactyls." *Brain Structure and Function* 220/4, pp. 2303–14.

Rizzolatti, G., and M. A. Arbib. 1998. "Language within Our Grasp." *Trends in Neuroscience* 21/5, pp. 188–94.

Rizzolatti, G., and L. Fadiga. 1998. "Grasping Objects and Grasping Action Meanings: The Dual Role of Monkey Rostroventral Premotor Cortex (Area F5)." *Novartis Foundation Symposium* 218, pp. 81–95; discussion pp. 95–103.

Rizzolatti, G., L. Fadiga, L. Fogassi, and V. Gallese. 1999. "Resonance Behaviors and Mirror Neurons." *Archives of Italian Biology* 137/2–3, pp. 85–100.

Rubinov, M., and O. Sporns. 2010. "Complex Network Measures of Brain Connectivity: Uses and Interpretations." *Neuroimage* 52/3, pp. 1059–69.

Sanfey, A. G., J. K. Rilling, J. A. Aronson, L. E. Nystrom, and J. D. Cohen. 2003. "The Neural Basis of Economic Decision-Making in the Ultimatum Game." *Science* 300/5626, pp. 1755–58.

Schilbach, L., B. Timmermans, V. Reddy, A. Costall, G. Bente, T. Schlicht, and K. Vogeley. 2013."Authors' Response: A Second-Person Neuroscience in Interaction." *Behavioral Brain Sciences* 36/4, pp. 441–62.

Schilbach, L., A. M. Wohlschlaeger, N. C. Kraemer, A. Newen, N. J. Shah, G. R. Fink, and K. Vogeley. 2006. "Being with Virtual Others: Neural Correlates of Social Interaction." *Neuropsychologia* 44/5, pp. 718–30.

Schilbach, Leonhard, Bert Timmermans, Vasudevi Reddy, Alan Costall, Gary Bente, Tobias Schlicht, and Kai Vogeley. 2013. "Toward a Second-Person Neuroscience." *Behavioral and Brain Sciences* 36/4, pp. 393–414.

Schleim, Stephan. 2015."How Empathy Became a Brain Function: A Neurophilosophical Case Study." *Philosophy, Theology, and the Sciences* 2/1, pp. 41–62.

Schlichting, M. L., and A. R. Preston. 2014."Memory Reactivation During Rest Supports Upcoming Learning of Related Content." *Proceedings of the National Academy of Sciences* 111/44, pp. 15845–50.

Sebanz, Natalie, Harold Bekkering, and Günther Knoblich. 2006. "Joint Action: Bodies and Minds Moving Together." *Trends in Cognitive Sciences* 10/2, pp. 70–76.

Singer, Peter. 2014. "Against Empathy." Forum Response. *Boston Review* September/ October, September 10, 2014. http://bostonreview.net/forum/against-empathy/ peter-singer-response-against-empathy-peter-singer/.

Singer, T., and C. Lamm. 2009."The Social Neuroscience of Empathy." *Annals of the New York Academy of Sciences* 1156, pp. 81–96.

Singer, Tania, and Olga M Klimecki. 2014. "Empathy and Compassion." *CURBIO* 24/18 R875–R78.

Spezio, Michael. 2011. "The Cognitive Sciences: A Brief Introduction for Science and Religion." In *The Routledge Companion to Religion and Science*, edited by James W. Haag, Gregory R. Peterson and Michael L. Spezio, 285–95. New York: Routledge.

———. 2015. "Embodied Cognition and Loving Character: Empathy and Character in Moral Formation." *Philosophy, Theology, and the Sciences* 2/1, pp. 25–40.

———. In press. "Forming Identities in Grace: Imitatio and Habitus as Contemporary Categories for the Sciences of Mindfulness and Virtue." *Ex Auditu*.

Sporns, O. 2011."The Human Connectome: A Complex Network." *Annals of the New York Academy of Sciences* 1224/1, pp. 109–25.

Srinivasan, R., P. L. Nunez, D. M. Tucker, R. B. Silberstein, and P. J. Cadusch. 1996. "Spatial Sampling and Filtering of Eeg with Spline Laplacians to Estimate Cortical Potentials." *Brain Topography* 8/4, pp. 355–66.

Stump, Eleonore. 2010. *Wandering in the Darkness: Narrative and the Problem of Suffering*. New York: Oxford University Press.

Szymanski, C., A. Pesquita, A. A. Brennan, D. Perdikis, J. T. Enns, T. R. Brick, V. Muller, and U. Lindenberger. 2017. "Teams on the Same Wavelength Perform Better: Inter-Brain Phase Synchronization Constitutes a Neural Substrate for Social Facilitation." *Neuroimage* 152, pp. 425–36.

Taylor, Michael. 2006. *Rationality and the Ideology of Disconnection*. Contemporary Political Theory. New York: Cambridge University Press.

Thompson, Evan, and Francisco J. Varela. 2001. "Radical Embodiment: Neural Dynamics and Consciousness." *Trends in Cognitive Sciences* 5/10, pp. 418–25.

Titchener, Edward Bradford. 1909. *Lectures on the Experimental Psychology of the Thought-Processes*. New York: Macmillan.

Toi, M., and C. D. Batson. 1982. "More Evidence That Empathy Is a Source of Altruistic Motivation." *Journal of Personality and Social Psychology* 43/2, pp. 281–92.

Toppi, J., A. Ciaramidaro, P. Vogel, D. Mattia, F. Babiloni, M. Siniatchkin, and L. Astolfi. 2015. "Graph Theory in Brain-to-Brain Connectivity: A Simulation Study and an Application to an Eeg Hyperscanning Experiment." *Conference Proceedings, IEEE English Medical and Biological Society* (August), 2211–14.

Van Essen, D. C., and K. Ugurbil. 2012. "The Future of the Human Connectome." *NeuroImage* 62/2 (February 25), 1–12.

Van Essen, D. C., K. Ugurbil, E. Auerbach, D. Barch, T. E. Behrens, R. Bucholz, A. Chang, *et al.* 2012. "The Human Connectome Project: A Data Acquisition Perspective." *Neuroimage* 62/4, pp. 2222–31.

Van Huyssteen, J. Wentzel. 2014. "From Empathy to Embodied Faith? Interdisciplinary Perspectives on the Evolution of Religion." In *Evolution, Religion, and Cognitive Science: Critical and Constructive Essays*, edited by Fraser Watts and Leon Turner, 132–51. New York: Oxford University Press.

Vygotsky, L. S. 1978. *Mind in Society: The Development of Higher Psychological Processes*. Translated by Arthur Luria. Edited by Michael Cole et al. Cambridge: Harvard University Press.

Waal, F. B. M. de. 2006. "Morally Evolved: Primate Social Instincts, Human Morality, and the Rise and Fall of 'Veneer Theory.'" In *Primates and Philosophers: How Morality Evolved*, ed. Stephen Macedo and Josiah Ober. Princeton, NJ: Princeton University Press.

Wang, Xiaoying, Marius V. Peelen, Zaizhu Han, Chenxi He, Alfonso Caramazza, and Yanchao Bi. 2015. "How Visual Is the Visual Cortex? Comparing Connectional and Functional Fingerprints between Congenitally Blind and Sighted Individuals." *The Journal of Neuroscience : The Official Journal of the Society for Neuroscience* 35/36, pp. 12545–59.

Zhou, G., M. Bourguignon, L. Parkkonen, and R. Hari. 2016. "Neural Signatures of Hand Kinematics in Leaders vs. Followers: A Dual-MEG Study." *Neuroimage* 125, pp. 731–38.

8

Towards a Minimal Social Ontology

Persons, Symbols, Artifacts in Interaction

Philip S. Gorski

T HE IDEA OF "INTERACTION" may be a new one in some of the natural
sciences, but it has a long lineage in the social sciences. However, an-
thropologists, economists, political scientists and sociologists do not generally use the term in quite the same way that the contributors to this volume
do. Qualitative social researchers mostly use it in a colloquial sense to refer
to interaction between people. Quantitative social researchers typically use
it in a technical sense to refer to "interaction effects" between statistical
"variables." So, while social scientists do talk a lot of about interaction, it's
not usually in reference to ontology.

In fact, there has not been much talk of "ontology" in the social sciences at all until very recently.[1] Historically, the various social science disciplines have generally been much more worried about epistemology than
ontology. That is, they have been more concerned about how we know than
about what there is. In this, of course, they have simply followed the lead
of modern Western philosophy, which abandoned metaphysics in favor of
epistemology at its inception.

The main goal of this chapter is to sketch out an interactive ontology
for the social sciences analogous to those developed for other disciplines
elsewhere in the volume. It is in three parts. The first concerns social substance. I argue that an adequate account of social structure must minimally
include the following three elements: persons, symbols and artifacts. The
second concerns social relations. I argue that these three building blocks

1. But see Archer, *Realist Social Theory*; and Bhaskar, *The Possibility of Naturalism*.

are connected via four main types of relationships: proximity, affordance, intentionality, and communication. The third section focuses on process. I contend that there are six principal types of social process: flow, drift, reform, revolution, conjuncture and emergence. In the conclusion, I briefly reflect on how the ontology of the social world differs from that of the physical and biological worlds, and on the implications of these differences for the social sciences.

Social Structure: A Minimal Ontology

Every social theory is premised on a social ontology of some kind, a set of assumptions about the basic constituents of the social world.[2] In my view, a satisfactory social ontology must minimally include at least three elements: human persons, cultural signs, and material artifacts.[3] Only an ontology that includes all of these elements under some description will be able to provide an adequate account of social structures.

I say "under some description" because social scientists use many different and roughly cognate terms to describe the basic elements of social structures. Why, then, do I prefer these particular descriptions? Not because I believe they are the only possible or best imaginable ones. Rather, because I believe they are better than the most influential descriptions currently in use. I will now try to explain why.

The term "person" is not very widely used in the social sciences—nowhere near as widely as in philosophy and theology, for example. This is not the place to review the literature on personalism or the various conceptions of personhood within it. Drawing on the work of Christian Smith,[4] and for purposes of the present analysis, I will define a human person as *an embodied center of reflection, purpose and relationships*. This definition is not meant to be complete; rather, it is intended to highlight certain contrasts with two alternative conceptualizations that are widely used in the social sciences: "individuals" and "actors." Both are beset by serious problems.

In the skeptical versions of Western epistemology as well as in the classical liberal versions of Western political philosophy that arose in the sixteenth and seventeenth centuries, the word *individual* has a very specific meaning. It refers to a monad that exists prior to and apart from relations

2. Some theories have fairly explicit ontologies; others are more implicit. Take neoclassical economic theories. They act on the assumption that the social world consists of strategic interactions between utility-maximizing individuals.

3. Gorski, "The Matter of Emergence."

4. Smith, *What Is a Person?*

with the external world and with other monads.[5] Now, this assumption has proven morally and politically useful at times. Amongst other things, it provided justifications for human rights and popular sovereignty.[6]

Still, we have ample grounds to regard it as both anthropologically and sociologically unrealistic. After all, more than any other animal, humans are born helpless and dependent on others.[7] They cannot survive, much less flourish, without care and nurturing.[8] Indeed, it is only through ongoing relationships with others that the human animal actually becomes an "individual" in any meaningful sense, that is, a human person possessed of a distinct and stable identity.[9]

What about the word "actor"? Is it better? It suggests the existence of a "stage," other "actors," and an "audience." It also implies the existence of a "script," the enactment of "performances" (verbal and physical), and the rendering of external judgment (aesthetic). And in dramaturgical and performative forms of social theorizing, the social world is explicitly conceptualized as a grand stage.[10] Insofar as such theories point to a wider social and cultural context, they are certainly more realistic than individualistic theories.

Still, the actor concept has serious problems of its own. For one thing, it implies that our social persona is "just an act," a mask that conceals a real self that exists in private. Indeed, some proponents of the dramaturgical approach to social theory suggest that there's nothing behind the mask, that we have no real self apart from our public performances. In addition, this approach suggests that the "audience" (i.e., other people) judges us based solely on the aesthetic quality of our public performances. Now it is certainly true that most humans engage in dissimulation sometimes, and that people often judge one another in aesthetic terms. But it is equally true that all normal

5. Hobbes, *Leviathan*; Macpherson, *The Political Theory of Possessive Individualism*.

6. See Elshtain 2. But *see* 008. The assumption was crucial to the development of modern epistemology, for example, insofar as it underlay skeptical and introspective methods such as Descartes'. It has also helped to underwrite a moral defense of the inherent dignity and "inalienable rights" of human persons by appealing to the human capacity for rational autonomy as in Kant's works. Finally, it has aided political thinking about social justice, via contractarian reasoning about the political order as in Rawlsian liberalism.

7. McIntyre, *Dependent Rational Animals*.

8. Gilligan, "In a Different Voice"; Held, *The Ethics of Care*.

9. Taylor, *Philosophical Papers*. Vol. 1, *Human Agency and Language*.

10. Alexander, *Cultural Pragmatics*; Goffman, *The Presentation of Self in Everyday Life*.

human beings have inner lives.[11] And it is also true that all normal humans evaluate themselves and each another in moral terms.[12]

The word "person" does not suffer from either of the above defects. It does not collapse our outer self into our inner self, or vice versa. Nor does it collapse ethical judgments into aesthetic ones. Moreover, in personalist philosophy, human beings become true individuals only in and through their myriad relationships with other persons. Human persons are likewise presumed to have an inner autonomy that confers some measure of outer freedom in their actions.

Like the notion of the person, the phrase "cultural symbols" has been chosen in lieu of several more widely circulating terms: "language" and "discourse." This is not the place to review the endless debates about best definition of culture or various theories of representation. In order to highlight certain contrasts with alternative conceptualizations, I offer the following definition: *a cultural symbol is an action, thing or utterance that enables collective activity, joint attention, or shared experience within a certain community.*

During the middle decades of the twentieth century, Anglo-American philosophy took a sharp "linguistic turn." The trailblazer was the Austro-Anglian philosopher, Ludwig Wittgenstein.[13] He emphasized the inter-relationship between ordinary language, social interaction and cultural context.[14] Specifically, he argued that a human utterance only means something in relationship to certain activities embedded within a particular culture.[15] In the closing decades of the twentieth century, some social scientists followed Wittgenstein's lead and started to explore the many and various ways in which human language influences social interactions.[16]

It was around this same time that some social theorists gave the linguistic turn in philosophy a much more radical twist. Inspired by post-modern literary critics and philosophers like Derrida[17] and Foucault,[18] they dropped the idea of "ordinary language" in favor of the term "discourse." Where Wittgenstein and his followers had argued that linguistic meanings are fixed by practical activity and cultural context, the post-modernists sought to sever

11. Archer, *Realist Social Theory.*

12. Taylor, *Sources of the Self.*

13. Wittgenstein, *Philosophical Investigations.*

14. Winch, *The Idea of Social Science.*

15. Kripke, *Wittgenstein on Rules and Private Language.*

16. Rorty, *The Linguistic Turn.*

17. Derrida, *Of Grammatology.*

18. Foucault, *The Order of Things.*

these links. They treated language as a self-contained system with its own internal logic. They argued that words acquired their meanings from their relations with other words. Thus, hard only means something in relation to soft, man in relation to woman, and so on. If that was all there was to it, then words could have stable meanings. The problem is that the meaning of the man/woman "binary" is also influenced by its relationship to other binaries such as hard/soft whose meanings are in turn connected to still other binaries in endless "chains of signification." Where Wittgenstein had emphasized the ways in which practice and culture stabilized linguistic meaning, the post-structuralists argued that "discourse" is inherently unstable and, what is more, that it envelops both practice and culture. In Derrida's (in)famous phrase: "There is nothing outside of the text."

The ordinary language and discursive approaches are both inadequate, albeit for different reasons. Wittgenstein's followers tended to bracket out non-linguistic sources of meaning, such as bodily rituals and artistic representations.[19] Because of their (overly) capacious understanding of "textuality," post-modern discourse theorists do not make this mistake. But they tend to exaggerate the degree to which "discourse" structures "subjectivity" and, conversely, to downplay the human capacity for cooperation and meaning-making.[20] The term "cultural symbols" avoids both these difficulties. The adjective "cultural" emphasizes the human capacities for cooperation and creativity. Meanwhile, the term "sign" is capacious enough to encompass both linguistic and non-linguistic sources of meaning.

Social scientists almost never use the term "artifact." Indeed, outside the fields of archaeology and metaphysics, the term is rarely even heard in academic discussions. The definition used here is analogous to those employed in these two fields. *An artifact is a material object fashioned by human beings for a specific purpose.* The paradigmatic example is a tool. But clothing, shelter, infrastructure, and even artworks would all count as artifacts under my definition.

Now, many social scientists today will argue that human societies are "socially constructed." But by this, they are not referring to the material construction of human societies; rather, they usually mean the discursive construction of social groups.[21] The central point is that many social categories (e.g., race and ethnicity) are not natural categories. This argument has a lot of merit. Consider race. There was a time when Irish immigrants

19. Winch, *The Idea of Social Science.*

20. Asad, *Formations of the Secular.*

21. Burr, *Social Constructionism.*

to the United States were considered "black" rather than white.[22] Meanwhile, in Brazil, there are many racial categories in between black and white that do not exist in the American racial system.[23] When social scientists argue that "race is a social construct," what they usually mean is that races are not natural kinds.

But some proponents of a radical version of social constructionism go much further than this. They contend that the social and even the natural worlds are *only* social constructs, by which they mean "effects" of "discourse." At bottom, this sort of radical social constructionism is a kind of idealist nominalism: the world is just what we say it is, nothing more and nothing less. Taken to its extreme, this position leads not only to complete cultural and moral relativism but also to an epistemic relativism in which there is no meaningful difference between, say, quantum mechanics and Azande magic.[24]

In recent years, exaggerated versions of social constructionism have provoked a materialist backlash. The "new materialism" or "neo-vitalism" is very different from old school, neo-Marxist, "historical materialism."[25] It is not about the "material bases" of human societies or the economic sources of political ideologies. Rather, it is about the active nature of inanimate matter. The new materialists argue that physical matter is neither completely passive nor perfectly pliable. Rather, it is continually acting and interacting. Water is evaporating and condensing, freezing and thawing, eroding streambeds and oxidizing iron. A hammer can pound in nails, but not screws; it can break glass, but not diamonds.

There is an important point here. As with social constructionism, however, this point can be and often is pushed too far. For instance, some versions of the new materialism make no distinction between the natural and the artificial, the found and the made. Of course, this distinction is not completely hard and fast. The super-clean water used in high-end manufacturing is made not found; if drunk in large quantities, it is actually fatal. The distinction between the at-hand and the to-hand is continuous, not dichotomous. Still, there is a meaningful difference between natural objects and man-made ones. Natural objects may afford certain human usages, but they are not designed for specific purposes the way that human-made objects are.

22. Roediger, *The Wages of Whiteness*.

23. Telles, *Race in Another America*.

24. Bloor, *Knowledge and Social Imagery*.

25. Bennett, *Vibrant Matter*; Coole and Frost, eds., *New Materialism*; Groff, *Revitalizing Causality*.

Speaking of "material artifacts" incorporates the insights of social constructionism and the new materialism but without accepting their more exaggerated claims. It acknowledges that the social world is (partially) constructed through linguistic categories while insisting that most social structures also have an artifactual dimension. Following the new materialists, the artifacts idea recognizes that matter is not entirely passive and pliable. However, it also insists on the difference between the natural and the artifactual, between the at–hand and the to–hand.

Thus far, I have explained why I prefer these particular terms to various alternative descriptions. In closing, let me briefly explain why I believe that any adequate account of social structure must include all three of them under some description. Social theories that omit the artifactual element will conclude that social structures are far less stable than they actually are. They will imply—even claim—that "deconstructing," "destabilizing," or "subverting" a "discourse," "binary," or "signifier" will be sufficient to tear down a social structure. This is a silly and self-congratulatory fantasy that only a cloistered, self-important academic could possibly believe.

If radical social constructionists err in treating artifacts as if they were just texts, positivistic social behaviorists err in treating human beings as if they were just material objects. Behaviorists imagine that human behavior is simply an effect of external stimuli of some sort. With enough data, and the proper methods, they promise, human behavior will submit to scientific explanations of the sort developed in the physical sciences. Alas, this promise has been broken again and again, as one behaviorist program after another has succumbed to the vagaries of human behavior. The reason for this is not far to seek: humans are not objects; they are persons with a capacity for reflection and re-orientation. As philosopher Donald Davidson famously put it, where human action is concerned, reasons can be causes.[26] And as his colleague John Searle rightly added, humans often have reasons for their reasons as well; that is, they may reject some reasons for action in favor of others, on grounds of morality, convention, or character.[27] This is why a social theory that treats persons as objects will inevitably fail.

Now, rational choice theorists cannot be accused of denying that reasons can be causes. For them, all human action and indeed all of social life results from individuals' efforts to maximize their "utility" based on some set of well-ordered subjective "preferences." The perennial problem for economistic accounts of this sort is the origin of preferences. In the most internally consistent versions of the rational-choice paradigm, preferences are

26. Davidson, *Actions, Reasons, and Causes.*
27. Searle, *Intentionality.*

treated as purely personal "tastes," whose origin is ultimately irrational and inexplicable.[28] This is clearly a case of professional training overriding common sense. One does not need to be a cultural sociologist or anthropologist to see that people's preferences and even their tastes are deeply influenced by cultural context and social relations. They are part of what makes us who we are, and what defines which "we" we're a part of. Preferences are cultural and social through and through. To say nothing of ethics, morality, and values, which are even more resistant to treatment as "preferences."

Structural Relations: An Expanded Ontology

A good social ontology must do more than inventory the building blocks of the social world. It must also catalogue the various ways in which they can be and typically are fit together into concrete social structures. It must attend to types of relations, and not just categories of substance.[29] In this section, I propose that internal relations in social structures are of four types: proximity, affordance, intentionality, and communication.

Some readers may object that I am engaging in "reification," that is, that I am treating social structures as thing-like. I am happy to confess to this crime, as I am in fact a philosophical realist about social structures. In my version of social realism, however, much hinges on the word "like" in the phrase "thing-like." Social structures are not things in quite the same sense as physical or biological structures are. I will revisit the charge of reification at the end of this section.

By "proximity," I mean a relationship of spatio-temporal contiguity. Two persons may be close together or far apart in space and time, in space but not time, in time but not space, or in neither the one nor the other. The same holds for material artifacts, such as a hammer and a nail. Relationships of proximity among and between persons and artifacts are often important in social life. They tend to be less important in relationships involving cultural signs.

By "affordance," I mean a relationship of means to ends that is accidental rather than essential.[30] Consider again the paradigmatic example of an affordance: a rock that can be used for sitting. The rock was not designed for sitting; and it would still be a rock if it were not possible to sit on it. Artifacts may also have affordances of course. A stiff spatula can be used as an ice scraper, for instance, and a large screwdriver can function as a chisel.

28. Becker, *Accounting for Tastes*.
29. Emirbayer, "Manifesto for a Relational Sociology"; Somers, "'We're No Angels.'"
30. Scarantino, "Affordances Explained."

Human language also generates various affordances. Indeed, the linguistic anthropologist Webb Keane has recently shown that second- and third-person locutions generate "ethical affordances."[31] In second-person speech we put ourselves in someone else's shoes, which affords reasoning about equity. And in third-person speech we are placed into a God's-eye perspective that affords reasoning about justice.

I use the word "intention" in the broader, philosophical sense, rather than the narrower, colloquial sense. Intention, in this sense, essentially means "focus."[32] The focus may be close up in time and space as when I focus my attention on one person in a crowded room or reach for one tool in a well-stocked toolbox. In both these cases, relations of attention coincide with relations of proximity. This is not always the case, however. Intentional objects may also be far away in time or space as when I focus on starting a family or saving up for a house. The human capacity for memory and imagination means that one's intentions may also be directed towards things that are in the past and even to non-physical "objects." As mainstream philosophers use the term, intentional relations always involve persons. Some philosophers argue that they may also obtain between material artifacts.[33] For example, one might argue that a hammer has an intentional relationship to a nail. Here, I adopt this slightly expanded usage.

The fourth and final type of social relationship that I will consider is "communication."[34] Such relationships involve the transmission or exchange of information and meaning. The most common type of communicative relationship is between persons, typically through the medium of human language or other cultural signs. But communication can often take non-verbal and non-linguistic forms, too, as with hand gestures and facial expressions. They may also be between persons and artifacts, insofar as those artifacts also function as cultural signs, as in the case of a road sign or instruction manual.

We are now in a position to revisit the subject of reification. Reification occurs when a social structure is (mis)conceptualized as a physical object. The most common and severe form today is what I will call behavioral determinism. It (mis)conceptualizes human persons as material objects that respond to external stimuli in highly predictable or even law-like ways. It is particularly common in rational-choice theory, but also in the cognitive sciences. The common denominator is a denial of inner freedom. Behavioral

---

31. Keane, *Ethical Life.*
32. Searle, *Intentionality.*
33. Harman, *Tool-Being.*
34. Habermas, *Lifeworld and System.*

determinism also comes in a macro sociological form. It treats social groups as unitary actors motivated by objective interests. Crude forms of Marxist theory treat social classes in this way. Behavioral determinism typically goes together with cultural epiphenomenalism, the idea that human culture is ex-post ideology, a secondary byproduct of "real" interests.

But in some of the social sciences, particularly anthropology and sociology, the reverse error of de-reification is actually far more common today. De-reification occurs when the social world is (mis)conceptualized as wholly immaterial. The most common and severe form of de-reification is what might be called cultural projectionism. It treats the social and some-times even the natural world as a blank screen onto which "discourses" project completely arbitrary and ultimately illusory images. This is why it is important to keep in mind the embodied character of human persons and the artifactual dimension of the social world.

Temporal Relations: An Interactive Ontology

Thus far, I have inventoried the basic elements and relations that constitute the social world. A truly interactive social ontology must also incorporate a temporal dimension. For social structures exist in and across time, just like physical and biological ones do. And any social science worth its salt must be capable of accounting for structural stability as well as change through time. In this third and final section, I distinguish five major types of social-structural processes: flow, drift, reform, revolution, conjuncture, and emergence.

A flow conserves a structure. To understand the specificities of social flows, it will be helpful to begin with physical and biological ones. First, consider a physical flow, such as water flowing out of a spring or an eddy in a stream. So long as the water flows at a more or less constant rate, and the shape of the spring or streambed does not change significantly, the flow will retain a certain shape or form, oscillating within some set of parameters. The matter that makes up the flow is continually changing, but the shape of the flow remains relatively constant. Physical flows are not self-sustaining, however. If the water runs dry or the stream silts up, the spring or eddy will simply disappear. By contrast, biological flows can be self-sustaining for some period of time (i.e., the life span of the organism). The paradig-matic instance of a biological flow is the metabolic process.[35] An organism takes in food, transforms it into energy, and excretes the waste products. As with a physical flow, the matter that composes an organism is continually

35. Jonas, *The Phenomenon of Life.*

replenished by the metabolic process. But it does so in a way that also conserves the structure that shapes the flow, in this case the "body" of the
organism. What is more, if the source of the flow "runs dry," many organisms are capable of searching for new "food" sources. Many organisms are
also able to repair or adapt to damage to their physical structures (i.e., to
"heal"), albeit within some limits. What biological organisms cannot do is
willfully create or reshape their bodies. By contrast, social flows can sometimes be willfully created and reshaped through conscious human activity,
though not always or easily. Social structures are neither naturally occurring, like physical flows, nor self-reproducing, like biological ones. Rather,
they are created and sustained through human activity. The stability of a
social flow can be maintained through various mechanisms: the routini-
zation of everyday activity, the creation of social norms, and the shaping
of the material environment to name a few. Durable social organizations
such as cities, universities, or businesses usually deploy all three of these
mechanisms in combination.

Drift refers to slow but significant changes in a social structure that
result from endogenous but non-intentional causes. Some of the distinctive
features of social-structural drift can be brought out through a brief contrast
with the biological phenomenon known as genetic drift. It occurs when the
gene pool of a particular species is altered by "chance occurrences," meaning
alterations that are not the result of normal evolutionary mechanisms (i.e.,
natural selection, migration, or mutation) or of non-biological events (e.g.,
natural disasters, human activity, or climatic change). The paradigmatic
example is the reproductive successes or failures of particular individuals
for reasons not having to do with fitness or the lack thereof, which alter the
frequency of a given gene. Now, social structures do not have actual DNA.
But they do have reproductive mechanisms of a sort. Three of the most important were enumerated above in the discussion above: routines, norms,
and infrastructure. Social drift occurs when small changes in routines,
norms, and infrastructure accumulate over time. For example, it might be
due to changes in the flow of persons through the structure. Changes in the
cultural background of new entrants into an existing organization (e.g., an
extended family, a business enterprise, or an educational institution) may
eventually transform the internal culture of that organization, especially
if strong socialization mechanisms are not in place. Or it might be due to
incremental reinterpretations of social norms. Think about how norms
about "proper attire" in a professional environment in the United States
have progressively loosened over the past half century. Finally, consider how
new infrastructure in an existing city (e.g., the construction of an interstate
highway) can lead to slow but cumulative changes in human activity (e.g., in
shopping patterns, housing choices) that may eventually change the city in

significant ways (e.g., by increasing levels of racial segregation).[36] Of course, such changes may also be intentional.

Reform and revolution both refer to rapid and significant social changes that result from endogenous and intentional causes. Both differ from drift in their speed and its intentionality. How then do they differ from each other? As I define these terms, a reform seeks to conserve a structure, while a revolution seeks to transform it. Since these are the most familiar social-structural process, I will not discuss either in great detail.

The four processes discussed so far all have endogenous causes. That is, they are brought about by changes within a given structure. Conjuncture, the fifth type, results from exogenous causes. It occurs when two flows intersect and alter one another. Sometimes the conjunctures and the resulting changes are both intentional. Wars provide a good example. The poor showing of the Prussian army in its clashes with Napoleon's forces led to the so-called Stein-Hardenberg reforms. The result was deep changes in the tactics and training of the much-vaunted Prussian military. Sometimes the conjuncture and the changes are both unintentional. Western colonialism provides an excellent illustration. The unequal encounter between colonial powers and indigenous people caused significant cultural change on both sides.[37] In other cases, an unintentional conjuncture leads to intentional reforms. During the 1960s, the conjuncture of the baby boom and the economic boom of the post-WWII decades led to a rapid expansion of Western systems of higher education, which fundamentally transformed universities from bastions of elite formation to sites of vocational training.

The sixth and final type of change process is emergence. There are many different definitions of emergence.[38] Here, I will use the term to refer to what is usually called "strong" or "ontological" emergence.[39] Emergence in this sense occurs when a whole has causal powers that are not possessed by its parts in isolation from one another. The textbook example is the power of H_2O to extinguish fires. Neither hydrogen nor oxygen has this power. Adding hydrogen to a fire will cause an explosion. Adding oxygen to a fire will only feed it. Hydrogen plus oxygen makes water, which *will* extinguish fires. Ontological emergence is a pervasive phenomenon in the social world. One is hard pressed to think of a social institution that does not have emergent powers of some kind that it would not have if its various parts were not related to one another in a particular way. Take the modern university. Amongst other things, it has the power to reproduce and generate scientific knowledge and to confer social status and educational credentials. Take

36. Roberto, *The Boundaries of Spatial Inequity*.

37. Sahlins, *Islands of History*.

38. Bedau and Humphreys, *Emergence*.

39. Elder-Vass, *The Causal Power of Social Structures*.

away one of its components—the faculty or the students, say—and it would lose some or all of these powers. Or change the relationship of its parts, by blocking communicative relations.

Conclusion

I elaborated my interactive social ontology in three steps. I began with substance, then turned to relations and finally added process. All three are necessary. A pure substance ontology of a neo-Aristotelian sort will not do, and for two reasons. First, because a substance is the kind of substance it is because of the internal relations between its parts. Second, because most substances—and all living and social substances—can only remain what they are by virtue of certain processes. A purely relational ontology of a neo-pragmatist sort is equally unsatisfactory, and also for two reasons. A substance is the kind of substance it is not only because of its internal relations but also because of its constituent parts. Relations alone do not define it. Further, most relations are dynamic rather than static, and therefore involve certain kinds of processes. Nor will a pure process ontology do the trick, and for reasons that should now be apparent: a process involves sustained relations between certain categories of substances across time.

At each step of the analysis, I argued for a minimal social ontology. Without this ontological minimum, I contended, a social theory will not be fully adequate to social reality. An adequate theory of social structure must include persons, symbols and artifacts under some description. It must also attend to certain types of internal relations within social structures, specifically, relations of proximity, affordance, intention and communication. Finally, it must include endogenous and exogenous and intentional and unintentional causes of social-structural stability and change. To this end, I enumerated six key mechanisms: flow, drift, reform, revolution, conjuncture, and emergence.

Throughout the analysis, I drew stylized comparisons between the physical, biological, and social worlds. My goal in doing so was to highlight the ontological differences among them and, in particular, to underline what is ontologically distinctive about the social world. I did not mean to suggest that these worlds are separable in practice or that the boundaries between them are sharp or impermeable. In the present era, the social world has an increasing impact on the other two, leading some observers to christen it as "the Anthropocene." Further, biologists have taught us that there are also animal social worlds that have more in common with the human social world than we previously imagined. With those qualifications in mind, it is still true that the human social world stands apart in various ways. It is unique insofar as it is co-constituted through cultural symbols. While some intelligent animals appear capable of learning human symbols systems, they do not have and are probably incapable of developing symbols systems of their own. Further, while many animals do produce artifacts (e.g., burrows and nests), and a few even make and use simple tools, none produce artifacts in the same quantity or quality as humans do. All of which is to simply restate what has long been known, namely, that human beings differ from other animals in their capacity for language and tool–making.

References

Alexander, J. C., 2004. "Cultural Pragmatics: Social Performance between Ritual and Strategy," *Sociological Theory* 22/4, pp. 527–73.

Archer, M. S., 1995. *Realist Social Theory: The Morphogenetic Approach*. Cambridge: Cambridge University Press.

———. 2000. *Being Human: The Problem of Agency*. New York: Cambridge University Press.

Asad, T. 2003. *Formations of the Secular: Christianity, Islam, Modernity*. Cultural Memory in the Present. Stanford: Stanford University Press.

Becker, G. S. 1996. *Accounting for Tastes*. Cambridge: Harvard University Press.

Bedau, M. A., and P. E. Humphreys. 2008. *Emergence: Contemporary Readings in Philosophy and Science*. Cambridge: MIT Press.

Bennett, J., 2009. *Vibrant Matter: A Political Ecology of Things*: Durham, NC: Duke University Press.

Bhaskar, R. 1998. *The Possibility of Naturalism: A Philosophical Critique of the Contemporary Human Sciences*. Critical Realism—Interventions. London: Routledge.

Bloor, D. 1991. *Knowledge and Social Imagery*. 2nd ed. Chicago: University of Chicago Press.

Burr, V. 2015. *Social Constructionism*. 3rd ed. London: Routledge.

Coole, D., and S. Frost, eds. 2010. *New Materialisms: Ontology, Agency, and Politics*. Durham, NC: Duke University Press.

Davidson, D. 1963. "Actions, Reasons, and Causes." *Journal of Philosophy* 60/23, pp. 685–700.

Derrida, J. 1976. *Of Grammatology*. 1st American ed. Baltimore: Johns Hopkins University Press.

Elder-Vass, D. 2010. *The Causal Power of Social Structures: Emergence, Structure and Agency*. Cambridge: Cambridge University Press.

Elshtain, J. B. 2008. *Sovereignty: God, State, and Self*. New York: Basic Books.

Emirbayer, M. 1997. "Manifesto for a Relational Sociology." *American Journal of Sociology* 103/2, pp. 281–317.

Foucault, M. 1970. *The Order of Things: Archaeology of the Human Sciences*. London: Tavistock.

Gilligan, C. 1977. "In a Different Voice," *Harvard Educational Review, 47/3*, pp. 365–78.

Goffman, E. 1978. *The Presentation of Self in Everyday Life*: Harmondsworth, UK: Penguin.

Gorski, P. S. 2016. "The Matter of Emergence: Material Artifacts and Social Structure," *Qualitative Sociology* 39/2, pp. 211–15.

Groff, R. 2008. *Revitalizing Causality: Realism about Causality in Philosophy and Social Science*. Routledge Studies in Critical Realism 18. London: Routledge.

Habermas, J. 1985. *The Theory of Communicative Action*. Vol. 2, *Lifeworld and System: A Critique of Functionalist Reason*. Translated by T. McCarthy. Boston: Beacon .

Harman, G. 2002. *Tool-Being: Heidegger and the Metaphysics of Objects*. Chicago: Open Court.

Held, V. 2006. *The Ethics of Care: Personal, Political, and Global*. Oxford: Oxford University Press.

Hobbes, T. 1968. *Leviathan*. Edited by C. B. Macpherson. Penguin Classics. Harmondsworth, UK: Penguin.

Jonas, H. 1966. *The Phenomenon of Life: Toward a Philosophical Biology*. Evanston, IL: Northwestern University Press.

———. 1985. *The Imperative of Responsibility: In Search of an Ethics for the Technological Age*. Chicago: University of Chicago Press.

Keane, W. 2015. *Ethical Life: Its Natural and Social Histories*. Princeton: Princeton University Press.

Kripke, S. A. 1982. *Wittgenstein on Rules and Private Language: An Elementary Exposition*. Cambridge: Harvard University Press.

MacIntyre, A. C. 1999. *Dependent Rational Animals: Why Human Beings Need the Virtues*. The Paul Carus Lecture Series 20. Chicago: Open Court.

Macpherson, C. B. 1964. *The Political Theory of Possessive Individualism: Hobbes to Locke*. Oxford: Clarendon.

Roberto, E. 2015. "The Boundaries of Spatial Inequality: Three Essays on the Measurement and Analysis of Residential Segregation." PhD diss., Yale University.

Roediger, D. R. 1991. *The Wages of Whiteness: Race and the Making of the American Working Class*. The Haymarket Series. London: Verso.

Rorty, R. 1992. *The Linguistic Turn: Essays in Philosophical Method*. Chicago: University of Chicago Press.

Sahlins, M. 2013. *Islands of History*. Chicago: University of Chicago Press.

Scarantino, A. 2003. "Affordances Explained." *Philosophy of Science* 70/5, pp. 949–61.

Searle, J. R. 1983. *Intentionality: An Essay in the Philosophy of Mind*. Cambridge Paperback Library. Cambridge: Cambridge University Press.

———. 2003. *Rationality in Action*. Cambridge: MIT Press.

Smith, C. 2010. *What Is a Person? Rethinking Humanity, Social Life, and the Moral Good from the Person Up*. Chicago: University of Chicago Press.

Somers, M. R. 1998. "'We're no Angels' Realism, Rational Choice and Rationality in Social Science." *American Journal of Sociology* 104/3, pp. 722–84.

Taylor, C. 1985. *Human Agency and Language*. Philosophical Papers 1. New York: Cambridge University Press.

———. 1989. *Sources of the Self: The Making of the Modern Identity*. Cambridge: Harvard University Press.

Telles, E. E. 2014. *Race in Another America: The Significance of Skin Color in Brazil*. My iLibrary. Princeton: Princeton University Press.

Winch, P. 1958. *The Idea of Social Science and Its Relation to Philosophy*. Studies in Philosophical Psychology. London: Routledge & Kegan Paul.

Wittgenstein, L. 2010. *Philosophical Investigations*. 4th rev. ed. by P. M. S. Hacker and Joachim Schulte. New York: Wiley.

Part 3

Interaction in Theology

9

Evolution of Religion, Evolution of Science

Their Interaction

MLADEN TURK

C ONSIDER THE FOLLOWING TWO questions: would we still be talking about the ways in which our traditional religious worldviews developed thousands of years ago, rooted in an even deeper evolutionary history of the human mind, if our modern scientific worldviews would exhaust our sense that there is more in our vision of who we are than accounted for in our modern scientific descriptions of ourselves? If our traditional religious worldviews would be sufficient to account for our descriptions of reality as described by modern science, would we still be trying to contribute novel interpretations of those views in order to account for newfound realities of our experience? We put demands on the world that no amount of scientific understanding of the world could answer. Contemporary approaches to the scientific study of religion, particularly the cognitive science of religion, do not sufficiently consider the interaction between religion and science throughout their history. When we look back at the important intellectual developments in the history of modernity, including movements and thinkers that produced modern science and modern religious reactions to our science-centered worldviews, we cannot overlook how interactive those developments are. If we want to get at 'the way things are' one thing is certain: it is never as simple as just stating it. Our sense of the world is rooted in our intellectual history and to understand it we must go over some interactions that led us to our current context.

This article clarifies the role of interaction in our understanding of scientific models for human religious behaviors. How is interaction to be understood and what difference does it make if we think of our knowledge of human evolutionary behaviors in interactive terms? The idea of universal determinism, recognized already by Durkheim as being of recent origin, seems to rule our current understanding of the physical world, and it exerts greater and greater influence on all modern ways of thinking including religion.[1] Determinism does not go unchallenged and numerous alternatives exist, but it still exerts a considerable influence in the contemporary context of modern science.[2]

Human religious behaviors can be traced back to the dawn of humanity and some of the earliest examples of material culture produced by *Homo sapiens* are often interpreted as "religious." For something to be defined as religious we must consider and interact with our present context and what this label means for us and then be careful not to apply it anachronistically to all instances of what we perceive as religious without being clear that we are using it in a presentist sense.[3] In every instance from history interaction between symbolic behaviors and how those behaviors were understood was dynamic.

Another important issue is that when we look back in time, we leave our familiar surroundings and we venture to the world practically unknown to us. It is in our interaction with the unknown that religious behaviors play a role because of the assumptions included in what we deem religious. Religious behaviors are systemic communal institutionalized discourse and practices that are related to powers or beings perceived as transcendent or set apart from ordinary humans. Understood that way, religious behaviors are, in part, what enabled our ancestors to have communal intentionality and the ability to respond to a new and uncommon environment in a synchronized and predictable way.[4]

What we call religion and what we call science are concepts that were formed over time and depend on historical and cultural context. The story of the scientific study of religion began to take shape in the wake of the Protestant Reformation. As Hans Schwarz points out, three figures exemplify the beginning of a new age: Johannes Kepler, Galileo Galilei,

---

1. Durkheim, *Elementary Forms of Religious Life*, 24.

2. Mitchell, *Complexity*, 4.

3. Wilson, "The Historiography of Science and Religion."

4. Mithen, *The Prehistory of the Mind*; Tomasello, *A Natural History of Human Thinking*.

and René Descartes.[5] Kepler's laws made our model of the solar system less harmonious than the model of antiquity and this situation helped to bring about the rethinking of those views in modernity. Galileo's questioning of prevailing Aristotelianism was perceived as disruptive by many of his contemporaries, and it strengthened a rethinking of traditional views that was already under way after the Reformation. Finally, with Descartes a new era of doubt was introduced, perhaps unwittingly, because of his quest to find a firm foundation for knowledge. To avoid what he perceived as an inadequate basis for knowledge, Descartes proposed that we should begin by doubting everything and only accept those truths that withstand our test of doubt.[6] Over time, this departure point became widely accepted. Thus, thinkers like Descartes effectively ushered in the modern age in which all traditional sources of authoritative knowledge were open to revision based on methodological doubt.

The relevance of reason had been elevated, but what reason provided was not the kind of certainty that Descartes might have hoped for. Instead, it is the modern trust in reason that eventually opens itself to doubt, and thus results in what Roberto Mangabeira Unger calls "the problem of groundlessness."[7] According to Unger—who follows Paul Tillich, Immanuel Kant, and others—we are not able to grasp the ground of being because in our reasoning one presupposition leads to another. There is always another question to be asked and answered and there is always another cause that can be pointed at.

Unger differentiates between speculative groundlessness and existential groundlessness. Speculative groundlessness is often expressed in philosophical/metaphysical questions raised by modern science. Existential groundlessness is the domain of what is in modern times understood as religion. Those two domains closely interact. As speculative groundlessness presents itself in existential questions, these in turn drive our speculative attempts to understand the ground of being. Unger is right when he writes that, in modern science, we try to "discern the immutable laws governing nature" in hopes that "these laws would then fix the outer limit to our comprehension of nature." However, as Unger points out, this quest has had serious limitations precisely because those methods are "suited to the exploration of parts of nature rather than of the universe as a whole."[8] This attitude is an insult to cosmology as it has developed since the 1920s.

---

5. Schwarz, *Vying for Truth.*

6. Descartes, *Meditations on First Philosophy.*

7. Unger, *The Religion of the Future.*

8. Ibid.

We propose that the interaction between speculative groundlessness and existential groundlessness is analogous to the interaction between the scientific study of religion and religious ways of understanding the world in modernity.

Another way to point at the groundlessness is, for example, that of anthropologist Richard Shweder.[9] In one of his lectures on cultural pluralism, Shweder points out a principle he, somewhat humorously, calls "confusionism." Shweder explains that confusionism states that "the knowable world is incomplete if seen from any one point of view, incoherent if seen from all points of view at once, and empty if you try to see it from nowhere in particular."[10] Yet another earlier influential way of formulating this came from philosopher of science Karl Popper, who realized how difficult it is to avoid what is called "the Munchhausen trilemma." Popper defined this problem and gave his answer to it. The trilemma can be stated simply that with every proof, we can ask for a proof of that proof and we can then resort to one of three possibilities. First is to produce a circular proof, second to offer a regressive proof, and the third is to present an axiomatic proof.[11] This persistent epistemological problem seems to have been identified even in antiquity by Sextus Empiricus[12] and again in the early nineteenth century by Jakob Friedrich Fries.[13] Those and other methodological issues are at the very core of modern science and as such they permeate all knowledge claims based on it.

Interaction between modern scientific ways of knowing and religious behaviors in modernity are also deeply transformed by the trilemma. Evolutionary and historical processes led to traditional religious ways of addressing our questions about the universe as a whole. However, our ground-of-being considerations of reality produced by evolutionary and historical processes are revised in light of our current rapid change in technologically expanded understanding, which is deeply rooted in assumptions that replaced those traditional religious views. If we put our "trust" in those assumptions we seem to be fine. But as soon as those assumptions are questioned, we find ourselves thrown out into the abyss of groundlessness.

Traditional religious worldviews proposed various ways to manage this groundlessness. As Unger suggests, there are three different families

9. Shweder, *Thinking through Cultures.*

10. Shweder, "Robust Cultural Pluralism."

11. Popper, *The Logic of Scientific Discovery.*

12. Sextus, *Outlines of Scepticism.*

13. Fries, *Neue Oder Anthropologische Kritik Der Vernunf.*

of attempts to address it.[14] Philosophically speaking, if we would abstract from religious behaviors it is possible to discern three different approaches to the issue of groundlessness. First, one is to assume that we have a friend in charge of the universe, as in Judaism, Christianity, and Islam, for example. This might be most desirable, but in our modern times perhaps most difficult to accept at face value. The second strategy is to emphasize the process of the universe in which everything changes, yet is united by a changeless unified being, as in Hinduism, Buddhism, and Jainism. The third way to approach this problem religiously is to assume that nature is meaningless but we create meaning though our mastery of a small part of it, as in Confucianism and Daoism. In the practice of most religious traditions, those three views are often combined in some way. On their own they exemplify specific religious traditions, but even when combined in some way, they are still only partially successful at addressing issues that they seem to have successfully addressed before.

In the transformation of the role of religion in the Western world, the ideas of certain figures had a major impact. As explained by J. Samuel Preus in his classic *Explaining Religion*, Jean Bodin and others like him led many to develop an apparently disinterested view of religion, becoming arbiters of its contribution to their lives.[15] Bodin differentiated between intellectual, political, and attitudinal realms of religion.[16] For Bodin, religious motivations and behaviors and their role in society were something to be analyzed and explained. No longer a source of meaning and a way of knowing whose authority transcended humanity, religion became a problem that must be addressed. During the sixteenth and seventeenth centuries, a series of conflicts in Europe was fought under the banner of religion. Perhaps it was the perception that those wars were fought because of minute theological differences that gave impetus to proposals to understand religion apart from its theological content. It seems that nobody expected a theological solution to a series of problems apparently caused by theological differences.

The assumption that was often taken for granted in early attempts to explain religion is that we must account for its origins first. In the context of sixteenth- and seventeenth-century Europe, it became more and more difficult to think of any theological solution to the conflict, and it was believed that all ways of being religious must have descended from some supposed primordial religion somewhere at the dawn of humanity. People began looking for that first religion so that they could find something to agree

14. Unger, *The Religion of the Future*, 11.
15. Preus, *Explaining Religion*.
16. Bodin, *Colloquium of the Seven*.

on. Another exacerbating factor for that time was religious pluralism in the
newly discovered world. Even though some new religions were practiced far
away, it was difficult for Europeans to account for the bewildering multiplic-
ity of perspectives that they were not familiar with. All religious forms of
the sixteenth and seventeenth centuries were understood as descendants of
some previous forms of religion from which they deviated. Finding what
religion was there in the beginning would determine which religions were
truer to their origin. For Bodin and others like him, original religion was
close to what they would see as an ancient form of Judaism. Preus asserts,
and probably rightfully so, that Bodin went even further and searched for
some hypothetical primordial religion of "the Great God of Nature." Other
authors—for example Edward Herbert of Cherbury—found that original
religion in a form of deism that broke away from the framework of biblical
antiquity or revelation.[17] For such thinkers, religion had its origins in God
but not in any specific religious tradition. For that reason, religion became
something to be studied and understood through methods like those of, at
that time nascent, modern science. Religious ways of thinking developed by
Herbert of Cherbury exalted reason above any other way of knowing about
religious matters; reason was seen as the way to recognize which forms of
religion are grounded in something that transcends human beings.

The spirit of the Enlightenment, as Kant wrote, is to have courage to
use your own reason.[18] Elevation of reason to the place formerly occupied
by traditional authorities is widely recognized as a major change but it is
not the only one. Besides reason, Kant emphasized autonomy. Other authors gave prominence to nature and progress, and it was all supposed to be
complemented by tolerant attitudes. All those characteristics of modernity
were interacting with both the science and the religious thought of that time.
Autonomy was a revolt against authoritarianism; reason was, following Descartes, the preferred way of liberating the mind from blind authority. Nature
was related to what is reasonable because what is natural was somehow also
what is reasonable and therefore grounded in the very nature of things. This
applied to both the universe and human affairs, including religious behaviors.
The idea of inevitable progress, which was observed in the world and paral-
leled in the development of human understanding of the world, permeated
both religious and scientific thought of that time.

All this helped the development of the religion of reason among people
like Herbert, John Locke, Voltaire, Christian Wolff, G.E. Lessing, and others.
According to Herbert, God bestows certain common notions or universally

17. Preus, *Explaining Religion*.

18. Kant, *Practical Philosophy*.

shared religious ideas to all people.[19] Those ideas included the beliefs that there is one God who ought to be worshiped by being virtuous, and abhorring evil, and that one will be rewarded or punished after death. What is interesting is that Herbert presented those ideas as axioms of a universal natural religion and did so in the manner of modern scientific assertions. This deist way of conceptualizing religion over time gained wide influence.

John Locke went further in the development of the religion of reason. He first introduced a distinction among beliefs that are according to reason, above reason, or contrary to reason.[20] He thought that religious knowledge is found by reason in those assertions that are according to reason or above reason but not in those contrary to reason. For Locke, religious ideas interact with naturalistic ways of thinking about the world.

A religion of reason was further popularized in France by thinkers like Voltaire, who even presented two arguments for the existence of God.[21] One of his arguments presented an analogy between God and a watchmaker; it was later famously adapted by William Paley.

German religion of reason is represented by figures like Christian Wolff, who insisted that reason be the criterion by which true religion is determined, and G. E. Lessing, who as a major figure in the German Enlightenment produced numerous works in which he emphasized the need for tolerance that the religion of reason dictates.[22] Lessing famously dismissed the validity of jumping from historical truths to metaphysical and moral ideas. Our metaphysics is not justified by history, he said. On the contrary, it is in history that we find examples of our moral and metaphysical ideas.

Despite a variety of views represented by a diverse group of thinkers, the religion of reason presents a coherent set of assumptions. The primary point of reference for religious behaviors was Christianity. Religion was often seen as a simple and effective way to ground morality. In addition, the religion of reason was presented as the religion of nature. Historical religion was but one example of the higher type of religion presented by the religion of reason.

The religion of reason was very soon exposed to a devastating set of critiques. First, Jean Jacques Rousseau introduced feeling, will, and the affections as intrinsic to human life. Then David Hume denied even a possibility of any respectable philosophical theology. In his discussion of nature, humanity, and religion, Rousseau made a complete shift

19. Edward Herbert, *De Veritate*, 117–18.

20. Locke, *An Essay Concerning Human Understanding*.

21. Voltaire, *Traité De Métaphysique (1734)*.

22. Lessing, *Lessing's Theological Writings*.

from cosmology and metaphysics to the realm of self-consciousness and doubt. Rousseau was a complete rationalist in his arguments, but at the same time his subject matter became the powerful force of feeling.[23] In every field of knowledge, Rousseau maintained, true knowledge comes only through personal experience. This claim, today somewhat obvious to many, has singlehandedly struck a death blow to the religion of reason. The interactions between religious traditions and the scientific study of religion that are taking place today are still at odds with this change. After Rousseau, it became widely acceptable to maintain that one can arrive at a religious point of view due to one's developmental trajectory and personal experience within the context of religious interpretations. There is no philosophical religious faith that is detached from, and not in interaction with, its ground in personal experience. Religious behaviors are what individuals arrive at in their encounter with the world.

Rousseau did not really go after any specific aspect of the religion of reason. He simply changed the point at which philosophical thought interacts with religious behaviors. Hume's *The Natural History of Religion* stands out practically on its own as a work after which no respectable philosophical theology is possible without somehow responding to its arguments.[24] In his treatise "Of Miracles," Hume maintained that we must proportion our belief to evidence that does not exceed probability. Finally, it was Immanuel Kant who, following Rousseau and Hume, realized that the mind asks metaphysical questions that it cannot answer. Kant extended Hume's critique of possibility to traditional natural theology, and at the same time he opened a possibility for faith or belief, which he opposed to empirical knowledge.[25] While Locke and Hume proposed a view in which the mind is passive and functions as a blank slate, Descartes did not find empirical evidence sufficient to pass his test of methodological doubt. Kant placed himself in the middle of those disputes by suggesting that our knowledge need not conform to objects, but objects must conform to our knowledge. Our a priori knowledge of objects does not come from our experience of them but from the active role that the mind has in construction of knowledge.

This hypothesis had significant epistemological consequences for modern science, but its influence was perhaps even stronger for theological reflections after that time. If the cognitive forms of experience determine the possibility of objects of knowledge, then our concept of time as well as our concept of God are determined by the conditions of knowledge.

23. Rousseau, *Emile*.

24. Hume, *Dialogues Concerning Natural Religion*.

25. Kant, *Critique of Pure Reason*.

We do not know objects, or things-in-themselves, apart from any knower; we know phenomena or how they are known to the human mind. Kant's epistemology is interactive in the sense that Kant conceives of the object as in some respect constituted by the a priori interaction with the knower. Kant established the possibility of knowledge of the phenomenal world as it interacts with the knower. All possible experience based on a priori categories can be known since it is the mind that knows them. Therefore, Kant thought, pure science of nature is possible. Kant went so far as to propose that such ideas as self, world, and God are regulative concepts necessary for any scientific inquiry since they provide a principle of systematization and unity that we cannot derive from our experience. From the way that the religion of reason dissolved, a new interactive way opened: such religious thinkers as Schleiermacher began to use religious concepts as interactive, or regulatory, in the Kantian sense. Both modern science, including the scientific study of religion, and much of religious thought encountered questions raised by modernity, including groundlessness; they interact dynamically and are as such interactively inseparable.

Religion often refers both to a group of people and to some dimension of culture that the group shares. Theoretical models developed by Western academic study of religion include psychological, sociological, anthropological, and historical approaches. They all are interconnected and complementary. They cannot differentiate between emotions, thought processes, and behaviors, as presented in psychological models, sociology, and the anthropology of pre-modern and modern societies. All are seen as just a part of what E. B. Tylor called "that complex whole."[26] Historical approaches are more explicitly involved with the interconnectedness of religious dimensions of human behavior; some look far into the human past and model the origin and development of all human beings. Various proposed models for the scientific study of religion, especially when seen from a perspective of non-Western religious traditions, have been characterized as blurring the boundary between academic study of religion and theology.[27] This blurring, regardless of how undesirable it is for the goals of the academic study of religion, is probably inevitable because the problem of groundlessness persists. Whether we deal with religion through its internal discourse, practice, and institutions or with religion as a part of culture, we find that the critical theoretical approaches to religion are actively cancelling each other out, whether based on the work of thinkers like Edward Said, Michel Foucault, and Jacques Derrida, on social scientific approaches, or on cognitive grounds.

26. Tylor, *Primitive Culture*.
27. Alles, "Study of Religion," 13.

While critical theoretical approaches reject the possibility of generalizations about religion, cognitive approaches are producing just such generalizations. At the same time, some traditional subfields of Christian thought such as systematic theology and even biblical studies may be practiced in a mode that resembles critical theoretical and the scientific study of religion.

In critical theoretical approaches to religion, as presented by Mark C. Taylor, the interaction of various aspects of religion is presented as a tension between its constructive and disruptive roles. Taylor writes "Religion is an emergent, adaptive network of symbols, myths, and rituals that, on the one hand, figure schemata of feeling, thinking, and acting in ways that lend life meaning and purpose and, on the other hand, disrupt, dislocate, and disfigure every stabilizing structure."[28] This example points at the elusive nature of religion but it also illustrates what Taylor calls dislocation, namely, that what is termed religion is about the horizon and boundary of experience and yet also concerns immediacy and closeness. We cannot know where precisely to look for religion because it is about that which slips from our ability to grasp.

This brings us to one of the most popular buzzwords within the larger field of religious studies: the cognitive science of religion. This field grew in popularity over the years, and it now has a developed set of research programs and paradigms,[29] springing from various fields of cognitive science ranging from philosophical to experimental. The field seems to be disinterested in postmodern claims that no such generalizations can be achieved in practically any field, let alone in the study of religion. Instead, cognitive science of religion provides explanatory theoretical models for religious behaviors. Justin Barret summarizes this program by pointing out four distinct contributions of such an approach: explanation of the prevalence of teleological reasoning about the natural world, children's acquisition of God concepts, the minimal counterintuitiveness of religious concepts, and the relationship of religion and pro-sociality. Cognitive approaches assume that religious phenomena, at least those that can be subsumed under those four categories, are common and universal not only cross-culturally but also historically. Cognitive studies of teleological reasoning about the natural world are presented as resonating with a persistent intuition of experiencing the natural world as designed and purposeful, which arises early in human development. Other studies in this field have pointed out that religious concepts are based upon the same innate, intuitive cognitive mechanisms that all other concepts use, except that they also minimally

28. Taylor, *After God*, 12.
29. Barrett and Burdett, "The Cognitive Science of Religion."

violate, or better, they are about the boundaries of such intuitions. A slight push on the boundaries of our ordinary cognition makes such concepts prone to replication and more memorable than they would be if they neatly fit within their respective cognitive domains. Here again we have interaction as a framework within which religion is understood and presented. Probably the most important part of cognitive approaches to religion is it s finding that religion emerges in human groups and promotes social behaviors. Such social religious behaviors are adaptive and relevant for the survival of those who behave this way.

Religious behaviors not only represent perhaps the deepest layers of our collective wisdom, but they might hold the key to our future. In his popular overview of natural scientific studies of religion, Nicholas Wade notes that in the past 50,000 years of human history, religion seems to have played a major role throughout, but in the last 350 years that began to change.[30] Even in that last period, it was only for some people that traditional religious behaviors came under critique and suspicion. Yet even in those cases, religion is still the defining factor since any critique is necessarily interactive with that which it attempts to explain away. We have a cognitive bias for binaries, like day and night or cold and hot, that have very little to do with the continuum of the natural world. Our modern attempt to differentiate between what is "really out there" and what is "believed" is similar. Our preference for binaries is based on our evolutionary history and probably has to do with our lateral symmetry, handedness, and our two-brain hemispheres. Cognitive theories of religion propose that religion is produced by the same cognitive mechanisms that all other cognitive capacities depend on. That said, religious behaviors are also about that part of our evolved cognitive mechanisms that suggests readiness of motivations and opportunities of experience on the boundary of the familiar. It is this possibility that we live with that then becomes as real as anything else. It does not matter whether what is possible is also literally true because its very possibility makes it sufficiently real so that it interacts with everything else. An interactive view of religious behaviors and scientific models of such behaviors gives us a two-sided relation to what is at hand. We are both outsiders and insiders when it comes to religion. Scientific theorizing about religion assumes its outsider status, but it is not exempt from the Munchausen trilemma.

We must recognize that all theoretical models are at best limited and perhaps even wrong. Religious behaviors are in part what shape our scientific understanding of them, because both modern science and traditional religious worldviews are based on interactions most visible to us today in processes of

30. Wade, *The Faith Instinct*, 276.

modernization, urbanization, globalization, and multiculturalism. The Enlightenment trajectory of categorical separation of religion from other ways of interaction is better understood as a point on a continuous complex cognitive landscape of which, over time, we interactively make constructive additions, and revise so as to fit our newfound concerns.

References

Alles, Gregory D. 2005. "Study of Religion: An Overview." In *Encyclopedia of Religion*, edited by Lindsay Jones, 13:8761–67. 2nd ed. 15 vols. Detroit: Macmillan Reference USA.

Barrett, Justin L., and Emily Reed Burdett. 2011. "The Cognitive Science of Religion." *Psychologist* 24/4, pp. 252–55.

Bodin, Jean. 2008. *Colloquium of the Seven about Secrets of the Sublime*. Translated from Latin by Marion Leathers Kuntz. University Park: Pennsylvania State University Press.

Descartes, René. 1996. *Meditations on First Philosophy: With Selections from the Objections and Replies*. Translated by John Cottingham. Rev. ed. Cambridge Texts in the History of Philosophy. New York: Cambridge University Press.

Durkheim, Emile. 1995. *The Elementary Forms of Religious Life*. Translated with an introduction by Karen E. Fields. New York: Free Press.

Fries, Jakob Friedrich. 1935. *Neue Oder Anthropologische Kritik Der Vernunft*. 3 vols. Berlin: "Öffentliches Leben."

Herbert of Cherbury, Edward Herbert. 1937. *De Veritate*. Translated with an introduction by Meyrick Heath Carré. University of Bristol Studies. Bristol, UK: Arrowsmith.

Hume, David. 2007. *Dialogues Concerning Natural Religion, and Other Writings*. Edited by Dorothy Coleman. Cambridge Texts in the History of Philosophy. Cambridge: Cambridge University Press.

Kant, Immanuel. 1996. *Practical Philosophy*. Translated and edited by Mary J. Gregor. The Cambridge Edition of the Works of Immanuel Kant. New York: Cambridge University Press.

———. 1998. *Critique of Pure Reason*. Translated and edited by Paul Guyer and Allen W. Wood. The Cambridge Edition of the Works of Immanuel Kant. New York: Cambridge University Press.

Lessing, Gotthold Ephraim. 1957. *Lessing's Theological Writings: Selections in Translation with an Introductory Essay by Henry Chadwick*. A Library of Modern Religious Thought. Stanford: Stanford University Press.

Locke, John. 2008. *An Essay Concerning Human Understanding*. Abridged with an introduction and notes by Pauline Phemister. Oxford World's Classics. New York: Oxford University Press.

Mitchell, Melanie. 2009. *Complexity: A Guided Tour*. New York: Oxford University Press.

Mithen, Steven J. 1996. *The Prehistory of the Mind: A Search for the Origins of Art, Religion, and Science*. London: Thames & Hudson.

Popper, Karl R. 1992. *The Logic of Scientific Discovery*. New York: Routledge.

Preus, J. Samuel. 1987. *Explaining Religion: Criticism and Theory from Bodin to Freud.* New Haven: Yale University Press.

Rousseau, Jean-Jacques. 1993. *Emile.* Translated by Barbara Foxley. The Everyman Library 518. Rutland, VT: Dent.

Schwarz, Hans. 2014. *Vying for Truth—Theology and the Natural Sciences, from the 17th Century to the Present.* V&R Academic. Göttingen: Vandenhoeck & Ruprecht.

Sextus, Julia Annas. 2000. *Outlines of Scepticism.* Edited by Julia Annas and Jonathan Barnes. Cambridge Texts in the History of Philosophy. Cambridge: Cambridge University Press.

Shweder, Richard A. 2012. "Robust Cultural Pluralism in the New World Order: Three Prophecies. Lecture presented at the University of Chicago Center in Beijing on May 8, 2012. https://www.youtube.com/watch?v=9Lunz9SVIvQ/.

———. 1991. *Thinking through Cultures: Expeditions in Cultural Psychology.* Cambridge: Harvard University Press.

Taylor, Mark C. 2007. *After God.* Religion and Postmodernism. Chicago: University of Chicago Press.

Tomasello, Michael. 2014. *A Natural History of Human Thinking.* Cambridge: Harvard University Press.

Tylor, Edward B. 1903. *Primitive Culture: Researches into the Development of Mythology, Philosophy, Religion, Language, Art, and Custom.* 2 vols. 4th ed. London: Murray.

Unger, Roberto Mangabeira. 2014. *The Religion of the Future.* Cambridge: Harvard University Press.

Voltaire. 1937. *Traité De Métaphysique (1734), Reproduced from the Kehl Text.* Preface, notes, and variants by Helen Temple Patterson. Publications of the University of Manchester. Manchester: Manchester University Press.

Wade, Nicholas. 2009. *The Faith Instinct: How Religion Evolved and Why It Endures.* New York: Penguin.

Wilson, David B. 2002. "The Historiography of Science and Religion." In *Science and Religion: A Historical Introduction*, edited by Gary B. Ferngren, 13–29. Baltimore: Johns Hopkins University Press.

10

Notes toward Understanding

The Mystical Dimension of Divine-Human Interaction

MARY GERHART

Introduction—
Overview of Mysticism and Science

PAUL RICOEUR ONCE SAID that the most difficult part of doing philoso-phy is to find an adequate starting point. That observation surely also applies to the work of understanding mysticism as a contribution to an on-tology of interaction between the divine and the human. To complicate mat-ters, since the seventeenth century mysticism has often been presented as being antithetical—sometimes even an offense to science and reason. At the same time many theologians and scientists recognize mysticism as comple-mentary to other fields of understanding and readily provide examples of a variety of mystical experiences. Lawrence Cunningham referenced both attitudes in an article entitled "Nearer to God: Demystifying Mysticism." Although the practice of mysticism is likely to have been prehistoric, he placed the origin of the word 'mysticism' around 500 CE when a branch of Christian theology was developed that indexed the hidden aspects of religious experience. In the Christian tradition, Scripture or the Eucharist was recognized as having "a plain sense which every literate person could understand and a hidden or a 'mystical' one discovered only through the eyes of faith."[1] However ancient the practice of mysticism, the popular use of the term 'mysticism,' as suggested by Cunningham's title, is today often associated with mystification.

1. Cunningham, "Nearer to God," 21.

In addition to an antipathy toward mysticism since the Enlightenment and even in some forms of religion today, there is an equally misleading and misplaced confidence that the pursuit of empirical sciences is sufficient for human and cosmic flourishing. Contrary to this kind of over-claim is Albert Einstein's preference for the larger view, stated in 1919—a view that relativizes the practice of empirical science:

> The simplest picture one can form about the creation of an empirical science is along the lines of an inductive method. Individual facts are selected and grouped together so that the laws that connect them become apparent . . . . However, the big advances in scientific knowledge originated in this way only to a small degree . . . The truly great advances in our understanding of nature originated in a way almost diametrically opposed to induction. The intuitive grasp of the essentials of a large complex of facts leads the scientist to the postulate of a hypothetical basic law or laws. From these laws, he derives his conclusions.[2]

The key claim in Einstein's description of how the big advances in science have originated is counterintuitive to the way empirical science is often understood: namely, advances are made, he claims, in an *intuitive* grasp of the essentials of a large number of facts rather than in a selection and grouping of facts so that their laws become apparent.

Thirty-three years later in a 1952 letter to a Brown University undergraduate who had written him a fan letter, Einstein observed that "the deeper we penetrate and the more extensive our theories become, the less empirical knowledge is needed to determine those theories."[3] On another occasion he said, "The most beautiful and most profound emotion we can experience is the sensation of the mystical. It is the sower of all true science."[4] And when Albert Einstein was asked toward the end of his life if he had any regrets, he is reported to have answered that he wished he had read more of the mystics earlier in his life. While these personal remarks from a famous scientist do not explicitly endorse mystical experience in itself, Einstein's remarks do challenge the common view of empirical science as capable of being verified or disproved conclusively or exclusively by observation or experiment; they also suggest that he was interested in mystical experience and may have had some familiarity with it. At the very

---

2. Albert Einstein, "Induction and Deduction in Physics," *Berliner Tageblatt*, Dec. 25, 1919, CPAE 7, as quoted in Isaacson, *Einstein: His Life and Universe*, 118.

3. Einstein to McCormack, Dec. 9, 1952, Albert Einstein Archives, 36–549 (as cited in Iasaacson, *Einstein: His Life and Universe*, 580 n. 30).

4. Lincoln, *The Universe and Dr. Einstein*, 108.

least, such accounts do suggest that we demystify some understandings of science—understandings that might at the same time encourage some better, even complementary understandings of mysticism.

In his thoughtful philosophical description of science in *Thematic Origins of Scientific Thought*, Gerald Holton created a conceptual framework for relating two distinct realms of what constitutes science—a framework that validates those aspects of science that frequently go unacknowledged or taken for granted. He pointed out that science is carried out in two different spaces which he called S_1 and S_2. He called S_2, the most visible part, public science. In public science, formulations are presented analytically and empirically. Holton proposed that another dimension of science, S_1, is "an active and necessary component" although it is often overlooked or ignored:

> There (in S_1) we are more likely to see plainly the illogical, non-linear, and therefore 'irrational' elements that are juxtaposed to the logical nature of the concepts themselves. Cases abound that give evidence of the role of "unscientific preconceptions, passionate motivations, varieties of temperament, intuitive leaps . . . , not to speak of the incredible tenacity with which certain ideas have been held despite the fact that they conflicted with the plain experimental evidence."[5]

An unlikely example of appreciation for S_1 can be found in *Chance and Necessity*, written by the philosophically objectivist Jacques Monod:

> Man [*sic*] is able to give voice to his subjective experiences: the fresh discovery, the creative encounter need not be buried along with him in whom it has been simulated for the first time. I am sure every scientist must have noticed how his mental reflection, at the deeper level, is . . . to be embarked upon an *imagined* experience, an experience simulated with the aid of forms, of forces, in interactions . . . and I know—for it has happened to me—that one may suddenly find oneself identifying with the object itself, with say, a molecule protein.

Monod enigmatically concludes that such an experience is "more rightly regarded . . . as the subjective and abstract 'reality' offered directly to imaginary experience."[6]

A parallel to Holton's S_1 and S_2 can be drawn between R_1 and R_2 where R_1 is religious experience and R_2 is public religion or

---

5. Holton, *Thematic Origins of Scientific Thought*, 11–44. See also a later book, Holton, *The Scientific Imagination*.

6. Monod, *Chance and Necessity*, 155–56.

theological-philosophical reflection on religion.[7] In particular, Holton's foregoing description of S1, i.e., scientific experience, is strikingly resonant with what can be understood as R1—i.e., religious experience. This resonance appears, for example, in the apt description of religious experience—and, in particular, of mystical experience—by William James in his classic book *The Varieties of Religious Experience*. There James writes that the religious experience is evidence of a wider self "through which saving experiences come, a positive content of religious experience which, it seems to me, is literally and objectively true . . ."

> We plunge, it seems to me, into an altogether other dimension of existence from the sensible and merely 'understandable' world. Name it the mystical region, or the supernatural region, whichever you choose. So far as our ideal impulses originate in this region (and most of them do originate in it for we find them possessing us in a way for which we cannot articulately account), we belong to it in a more intimate sense than that in which we belong to the visible world.[8]

William James saw mysticism as the most intense form of religion and thought.

Despite the resonances between S1 and R1 in accounts of relatively private but essential discoveries by both scientists and non-scientists, the prominence of published S2 and R2 (public science and public religion) may deter both scientists and non-scientists—particularly in our culture—from publicly disclosing the seemingly odd circumstances of receiving an insight or of certain extraordinary personal revelations. Abraham Maslow, a psychologist, studied this reluctance by conducting a number of extensive interviews. He found that if individuals were repeatedly invited to reflect on their own lives they were more likely than not to come to recognize and identify some of those previously suppressed experiences as "peak-experiences": i.e., experiences which had a "sense of sheer unpreparedness and surprise" and which had turned out, in spite of the individual's own contrary philosophies, to be life-transforming. One person originally classified her experience as some kind of "peculiar but unimportant thing that had happened but that had best be forgotten because this experience conflicted with her whole materialist philosophy of life."[9]

From the perspective of cultural and historical diversity over the ages, what is human in terms of individuals or societies is not unchanging. For

7. Gerhart and Russell, *Metaphoric Process*, 95–96, 107.

8. James, *The Varieties of Religious Experience*, 388–89.

9. Maslow, *Religions, Values, and Peak-Experiences*, xv, 23.

this paper I am assuming that in general a mystic experiences an expansion and a deepening of what is and has been affirmed in many ways, for example as the divine, as spirit, as cosmic creator and sustainer. Mystical understandings are also constituted by the perception of new relationships in what exists—new ways of understanding, relating to, and formulating the empirical and extra-empirical natural powers of diverse things. Mystical understanding is often expressed in relation to the divine, most often understood as preternatural or supernatural. Insofar as human beings see themselves as related to the divine from the epochal beginning of their existence, their mystical understandings, however particular, include the cosmos as the frame for all that has been found to exist. As a result, this mystical relationship relativizes the question of whether the physical universe originated from a material substance or from some kind of interaction. For even if the physical universe is understood as originating from matter, the most appropriate understanding of its origin need not be a materialist philosophy. Hildegard of Bingen, a twelfth century scientist and mystic, for example, interpreted the 'material' of the original creation story as 'holy material.'[10] She thought that the work of human beings was to recreate the visible world's viridity (*viriditas*) abounding in the natural world—that is, to make God materially present in themselves and in the world. Such an understanding of the mystical dimension of divine-human interaction offers a surprising alternative to a philosophy of materialism.

It is apparent that any study of mysticism must distinguish between having mystical experiences and trying to understand the experiences in relation to whatever else is known and acknowledged to be the case. This distinction between experience and theory is affirmed in the sciences as well: in the field of physics, for example there are experimental physicists and theoretical physicists. In mysticism, there are those individuals who are known through accounts of their mystical experiences and others who are known for understanding mystical experiences in relation to other fields of understanding. W.H. Auden, for example, wrote a lengthy introduction[11] to a book entitled *The Protestant Mystics* but left no evidence that he may have had this kind of experience himself.

By contrast, T. S. Eliot never wrote about mystical experience but provides some evidence of his having one in a poem written after he had been hospitalized for a serious illness. Edward Mendelson, in "A Different T. S. Eliot" (a review of a biography by Robert Crawford and two edited collections of Eliot's poetry) noted that at Harvard Eliot loafed through his

10. Ritchey, "*Viriditas* and *Virginitas*," especially 56–57.
11. Auden, "Four Kinds of Mystical Experience."

first year, was placed on academic probation, and became serious about his classes only when he began studying ancient and modern philosophy and reading languages, including Buddhist and Hindu scriptures. Shortly before he graduated, he wrote a two-stanza poem, "Silence," which he never published, about an experience "for which we waited," one that overwhelms his consciousness of everything else. Following are the lines that refer to his having the experience:

> This is the ultimate hour
> When life is justified.
> The seas of experience,
> That were so broad and deep,
> So immediate and steep,
> Are suddenly still.
> You may say what you will,
> At such peace I am terrified.
> There is nothing else beside.[12]

Auden, Crawford, and Mendelson all comment on the autobiographical aspect of Eliot's poem. Auden told friends that Eliot had mystical visions of which he never spoke and inferred Eliot's mystical experience from poems like the foregoing one. Crawford sees this poem as prompted by Eliot's recent hospitalization for scarlet fever and describes it merely as a poem that "registers emotional disturbance" about something "fearful." Mendelson takes issue with Crawford's assessment and suggests that the poem describes a moment of *religious* awe, a terrifying vision of the "peace that passeth understanding," a mystical experience that Eliot did not forget:

> . . . my eyes failed, I was neither
> Living nor dead, and I knew nothing,
> Looking into the heart of light, the silence. . . .
> ("The Waste Land," pp. 39–41)

> And the lotos rose, quietly, quietly,
> The surface glittered out of heart of light.
> ("Four Quartets," pp. 36–37)[13]

Mendelson thinks that Eliot recalled the experience later as in this moment of visionary intensity.

---

12. Mendelson, in "A Different T. S. Eliot," 2.

13. Eliot as quoted in ibid.

Historical and Cultural Variations
in the Term "Mysticism"

With respect to understanding Christian mysticism, a radical change has taken place since the fifteenth century. The change can be perhaps best appreciated in a linguistic comparison between what it was named four centuries ago and how it is named now. Until the seventeenth century, the alignment of mysticism with other disciplines was much less rigid, suggesting that to appreciate mysticism today we need to loosen some associations and forge new ones. It is surprising to learn that, according to Michel de Certeau, the field of study today called "mysticism" (in the seventeenth century called "la mystique") had the same linguistic form then as the names of two other sciences: namely, "mathématique" and "physique." Today the linguistic similarity has disappeared. "Mathematics" and "physics" (but not "mystics") are legitimated fields of understanding, and the term "mystics" no longer designates a field of understanding of a particular kind of human experience; the term instead denotes particular persons. Certeau's use of the term 'la mystique' (according to the translator of his book) "has no precise equivalent in today's English, which regularly uses 'mysticism' for both 'la mystique' and 'le mysticisme.'" To preserve Certeau's meaning of 'la mystique' (i.e., "the mystical" as a noun), Michael Smith (the translator of Certeau's richly documented work) substitutes the term "*mystics*" (italicized) for the study, field, theology, or philosophy of what in English today is commonly referred to as "mysticism."[14] I have adopted his usage, and from this point "*mystics*'" (italicized) will refer to the discipline or field of study and the term "mystics" (un-italicized) will refer to persons. Smith's rather cumbersome "grammatical promotion" of the original term "the mystical'" nevertheless restores and achieves a diacritical parallelism between '*mystics*' and the terms 'mathematics' and 'physics.' (One further difference is that "mathematical" and "mystical" are still used as adjectives, but the equivalent form of "physics"—i.e, "physical"—now designates a generic description of a category of observation rather than a particular scientific field.)

Regardless of what it is called, the science (or discipline or field) of *mystics* has a long and distinguished history in the major religious traditions. In Christianity, *mystics* is most often referred to as "mystical theology" and goes back to Dionysius the Areopagite, one of the first theorists to use that term. We get a sense of the scope and importance of the field in Bernard McGinn's five-volume series on Christian *mystics*, sub-titled "The Presence of God." McGinn provides a comprehensive historical-theological study of

14. Certeau, *The Sixteenth and Seventeenth Centuries*, ix–x et passim.

different forms of Christian *mystics*: from its inception in Jewish context and Greek ideals; through the dramatic portrayals of Jesus in New Testament writings and ancient Christian and monastic ideals; with its growth through the twelfth century; in the periods of "flowering" to 1350, its "harvesting" to 1500, and in the Reformation up to 1650. A sixth volume, forthcoming in 2017, is on successive vernacular forms of *mystics*.

In his introduction to the first volume, entitled *The Foundations of Mysticism*, McGinn asserts the importance of mystical experience, emphasizing that "mysticism is only one part or element of a concrete religion and of any particular religious personality . . . . [In this sense,] no mystics (at least before the present century) believed in or practiced 'mysticism.' They believed in and practiced [some religion] . . . that contained mystical elements as parts of a wider historical whole."[15] This observation, here pertaining to Christian *mystics*, in varying degrees may apply to *mystics* in other religions and mitigates some of the historical-cultural differences apparent among those religious sketched below and others.

In Judaism, Kabbalah refers to distinctive experiences of visions and dreams found in the Torah as well as teachings of the existence of souls in relation to the essence of God. Knowing this essence is impossible except in knowing what it is not. The emanations of God (e.g., wisdom, mercy, strength, splendor) are perceived as ways that God interacts with the universe.

In Islam, at the deepest levels of being religious, Sufi mystics seek the realm of *ihsam*, i.e., the realm of instantiating beauty as a way of seeing the divine in loveliness. Purification of the heart precedes *ihsam* by wholehearted submission to God. The aims of Sufism include the experience of ecstatic states (*hal*) and overcoming the lower self (*nafs*).

In the many forms of Buddhism, the practice of meditation aspires to *nirvana*, a state in which the subject is released from the effects of "dependent arising," i.e., the conditions created by a plurality of causes (not limited to physical causes) and into or beyond a cycle of deaths and rebirths.

Taoists see *Tao*, i.e., "the Way," as the "ineffable cosmic principle" by which seemingly opposed but interdependent elements in darkness and the unconscious, referred to as yin and yang, point toward and can achieve harmony with *Qi*, the life force. Through Taoist exercises and rituals, some of which have been formalized in the West into *Tai chi*, one's body and soul are transformed and dissolved into the cosmos. The person moves from being an individual to becoming immortal as heaven and earth.

---

15. McGinn, *The Foundations of Mysticism*, xvi. Elizabeth Jeep recalls Richard Rohr's helpful definition of a mystic: A person who has moved from mere belief or belonging systems to inner experience.

Mystical experiences and understandings include well-known rituals and practices, such as the sweat lodge, dream-quest and initiation rituals of native American Indians.[16]

Modeling Mystical Experience

What kinds of understandings would make it possible for mystical experiences to be acknowledged and affirmed with scientific discovery as complementary sources of insight and understanding of human beings in a cosmic context? Following is a list of some kinds of experiences that have been referred to as mystical.

1. Mystical experiences are sometimes attested to in everyday language, for example, when someone spontaneously gives an account of having been given, from no ostensible source, a momentous insight into a problem that one hitherto could not solve; or the sense of a "call" to a particular way of being in the world; or "a consolation without prior cause" (Ignatius of Loyola); or a concurrence of unlikely events that unexpectedly gave direction to one's deepest desires. The following is an unpublished account of Paul Dirac's experience of receiving his most important scientific insights:

> Paul Dirac used to describe the experiences that led to his most important discoveries. After long and intense thought about some problem, he would have a vision of an arm coming from above, with its hand holding a small silver tray. On the tray was a card, which Dirac was invited to inspect. He took the card and looked at it, and it had the answer written on it. He replaced the card on the tray, and the vision withdrew upward. Then he would work out the mathematics needed to establish the correctness of the answer that he had been given. His great ideas, such as the Dirac equation, magnetic monopoles, the prediction of antimatter, the establishment of field theory, the statistical distribution now called Fermi-Dirac statistics—all came to him in this way.[17]

16. See also *inter alia*, Aumann, "Mystical Phenomena," 171–74; Brück, "Mysticism," 656–58; Marcoulesco, "Mystical Union," 239–45; Dupre, "Mysticism," 245–61.

17. "The outstanding exception to this "mystical" gift was the transformation theory of 1926. In that case Dirac struggled with the mathematics without knowing the outcome. He finally pushed it through and showed how to transform the equations so that they could depend on momentum rather than position. In the process he developed the use of the generalized function that is now called the Dirac delta, thereby opening a new branch of mathematics. In later years Dirac called the transformation theory his 'darling' because he really felt it belonged to him and had not been a gift from above." (This entire unpublished account is by John Albright, who as Paul Dirac's colleague at

The distinguishing feature of this kind of mystical experience is the sense of improbability that the insights are the results of one's own best efforts.

2. In explicitly theoretical and theological language, mystical experience can be understood as a limit-experience in which one is made newly aware of a *limit-to* ordinary experience, and of a *limit-of* character of experience possibly opening into a basic trust regarding the fundamental actualities of one's life (e.g., Karl Jaspers, David Tracy).[18] This fundamental trust is often experienced as living in the presence of an otherwise unaccounted-for divine graciousness—theologically expressed, for example, as God. For Charles Hartshorne, the idea of God is equivalent to "the idea of a cosmic totality conceived as an integrated individual."[19] He argued that this idea of God is always directly though vaguely present to human beings—i.e., in all human experience, including "non-divine" experience. In this sense, a mystic's avowal to have had an experience of God is compatible with a theistic as well as several other understandings of God.

Moreover, in some first-person written or oral accounts of ecstatic or visionary experiences (e.g., Teresa of Avila, John of the Cross), a unitive relationship with the divine is described. Saint Athanasius of Alexandria, for example, wrote that Christ became 'incarnate' that we might be 'ingodded.'[20] Classically, the mystic was understood to enter the "unitive" way or path only after passing through the purgative way (divesting from all that keeps oneself from union with the divine) and the illuminative way (becoming spiritually enlightened). *Mystics* can be found in all three major Christian traditions—Orthodox, Catholic, and Protestant. The new Finnish School of Luther research, for example, maintains that Luther infrequently referred to *theosis*—a category of divine union (*unio Christi*) for justification.[21]

3. Philosophically, mystical experience is better understood in the field of phenomenology than in that of psychoanalysis although both fields have resources for interpreting phenomena having a high surplus of meaning. In *Freud and Philosophy* (1970), Paul Ricoeur calls attention to the wide range of phenomena that typically embody a double meaning. Many instances of double meaning are dissimulations of desire, e.g. fantasies and hallucinations and some dreams. Others, such as symbols, myths, fables, rituals, beliefs are expressions of "a particular way in which man places himself in relation to

---

Florida State University had many conversations with him.)

18. See Tracy, *Blessed Rage for Order*, esp. 92–94, 105–9, 179.

19. Hartshorne, *Beyond Humanism*, 284–86.

20. Ware, "Symeon the New Theologian," 235.

21. See Braaten and Jenson, eds., *Union with Christ*; see also Mannermaa, *Two Kinds of Love*.

fundamental reality, whatever it may be."[22] Ricoeur does not expect psycho-analysis to illuminate mystical experience. In his view, *mystics* is best under-stood in the context of the history of religions.

Neurology like psychoanalysis is another field which affords inter-esting associations but may have limited success in interpreting mystical experience. One example of the limits of a neurological approach to *mystics* is Charles Singer's 1917 analysis of Hildegard of Bingen's mystical visions as caused by migraine headaches in a chapter entitled "The Visions and Their Pathological Basis." But after comparing her visions with those documented by one of his clients who kept a record of what he saw during pathological states, Singer decided that even if Hildegard suffered migraines, her visions did not spring from a pathology and that a better comparison would be with William Blake for the "great originality and creative power of both her and his visions."[23] Similarly, Oliver Sacks concluded (perhaps hyper-bolically), in his study of Hildegard's visions in Part Three of his hugely popular *The Man Who Mistook His Wife for a Hat and Other Clinical Tales*, that Hildegard's visions are "the single notable exception" to appropriately assigning most visions to neurological disorders.[24] Neurological analyses tend to create more suspicion about the authenticity of mystical claims rather than explain their originality.

4. Complementary to philosophical approaches, artistic and literary representations and expressions of mystical experience perennially amaze and inspire: for example, Dante's initially hellish journey toward consum-mate beauty epically envisaged in his *Divine Comedy*, the arresting "St. Te-resa in Ecstasy" in Santa Maria della Vittoria in Rome, sculpted by Bernini, or the high lyricism in the great thirteenth- century Islamic mystical poem, *Mathnavi*, written by the Sufi Jalal al-Din Rumi. Literary expressions of mys-ticism—however extraordinary and variously named—abound in startling images that expose the depths, heights and reaches of consciousness and experience. Other images present logical contradictions or oxymoronic co-nundrums, as in T. S. Eliot's "hints and guesses" of

> The impossible union
>
> Of spheres of existence . . . [where] the past and future
>
> Are conquered and reconciled . . . .

22. Ricoeur, *Freud and Philosophy*, 7–8 and 89n3.

23. Singer, "The Scientific Views and Visions of Saint Hildegard," 79–164.

24. Sacks, *The Man Who Mistook His Wife for a Hat*. The most intriguing part of Sacks's work is the addition in his coauthored, expanded edition of *Migraine* of a new part 4, titled "Migraine as a Universal," which points to a universal self-organizing power in nature (or God), creating order and complexity (291).

These are spheres, he suggests, in which action includes the "source of movement"—as distinct from action that is "only moved."[25] Eliot calls the transience and elusiveness of this "impossible union" of past and future a "sudden illumination"—a realization that "[w]e had the experience but missed the meaning."[26]

Eliot's poetic vision of the conjunction of the timeless with time teases us out an experience of time as a measurable phenomenon and relates us to some perhaps mystical unknown beyond our consciousness of time. Theologically, this vision relativizes a regression toward an originating substance as well as an advance toward a determinate dissolution of time. Scientifically, this vision stimulates new questions about the known known as well as the known unknown. Most dramatically we sense there are questions we have not even begun to ask, either personally or perhaps even as a species.

Bridging the Conflict between Mystics and Mystification

Are claims about a mystical dimension of common human experience suspect because they are susceptible to misrepresentation or misunderstanding? Although this danger is not irrelevant to the topic, it would seem sufficient to point out that principles and canons in both the sciences and the religions exist to help discern the difference between authentic and fraudulent claims even if neither science nor religion can prevent instances of misperceptions or misrepresentations of experience. The need for discernment, validation and verification of claims is complicated in either science or religion.

> Bernard Lonergan explored this need in *Insight: a Study of Human Understanding*. There he focused on the knower as the one who discerns, validates, and verifies. Indeed, a consciousness of one's being a knower is an experience of an intellectual "conversion." Already in his early thinking Bernard Lonergan linked knowing that we know (which he called an "immanent act") with mystical experience. "The theory of intellection as immanent act fits in with a philosophy of mystics . . . . [T]he mystical experience is . . . an experience, a transcendence, of the soul as soul and not merely as related to the body."[27] In his later work, *Method in Theology,* Lonergan understands as-

25. Eliot, "Third Quartet," ll. 216–22, in Eliot, *Four Quartets*.
26. Ibid., l. 93.
27. Liddy, *Transforming Light*, 82.

ceticism and mysticism as modes "of a religiously differentiated consciousness, teaching the way to total other-worldly love and warning against pitfalls on the journey": one is in love with someone transcendent "without qualifications or conditions or reservations or limits . . . ."[28]

Einstein, too, saw mystical experience as a form of knowing:

> He to whom this emotion [i.e., the sensation of the mystical] is a stranger, who can no longer wonder and stand rapt in awe, is as good as dead. To know that what is impenetrable to us really exists, manifesting itself as the highest wisdom and the most radiant beauty which our dull faculties can comprehend only in their most primitive forms—this knowledge, this feeling is at the center of true religiousness.[29]

Einstein was unstinting in his affirmation of the mystical, once declaring, "The cosmic religious experience is the strongest and noblest mainspring of scientific research."[30]

Many scientists, when referring to the mysteries of the universe, its vast forces, its origins, and its rationality and harmony, stop short of calling these transcendental qualities "divine" and avoid using the word *God*. Yet Einstein, who has been called an atheist, had no such inhibitions. "My religion," he says, "consists of a humble admiration of the illimitable superior spirit who reveals himself in the slight details we are able to perceive with our frail and feeble minds. That deeply emotional conviction of the presence of a superior reasoning power, which is revealed in the incomprehensible universe, forms my idea of God."[31]

Pierre Teilhard de Chardin, an eminent paleontologist, achieved an enviable balance in explicating what Kathleen Duffy calls the "intimate interaction" of scientific observation and imaginative intuition. He saw nature as impenetrable by science alone and mysticism as ignorant unless informed by a knowledge of the dynamics of nature. For him, the "flame of desire attracts all things into ultimate unity: physical forces (in matter), psychological forces (in human interactions) and a super-personal Force at the heart of matter."[32] In his book *The Divine Milieu* (which was not approved by church authorities and was published only privately during his

---

28. Lonergan, *Method in Theology*, 118, 109.

29. Albert Einstein in Barnett, *The Universe and Dr. Einstein*, 108.

30. Ibid.

31. Ibid., 109.

32. Duffy, *Teilhard's Mysticism*, 125.

lifetime), Teilhard asserted that "God reveals himself everywhere, beneath our groping efforts, as a *universal milieu,* only because he is the ultimate point upon which all realities converge."[33]

Conclusion:
A Philosophical Argument for an Ontology of Interaction

Hans-Georg Gadamer's proposal to replace the concept of "substance" with the concept of "structure" removes many of the philosophical obstacles to the adoption of an ontology of interaction. His proposal also resists the bias toward materialism in empirical science and popular understanding.

In his book *The Beginning of Philosophy,* Gadamer argues that the empirical alone overly depends on the principles of "causality" and "development." Gadamer points out a fundamental contradiction in the notion of "historical development." History, strictly speaking, is built on what is "decisively new" in a sequence of events, whereas "development" is understood as "merely a becoming visible," a "maturing process as it plays itself out [paradigmatically] in the biological growth of plants and animals." The contradiction in the clichéd phrase "historical development" brings to expression the "fundamental difference that exists between the process-quality of nature and the fluctuating accidents and incidents of human life." In this difference, Gadamer sees "a primordial opposition between nature and spirit."[34]

Gadamer proposes "structure" as an alternative to "cause" for understanding what is real and what is true:

> Structure denotes a connectedness among parts in which no one part is thought of as having priority . . . in a living organism no part occupies the first position while the others are all secondary. On the contrary, all the parts of the organism are unified, and they all serve it . . . . Structure does not mean that there is first a cause and then an effect; rather it has to do with an interplay of effects."[35]

Gadamer also proposes that Dilthey's concept of a "matrix of effects" replaces "cause and effect" by focusing "on the connection that each and every effect has relative to the others." In a work of art as well as in a living organism we deal not with a mere collection or sequence of elements:

---

33. Teilhard de Chardin, *The Divine Milieu,* 114.

34. Gadamer, *The Beginning of Philosophy,* 16. (I am thankful to David Tracy for calling my attention to this and other resources.)

35. Ibid., 23.

"there can . . . be no question of the artwork having a causal explanation; rather an explanation must be based on such concepts as harmony and interaction, thus it must be based on structure." For example, "a melody is not a mere sequence of tones. A melody has a [structure and] a conclusion, and an audience recognizes by applauding when the melody finds its fulfillment in this conclusion."[36]

Gadamer points out that "in [s]cience, 'the problem' is something that demands that we not be satisfied with hitherto accepted explanations but continue on and seek out new experiences and new theories." In philosophy, where 'the problem' comes from is a different kind of question: in philosophy, some problems do not yield solutions, yet they continue to present questions for the thinker. Freedom, for example, is a good example. Besides meaning "not being a slave," "not desiring things which we cannot have," "being wise even though one is in chains," or "freedom of choice," freedom also means being subject to nature.[37] For the philosopher, mystic and activist, this latter freedom is a problem essential for being authentically moral and social.

Regarding the problems that do not admit of a solution, Gadamer notes, "We all stand in the life-stream of tradition and do not have the . . . distance that the natural sciences maintain in order to conduct experiments and to construct theories. . . . W]e are always on the inside of the history that we are striving to comprehend" and necessarily stand within a dialectic with ongoing problems with no permanent solutions.[38] For Gadamer, method in both science and philosophy "is not a tool for objectifying and dominating something; rather it is a matter of our participating in an association with the things with which we are dealing." This method of "going along with" or interacting "presupposes that we . . . already find ourselves in the middle of the game and can occupy no neutral standpoint—even if we strive very hard for objectivity and put our prejudices at risk."[39]

Gadamer's substitution of the concept of 'structure' for the concept of 'cause' can prompt a new understanding of roles of the mystical and the scientific together, thus achieving what Hildegard called a kind of "resplendent reason"[40] in overcoming hubris in science and religion.

36. Ibid.
37. Ibid., 27.
38. Ibid., 28.
39. Ibid., 30.
40. See Hildegard, *Liber Divinorum Operum*, I, 2, xlii.

Cultures of understanding can be built by fostering better ways of treating what we don't understand. *In media res,* we shore these notes against our failures.

*I am indebted to Elizabeth Jeep and Carol R. Albright for dis cussions and suggestions regarding this essay.

References

Auden, W.H. "Introduction" to *The Protestant Mystics,* edited by Anne Fremantle. London: Weidenfeld and Nicholson, 1964. Reprinted and abridged as "Four Kinds of Mystical Experience," in *Understanding Mysticism,* edited by Richard Woods. 379-99. New York: Doubleday, 1980.

Barnett, Lincoln. *The Universe and Dr. Einstein.* New York: Harper & Brothers, 1948.

Braaten, Carl E. and Robert Jenson, eds. *Union with Christ: The New Finnish Interpretation of Luther.* Grand Rapids: Wm. B. Eerdmans, 1998.

Cunningham, Lawrence. "Nearer to God: Demystifying Mysticism." *Commonweal* 138 (2011) 21.

de Certeau, Michel. *The Mystic Fable.* Volume I, The Sixteenth and Seventeenth Centuries. Translated by Michael B. Smith. Chicago: University of Chicago Press, 1982.

Duffy, Kathleen. *Teilhard's Mysticism: Seeing the Inner Face of Evolution.* Maryknoll NY: Orbis, 2014.

Einstein, Albert. "Induction and Deduction in Physics." *Berliner Tageblatt.* Dec. 25, 1919, CPAE 7.

———. Einstein to McCormack. In Isaacson.

Eliot, T. S. "Third Quartet." In *Four Quartet,* 11.216-22. . New York: Harcourt, Brace & World, 1943.

Fox , Matthew. *Christian Mystics: 376 Readings and Meditations.* Novato, CA: New World Library, 2011.

Gadamer, Hans-Georg. *The Beginning of Philosophy.* New York: Continuum, 2001.

Gerhart, Mary, and Allan M. Russell. *Metaphoric Process: The Creation of Scientific and Religious Understanding.* Fort Worth: Texas Christian University Press, 1984.

Hartshorne, Charles. *Beyond Humanism: Essays in the New Philosophy of Nature.* Chicago: Willett Clark, 1937.

Hildegardis Bingensis. *Liber Divinorum Operum.* Edited by A. Delorez and P. Dronke. Corpus Christianorum Continuato Mediaeualis XCII. Brepolis: Editores Pontificii, 1996.

Holton, Gerald. *Thematic Origins of Scientific Thought.* Cambridge: Harvard University Press, 1973.

———. *The Scientific Imagination: Case Studies.* London: Cambridge University Press, 1978.

Isaacson, Walter. *Einstein: His Life and Universe.* New York: Simon & Schuster, 2007.

James, William. *The Varieties of Religious Experience: A Study in Human Nature.* New York: New American Library, 1958.

Liddy, Richard M. *Transforming Light: Intellectual Conversion in the Early Lonergan.* Collegeville: The Liturgical Press, 1993.

Lonergan, Bernard. *Method in Theology.* New York: Herder & Herder, 1972.

McGinn, Bernard. *The Foundations of Mysticism: Origins to the Fifth Century.* The Presence of God: A History of Western Christian Mysticism. Vol. I. New York: Crossroad, 1991.

Maslow, Abraham. *Religions, Values, and Peak-Experiences.* New York: Viking, 1970.

Mannermaa, Tuomo and Kirsi Irmeli Stjerna. *Two Kinds of Love: Martin Luther's Religious World.* Translated by Kim I. Stjerna. Minneapolis: Fortress, 2010.

Mendelson, Edward. "A Different T.S. Eliot." *New York Review of Books* 63 (2016).

Monod, Jacques. *Chance and Necessity: An Essay on the Natural Philosophy of Modern Biology.* New York: Random House, 1971.

Ricoeur, Paul. *Freud and Philosophy: An Essay on Interpretation.* New Haven: Yale University Press, 1970.

Ritchey, Sara. "Viriditas and Virginitas." In *Holy Matter: Changing Perspectives of the Material World in Late Medieval Christianity.* Ithaca: Cornell University Press, 2014.

Sacks, Oliver. "Migraine as a Universal" in *Migraine.* New York: Vintage, 1999.

———. *The Man Who Mistook His Wife for a Hat and Other Clinical Tales.* New York: Perennial Library, 1987.

Singer, Charles. "The Scientific Views and Visions of Saint Hildegard: The Visions and Their Pathological Basis." *Studies in the History and Method of Sciences.* 79-164. London: Clarendon Press, 1917.

Teilhard de Chardin, Pierre. *The Divine Milieu.* New York: Harper and Row, 1965.

Tracy, David. *Blessed Rage for Order: The New Pluralism in Theology.* New York: Seabury, 1975.

Ware, Kallistos. "Symeon the New Theologian." In *The Study of Spirituality.* edited by Cheslyn Jones, Geoffrey Wainwright, Edward Yarnold. New York: Oxford University Press, 1986.

11

Emergent Monism and the Classical Doctrine of the Soul

Joseph Bracken, S.J.

I N *WHATEVER HAPPENED TO the Soul?* Warren Brown, Nancey Murphy, H. Newton Malony, and their collaborators argue that the classical distinction between soul and body as respectively spirit and matter is a form of dualism which has been repudiated by the findings of natural science, above all, neurophysiology.[1] Consciousness and other mental operations can be closely correlated with neuronal activity within the human brain; hence, there is no empirical evidence to postulate an independent spiritual substance corresponding to the classical notion of the soul as the subject of mental properties. At the same time, they are opposed to reductive physicalism or ontological materialism with its philosophical premise that all allegedly mental activities are nothing but the byproducts of purely physical energy-events within the human brain. Hence, they espouse what they call "non-reductive physicalism," the belief that "the human nervous system, operating in concert with the rest of the body in its environment, is the seat of consciousness (and also of human spiritual or religious capacities)."[2] In effect, then, for Brown, Murphy and Malony there is no "mind" or "soul" as a spiritual entity over and above the brain or nervous system but only these higher-level, "supervenient" functions of the brain. In this way, they can claim that the human being is a unitary psycho-physical reality whose mental functions are emergent out of a properly disposed neuronal base in the brain. Ontological dualism has

1. Brown et al., eds., *Whatever Happened to the Soul?*, esp. 127–48.
2. Ibid., 131.

been overcome in favor of an emergent monism whereby matter properly disposed becomes capable of higher-order spiritual functions.

Brown, Murphy, and Malony, to be sure, do not wish to cast doubt upon traditional Christian belief in the resurrection of the body and life after death as a result of their theory of "non-reductive physicalism." As they make clear elsewhere in their book, they argue for the continuance of personal identity or life after death as a result of the power of God: "The identity for self as a body/soul unity is now dependent upon a source or power beyond its own capacity for survival."[3] Similar sentiments were expressed recently by John Polkinghorne in *The God of Hope and the End of the World*:

> [T]here is indeed the Christian hope of a destiny beyond death,
> but it resides not in the presumed immortality of a spiritual soul,
> but in the divinely guaranteed sequence of death and resurrec-
> tion . . . The only ground for this hope . . . lies in the faithfulness
> of the Creator, in the unrelenting divine love for all creatures.[4]

While I am sympathetic to the concerns of Brown, Murphy and Malony, on the one hand, and Polkinghorne, on the other hand, that human psychosomatic unity be affirmed in opposition to any form of metaphysical dualism, yet I am uneasy that they appeal simply to the power of God to resurrect the human person somehow in altered form after death. *Quod gratis asseritur, gratis negatur* (What is gratuitously asserted is [or at least can be] gratuitously denied). There is no philosophical common ground here with the non-believer in arguing for the plausibility of life after death.

Admittedly, as Philip Clayton claims in *God and Contemporary Science*, trans-empirical truth-claims play a role in science as well as in religion.[5] That is, scientists make use of theories which cannot be directly verified through appeal to empirical evidence; yet these same theories have considerable value for them in helping to organize and control the empirical data within their disciplines. Hence, theologians should likewise be privileged to employ trans-empirical hypotheses about the possibility of life after death. Yet the trans-empirical hypotheses employed by scientists can be indirectly verified through appeal to the way in which they make sense of the empirical data under investigation. No such indirect form of verification, however, seems to be possible for the claim of Brown, Murphy and Malony, on the one hand, and Polkinghorne, on the other hand, that God (in some way unknown to us human beings here and now) will resurrect human beings to

---

3. Ibid., 189.

4. Polkinghorne, *The God of Hope and the End of the World*, 108.

5. Clayton, *God and Contemporary Science*, 258–60.

a new life free from all suffering and no longer subject to mortality. Nothing in this world suggests that this could eventually happen. One must simply trust in God's faithful love for us.

Accordingly, in the space available to me here, I will propose an alternative theory for an understanding of the human person which, on the one hand, offers a philosophical rationale for traditional Christian belief in life after death, but which, on the other hand, is consistent with an overall metaphysics of creation and the God-world relationship. Hence, while it too is a trans-empirical hypothesis, its range of application goes well beyond the specific issue of life after death for human beings and thus stands a better chance of being indirectly verified by appeal to empirical evidence on a wide variety of fronts. In brief, what I will be proposing is that the dichotomy between matter and spirit will never be overcome unless and until one concedes that either spirit is to be understood as a byproduct of interactions on the material level or that, on the contrary, matter is to be understood as a byproduct of interactions on the spiritual level. Either matter or spirit must be ontologically derivative from its opposite. Materialistic scientists, therefore, who insist that the mental or spiritual capacities of human beings and other higher-order animal species are to be explained exclusively in terms of neuronal interactions within the brain of the individual are thus in my judgment more consistent in their thinking than philosophers and theologians who maintain that at a certain point in the evolutionary process matter spontaneously gives rise to spirit. Either spirit in some attenuated form has been present in material creation from the beginning or it is simply not there at all, appearances to the contrary notwithstanding. The big question, of course, is how spirit in an attenuated form can be present even in clearly inanimate material reality.

One thinks immediately of the celebrated hypothesis of Pierre Teilhard de Chardin that, corresponding to the "Without" or external appearance of things in this world, there is a "Within" or interior reality that develops in proportion to the growth in complexity and self-organization in the outer world.[6] My recourse, however, will be to the philosophy of Alfred North Whitehead with his presupposition that "the final real things of which the world is made up" are actual entities or actual occasions, that is, momentary immaterial subjects of experience which by their dynamic interrelation from moment to moment make up all the material things of this world (both animate and inanimate).[7] In my judgment, Whitehead is more logically rigorous than Teilhard de Chardin in working out his metaphysical scheme

6. Teilhard de Chardin, *The Phenomenon of Man*, 54–58.

7. Whitehead, *Process and Reality*, 18.

and thus less open to the charge of romantic mysticism on the part of empirically minded critics. At the same time, I will inevitably have to modify
Whitehead's scheme in order to use it as a philosophical underpinning for a
metaphysics of creation and the God-world relationship in which belief in
life after death for human beings and in the eschatological transformation of
the material universe are to have a place.

Whitehead's proposal that the material world is ultimately made up
of immaterial subjects of experience in dynamic interrelation is, of course,
itself partially derivative from the philosophy of Leibniz in his controversial
work *The Monadology*.[8] Therein Leibniz solved the long-standing philosophical conundrum whether matter is infinitely divisible by stipulating
that matter in the common sense understanding of the term is a byproduct
of the interplay of countless immaterial "monads" or unified centers of
force within a common field of activity. Matter is thus divisible into a finite
number of monads but the monads themselves as immaterial entities are
not further divisible.[9] Whitehead's counter-proposal was to retain the insight that immaterial entities ultimately make up the material things of this
world but to insist that these monads are not "windowless" as in Leibniz's
scheme nor are they permanently constituted one way rather than another
by God the Creator.[10] Rather, for Whitehead actual entities are strictly momentary subjects of experience which spontaneously constitute themselves
by "prehending" (literally, grasping on a feeling-level) other actual entities
in the environment or world out of which they are arising. Whitehead,
therefore, does not have to appeal to a "pre-established harmony" between
monads as determined by God but can instead stipulate that the actual entities create their own patterns of interrelation at every moment through
prehension of their predecessors and the explicit or implicit patterns of
behavior operative over time among them.

What Whitehead inherited from Leibniz, however, was a predisposition
to philosophical atomism, namely, the belief that all macroscopic realities, the
persons and things of this world, are nothing more than aggregates of actual
entities in dynamic interrelation. He recognized, to be sure, that since actual
entities come and go in rapid succession there must exist what he called "societies" of actual entities which would carry forward the pattern of interrelation
among successive generations of actual entities and thus serve as a principle
of continuity in the midst of change (much akin to the classical notion of

---

8. Leibniz, "The Monadology," 215–77.

9. Ibid., 217–18 nn. 1–3.

10. Ibid., 219 n. 7, 244–47 nn. 48–52.

substance).[11] But he apparently had no clear idea of how societies as such objective higher-order ontological unities were different from the process of subjective self-constitution or self-unification characteristic of actual entities. Yet, as I shall indicate below, it is precisely this dimension of Whiteheadian societies as objective higher-order ontological unities different from their constitutive actual entities which is necessary to justify on Whiteheadian grounds belief in a soul as emergent out of the brain as a physical organ and yet as distinct from it. Likewise, only on the basis of this revised understanding of Whiteheadian societies can one affirm the logical possibility of subjective immortality not simply for individual actual occasions or fleeting moments of experience for human beings (as Marjorie Suchocki worked out some years ago in her book *The End of Evil*[12]) but for a redeemed self which represents the totality of an individual's life-history or sum of its experiences. I will begin with a summary exposition of my reinterpretation of Whiteheadian societies and afterwards indicate how it applies to an understanding of the soul which, as noted above, is emergent out of the neural infrastructure of the brain and yet distinct from it.

There are relatively few passages in *Process and Reality* where Whitehead speaks at length about the nature of societies. In one of those passages, he describes societies in their dynamic interrelation as "environments" and "layers of social order" for their constituent actual occasions:

> Thus a society is, for each of its members, an environment with some element of order in it, persisting by reason of the genetic relations between its own members. Such an element of order is the order prevalent in the society. But there is no society in isolation. Every society must be considered with its background of a wider environment of actual entities, which also contribute their objectifications to which the members of the society must contribute. . . . Thus we arrive at the principle that every society requires a social background, of which it is itself a part. In reference to any given society the world of actual entities is to be conceived as forming a background in layers of social order, the defining characteristics becoming wider and more general as we widen the background.[13]

11. See Whitehead, *Adventures of Ideas*, 204: "A society has an essential character, whereby it is the society that it is, and it has also accidental qualities which vary as circumstances alter . . . . But an actual occasion has no such history. It never changes. It only becomes and perishes."

12. Suchocki, *The End of Evil*, 81–114.

13. Whitehead, *Process and Reality*, 90.

By "genetic relations" among actual entities Whitehead means that later actual entities derive the pattern for their mutual self-constitution from their immediate predecessors in the same society. Thereby a "common element of form"[14] or pattern of behavior is transmitted from one set of actual occasions to another within that society. My focus in this paper, however, is on Whitehead's description of a society as "an environment with some element of order in it." I would prefer to use the term "field" even though I am well aware of how the notion of field is itself a generic term, defined differently in different disciplines. I define it simply as an objective context for the interaction of entities which is itself somehow structured by the interplay of those same entities. In this sense, it is akin to another generic notion, namely, that of system.[15] Both fields and systems, moreover, as the above-cited text from Whitehead also suggests, can be readily seen as "layered" within one another, thus conditioning their ongoing mutual operation. The defining characteristics of an animal organism, for example, influence and thereby condition the existence and behavior of individual cells within the organism even as the cells by their dynamic interplay limit the functioning of the animal organism as a whole.

Still another reason to think of Whiteheadian societies as fields rather than simply as aggregates of actual entities (actual occasions) with an "element of order" between and among them is that the field, unlike an aggregate, can be said to perdure over time as successive generations of actual entities come and go. With each new generation of actual entities there must be a new aggregate. A field, on the other hand, as the context or "place" for the interplay of actual entities does not come and go with each new generation of actual entities. Rather, the field endures as the objective context or environment out of which each new generation of entities arises and to which each generation contributes its own very modest modification of the pattern which it inherited from its predecessors. Whitehead seems to confirm this hypothesis as follows:

> The causal laws which dominate a social environment [read, field] are the product of the defining characteristic of that society. But the society is only efficient through its individual members. Thus in a society, the members can only exist by reason of the laws which dominate the society, and the laws only come

14. Ibid., 34.

15. Ervin Laszlo defines a "natural system" as "a nonrandom accumulation of matter-energy, in a region of physical space-time, which is nonrandomly organized into coacting interrelated subsystems or components" (*Introduction to Systems Philosophy*, 30. Cf. also ibid., 23 where he links his notion of systems with field theory in physics.

into being by reason of the analogous characters of the members of the society.[16]

A field, in other words, as simply a context for the interaction of entities has no reason to exist if it is totally empty, devoid of entities. But, on the other hand, the entities (or more specifically Whiteheadian actual entities as momentary subjects of experience) need a structured or lawlike field of activity out of which to arise in order to pattern themselves in their individual self-constitution along the lines of predecessor actual entities in the same society.[17] Hence, there must always be such a context or lawlike environment for successive generations of actual entities even though the field itself initially came into existence and is here and now sustained in existence only in and through successive generations of actual entities with roughly the same pattern of existence and activity. Thus the field and its constituent actual entities mutually condition one another from moment to moment.

Given this field-oriented reinterpretation of Whiteheadian societies, how are we to understand the God-world relationship? First of all, as I shall explain below, a field-oriented interpretation of Whiteheadian societies allows one to affirm a trinitarian understanding of God as a community of divine persons. Secondly, it allows one to affirm the world of creation in terms of the doctrine of panentheism. That is, one can legitimately propose that the world of creation at every moment comes into being within the field of activity proper to the divine persons and is then sustained in existence through incorporation into the divine communitarian life. Finally, this field-oriented approach to Whiteheadian societies allows one to affirm the existence of the soul as an entity distinct from the brain which enjoys its

16. Whitehead, *Process and Reality*, 90–91.

17. As already noted, a more conventional Whiteheadian solution would run as follows: actual entities prehend the pattern exhibited by their predecessors through a process which Whitehead calls "objectification" (cf. Whitehead, *Process and Reality*, 23). That is, physical influences (prehensions) derived from antecedent actual entities are evaluated positively or negatively in terms of various conceptual prehensions derived partly from those same antecedent actual entities and partly from other sources. Finally, there is a "transmutation" of these suitably modified physical and conceptual influences so as to attain a unified physical "feeling" of the nexus or aggregate of actual entities from which the original physical feelings or prehensions in all their diversity were derived (ibid., 244–55). As I have argued elsewhere, however, it would be a much simpler process if newly concrescing actual entities immediately prehended the structure of the field out of which they were originating (cf. Bracken, "Proposals for Overcoming the Atomism in Process-Relational Metaphysics," 10–24, esp. pp. 16–17). That is, they would prehend the structure of the nexus as a whole directly rather than indirectly through an elaborate analysis and comparison of the structure or pattern proper to individual parts or members. In the end, the results would presumably be the same, but the process of transmission of form would be far more objective and reliable.

own special form of subjective immortality even as it shares in the overall transformation of material creation in virtue of the latter's progressive incorporation into the divine life.

How is it then that one can legitimately propose a trinitarian understanding of God within this neo-Whiteheadian framework without danger of tritheism, belief in three gods in close collaboration rather than one God in three persons. Key to my argument here is the philosophical claim that the objective unity proper to a Whiteheadian society is qualitatively different from the purely subjective unity of its constituent actual occasions, taken both individually and collectively. A Whiteheadian society, in other words, is not the agent of its own self-constitution like an individual actual occasion nor is it simply an aggregate of actual occasions for the reasons cited above. Rather, in Whitehead's language, it is an environment or objective context in virtue of which an ongoing succession of actual occasions can retain over time basically the same pattern of interaction or "common element of form." As such, it represents a higher-order unity or form of existence than that proper to its constituent actual occasions even though, as noted above, it only comes into being and is sustained in existence by the ongoing interplay of successive generations of such actual occasions.

Thus it is relatively easy to conceive the unity of the triune God in terms of a common field of activity which serves as the ground of their being or their divine nature. Each of the divine persons is to be considered as a "personally ordered society" of actual occasions whose structured field of activity overlaps perfectly with the fields of activity proper to the other two divine persons. Since the field of activity for each of the divine persons is by definition infinite, together they must constitute only one all-embracing field of activity. This accounts for their unity as one God, namely, an ongoing intersubjective community in which each divine person is totally immanent in the very existence and activity of the other two persons. As I see it, this is basically what Thomas Aquinas also had in mind with his description of the three divine persons as "subsistent relations" who share everything in common except their relational differences as distinct persons.[18] In both cases, the divine persons are a unitary reality in virtue of their possessing one and the same nature (or, as I see it, shared field of activity).[19]

18. Cf. Thomas Aquinas, *Summa Theologiae*, I, Q. 29, a. 4 resp.

19. Creaturely societies of actual occasions, by way of contrast, are separate from one another because their respective fields of activity in some respects overlap and in other respects are different from one another. Even husbands and wives after many years of marriage, for example, never completely share the same field of activity; each has a sphere of activity proper to himself/herself which defines him/her as a separate individual. In that sense, the persons of the Trinity are distinct from one another in that

Moreover, if one conceives this shared divine field of activity as a "matrix" or ontological ground for the world of creation, then one is in possession of a model for the God-world relationship which can be rightly regarded as panentheistic rather than pantheistic. For, in line with the notion of panentheism, God must be transcendent of the world as well as immanent within it. Yet the guiding presupposition of this model for the God-world relationship is that the three divine persons co-constitute a common field of activity which is theirs alone apart from the decision to create finite beings who could share in their divine life, albeit in a necessarily limited way. Yet, within this divine matrix proper to the persons of the Trinity, creation can gradually come into existence as an ordered hierarchy of ever more complex Whiteheadian societies of actual occasions, each with its specific "common element of form" or shared pattern of existence within a circumscribed field of activity.

How the original created actual occasions came into existence can in my judgment be explained as follows. If one stipulates that the divine initial aim to the creaturely actual occasion both empowers it to become itself and gives direction to its process of concrescence, then one can affirm the classical Christian doctrine *of creatio ex nihilo* not just at the first moment of the cosmic process for the initial set of actual occasions but at all subsequent moments and for every subsequent set of actual occasions. I presume here that even at the dawn of the cosmic process sets of creaturely actual occasions would co-exist so as to provide a basis for the formation of societies at a later stage. One can, for example, project the following scenario for the early stages of the cosmic process. There existed at first only coincidental nexuses of actual occasions with little or no coherence or persistence over time. Then by degrees the components of atoms (electrons, protons, neutrons) came into being, each as a temporal series of actual occasions with a distinguishable form. Then over an extended time first atoms, then molecules as more complex societies of actual occasions came into being. Finally, at least on this earth, if not elsewhere in the universe as well, life came into existence as still more organized societies of actual occasions in the form of proto-organisms with a "soul" or dominant subsociety of actual occasions. From these proto-organisms followed by degrees all the other forms of life, including human life, as still more organized and interconnected Whiteheadian societies.

---

they represent three different but necessarily interrelated subjectivities who together constitute a unique corporate reality or divine community. But they are in no sense separate individuals who here and now choose to coconstitute a community but who can separate from one another at will without loss of personal integrity.

The end-result, of course, is a strictly communitarian model of the God-world relationship. That is, not individual actual occasions but societies of actual occasions are, if not the *final* real things of which the world is made up, at least the *conventional* or *normal* things of which the world is made up. Yet, as already noted, within this communitarian understanding of the God-world relationship, one can logically affirm the priority of the divine community to all created communities or finite societies of Whiteheadian actual occasions so that the divine persons are genuinely free to create or not create, to give creatures a share in their communitarian life or not. At the same time, since all these finite societies of actual occasions exist within the divine matrix as their ontological ground of existence and activity, then one can with equal logic assert for this model of the God-world relationship the doctrine of panentheism, whereby creatures live in God but have at the same time their own existence and activity. In this way, one avoids the logical extremes of monism (pantheism) or dualism (the classical God-world relationship in which God is seen as separate from the world as its transcendent Creator).

At this point we are ready to take up the special case of the human soul as distinct from the brain and the rest of the human body. The human embryo during gestation gradually develops in complexity as a physical organism. In Whiteheadian terms, there is a slow buildup of more and more complex societies of actual occasions. From a philosophical point of view, what is key here is the *emergence of higher-order Whiteheadian societies out of the interplay of actual occasions within lower-level Whiteheadian societies. Successive generations of actual occasions, in other words, gradually evolve in terms of the complexity of the pattern governing their mutual interrelation. When the pattern reaches a certain stage of complexity, a new society or higher-level ontological unity emerges and with it a new regnant nexus of actual occasions to preside over that newly formed "structured society."[20] Eventually that regnant nexus can become a personally ordered society of living actual occasions or "soul" for the entire "structured society" or society made up of subsocieties.[21]

In this way, we can understand the emergence of the rational soul in human beings out of the developing infrastructure of the brain and central nervous system. It is not inserted into the organism by direct divine intervention but is, so to speak, a further development of the organism's own process of self-development or complexification. The actual occasions constitutive of the soul are different in degree but not in kind from the actual occasions at

20. Whitehead, *Process and Reality*, 103.
21. Ibid., 107.

work in the infrastructure of the brain. That is, as Whitehead explains, "the brain is coordinated so that a peculiar richness of inheritance is enjoyed now by this and now by that part; and thus there is produced the presiding personality [read, soul] at that moment in the body. Owing to the delicate organization of the body, there is a returned influence, an inheritance of character derived from the presiding occasion and modifying the subsequent occasions through the rest of the body."[22] Yet these actual occasions constitutive of the "presiding personality" or soul within the brain are still in the end momentary self-constituting subjects of experience like any other actual occasion within the human body or in the world at large.

At the same time, if one likewise claims that divine initial aims not only give direction to created actual occasions but also empower them to become themselves by a spontaneous self-constituting decision, we may legitimately say that God creates and sustains the human soul as it emerges out of the infrastructure of the brain and central nervous system. But God's creative activity is then at work, so to speak, from the inside of the organism's own process of self-development rather than operative from the outside by way of an extrinsic intervention into that same process. Likewise, God's creative and sustaining activity for the society of personally ordered actual occasions constitutive of the human soul is no different from God's creative and sustaining activity for every other created actual occasion in this world. Hence, there is no special divine intervention in the cosmic process so as to create the human soul as a strictly immaterial reality. Metaphysical dualism is thereby avoided, and emergent monism instead affirmed.

Finally, we take up the issue of life after death for human beings and the transformation of the physical universe through progressive incorporation into the divine communitarian life. For, if one concedes that the three divine persons by their dynamic interrelation co-constitute a conjoint field of activity for the workings of the divine life, and if one further concedes that this divine matrix likewise serves as the ontological ground of being for the world of creation, then one has at hand the ontological basis for asserting that the divine persons and their creatures can co-exist in their separate subjectivities and yet share the same divine life, albeit in different degrees. For, both the divine persons and all created subjectivities together co-constitute the divine matrix or common ground of being at any given moment. In its fundamental structure, of course, it is constituted by the ongoing relationship of the three divine persons to one another. But, in line with Whitehead's notion of the divine consequent nature, what happens in the world is thereby progressively incorporated into the divine life:

22. Ibid., 109.

"The revolts of destructive evil, purely self-regarding, are dismissed into the triviality of merely individual facts; and yet the good they did achieve in individual joy, in individual sorrow, in the introduction of needed constrast, is yet saved by its relation to the completed whole."[23]

Martin Buber in his celebrated book *I and Thou* took note of the fact that two human beings by their dynamic interrelation co-create what he called "the Between" (*das Zwischen*),[24] a meeting-place where the two subjectivities can influence and affect one another without danger of the one being absorbed into the other as an accidental modification of the other's existence and activity. Intersubjectivity, in other words, requires such an intentional common ground which is structured by the ongoing exchange between two or more participants and which perdures as an objective reality as long as they remain in living contact with one another. Applied to the God-world relationship as envisioned above, this means that the divine matrix is *das Zwischen*, the intentional common ground between the three divine persons and their creatures as created subjects of experience. Each of the self-constituting decisions of these created subjects of experience contributes in some small way to the further structuring of this objective reality which they share with the divine persons.

Unlike the divine persons, however, human subjects of experience at the moment of their self-constitution in this world are not fully aware of their co-participation in this all-encompassing divine matrix. Only at the moment of death when the personally ordered society of actual occasions constitutive of the "soul" wins freedom from the normal constraints of life in the body, does the actual occasion operative in this final moment presumably achieve enlightenment through the action of God's enabling grace. Where Suchocki, in other words, claims that every actual occasion in its moment of "enjoyment" or fulfilled subjectivity experiences transformation through incorporation into the divine life, I contend instead that, while the personally ordered society of actual occasions constitutive of the human person is progressively being incorporated as a given finite field of activity into the all-encompassing divine field of activity, only the final actual occasion within that same field will actually experience this transformation through the action of divine grace.[25] Yet in and through thus appropriating

23. Ibid., 346.

24. Buber, *I and Thou*, 37–72. Cf. also Desmond, *Being and the Between*, esp. 200–207. Desmond likewise sees the necessity of exploring the "between" or the common ground between dynamically interrelated subjects of experience as the true basis for understanding what it means to be.

25. What is ultimately at stake here between Suchocki and me is the philosophical issue of the continuity of the human self within the parameters of process-relational

more fully its own history, namely, the structured field of activity already constituted by the decisions of its predecessors, this final actual occasion will be in a position uniquely to evaluate and appreciate the significance of its life both for itself and others, and thus come to an abiding sense of "transformation, redemption and peace."[26]

All these remarks, of course, apply only to human beings in their successive moments of self-consciousness. Yet all other created realities, including the bodies of human beings, as noted above, are likewise constituted by the dynamic interplay of momentary subjects of experience and are likewise being taken up at every moment into the all-encompassing divine matrix. For, in terms of my adaptation of Whitehead's thought, they are finite structured fields of activity which can be progressively incorporated in terms of their basic pattern or structure into that same divine matrix. Yet, for the same reason, these finite fields of activity require a final set of actual occasions as their subjective focus in the moment before the death of the organism or the dissolution of the inanimate compound. This final set of actual occasions, moreover, will experience in varying degrees something like the transformation of the human soul at the moment of death. That is, to the degree that the actual occasions constitutive of these societies experienced spontaneity or even rudimentary self-awareness in this life, they will presumably experience a transformed existence within God. Our human bodies, in other words, will be renewed through participation in the divine life. All animals and plants that have ever existed on this earth will be likewise present within the divine life as alive in a new strictly immaterial way. Even the subatomic components of inanimate Nature with their ceaseless movement even within the present order

---

metaphysics. Suchocki as an orthodox Whiteheadian is logically obliged to accord subjective immortality to each individual actual occasion or moment of experience within a person's lifetime as it is prehended by God into the divine consequent nature. As a result, there is the unresolved problem of the "million Marjories" all enjoying the risen life but with no indication of how they together constitute the unitary reality of the redeemed human self. I, on the contrary, argue that the human self is a structured field of activity for successive moments of consciousness, which endures as individual actual occasions come and go. Hence, only a final actual occasion is needed to allow the personally ordered society of actual occasions, which is the human person, to experience full incorporation into the divine life.

26. Suchocki, *The End of Evil*, 109. See also Volf, "Enter into Joy!" In *The End of the World and the Ends of God*, 263, Volf writes, "The doctrine of justification presupposes *continued life and agency* of human beings precisely in the passivity of their being justified." The saved individual, in other words, is simultaneously both passive (i.e., saved by God's grace) and active (experiencing himself/herself in a new way). In neo-Whiteheadian terms, this would mean that the final actual occasion would be fully self-constituted and yet ever more able to enjoy what it has contributed to salvation history.

will not be present within God as something purely static or lifeless but as endowed with new energy. For, as promised in the Apocalypse or Book of Revelation (21:1–4), the old order will have passed away and there will be a new creation, a new heaven and a new earth.[27]

Here, of course, we encounter the problem of the Christian doctrine of the Last Judgment. If the resurrection of the body and the transformation of the material universe are taking place at every moment in the history of the universe, then how can one properly speak of the end of time and the Last Judgment? As I see it, what is key to the doctrine of the Last Judgment is that God's justice and mercy will simultaneously be vindicated in a way that all human beings can experience and understand. In a sense, within the scenario which I have sketched above, the Last Judgment is taking place at every moment in the cosmic process, at least since the origin of the human species. But certainly at the moment when the human species ceases to exist (either on this earth or elsewhere in the universe), the Last Judgment in the Biblical sense will already have taken place. Every human being will know his or her place in that cosmic drama and, if saved, give everlasting thanks to God for the wonders of God's creation.[28] As for the end of the physical universe, one can only say that it emerged by degrees from the divine matrix and will forever remain linked with it, however it naturally comes to an end or is transformed into still another universe at some future date.[29]

27. In *The God of Hope and the End of the World*, Polkinghorne likewise affirms in line with the teachings of Saint Paul that in the world to come there will be a "new creation" such that non-human creation will likewise share in the divine life (pp. 113–23). The weakness of his position, of course, is that Polkinghorne offers no philosophical justification for that belief. By the same token, my neo-Whiteheadian metaphysics of universal intersubjectivity offers such a philosophical justification. That is, if in line with Whitehead's dictum that "the final real things of which the world is made up" are actual occasions or momentary subjects of experience, then what ultimately survives is the divine matrix, an all-encompassing field of activity structured by subjects of experience (both divine and created) in ongoing dynamic interrelation. There is no dichotomy between matter and spirit which must be overcome by the power of God in the world to come. In the final analysis, all is spirit, i.e., immaterial subjects of experience in dynamic interplay within a common structured field of activity.

28. Cf. Tanner, "Eschatology without a Future?" I agree with Tanner that, properly understood, Christian eschatology has no more to do with the physical end of the universe than the doctrine of creation has to do with its temporal beginning: "Eternal life is a present reality; we possess now, in an unconditional fashion, life in God as the source of all good and need not wait for death to pass from the realm of death to that of life."

29. See Polkinghorne, *The God of Hope and the End of the World*, 140–45: unlike most contemporary systematic theologians, scientist-theologians like himself fully expect "that cosmic history will continue for many billions of years and that, before its foreseeable end, humanity and all forms of carbon-based life will have vanished from the universe."

To sum up, then, it is my contention that one can justify traditional Christian belief in the existence of the human soul and the possibility of life after death for human beings within a transformed material universe if one chooses carefully the philosophical scheme underlying those claims. One cannot, to be sure, rationally prove these beliefs beyond the shadow of a doubt, but one likewise should not have to appeal to the power of a loving God to make them happen as promised. Midway between these logical extremes is my own position that a properly conceived metaphysical scheme such as my own revision of Whitehead's philosophy should allow one to render these classical Christian beliefs at least plausible to the non-believer. In this way there can exist some sort of common ground between the believer and the non-believer about the nature of reality. Neither party may ultimately win the argument, but the intervening discussion will in any case keep both sides honest about the inevitable limitations of their own position and the rational plausibility of the opposing position. Given the finite character of the human mind, this may be all that one can reasonably expect from honest exchange of views.

References

Bracken, Joseph A., SJ. 1994. "Proposals for Overcoming the Atomism in Process-Relational Metaphysics." *Process Studies* 23, pp. 10–24.

Buber, Martin. 1970. *I and Thou*. Translated by Walter Kaufmann. New York: Scribner.

Brown, Warren, et al., eds., 1998. *Whatever Happened to the Soul? Scientific and Theological Portraits of Human Nature*. Theology and the Sciences. Minneapolis: Fortress.

Clayton, Philip D. 1997. *God and Contemporary Science*. Edinburgh Studies in Constructive Theology. Grand Rapids: Eerdmans.

Desmond, William. 1995. *Being and the Between*. SUNY Series in Philosophy. Albany: SUNY Press.

Laszlo, Erwin. 1972. *Introduction to Systems Philosophy: Towards a New Paradigm of Contemporary Thought*. New York: Gordon & Breach.

Leibniz, G. W. 1898. "The Monadology." In *The Monadology, and Other Philosophical Writings*, 215–77. Translated by Robert Latta. London: Oxford University Press.

Polkinghorne, John. 2002. *The God of Hope and the End of the World*. New Haven: Yale University Press.

Suchocki, Marjorie Hewitt. (1988) 2005. *The End of Evil: Process Eschatology in Historical Context*. Eugene, OR: Wipf & Stock.

Tanner, Kathryn. 2000. *The End of the World and the Ends of God: Science and Theology on Eschatology*. Edited by John Polkinghorne and Michael Welker. Theology for the Twenty-First Century. Harrisburg, PA: Trinity.

———. 2000. "Eschatology without a Future?" In *The End of the World and the Ends of God: Science and Theology on Eschatology*, edited by John Polkinghorne and

Michael Welker, 222–37. Theology for the Twenty-First Century. Harrisburg, PA: Trinity.

Teilhard de Chardin, Pierre. 1965. *The Phenomenon of Man.* Translated by Bernard Wall. New York: Harper.

Volf, Miroslav. 2000. "Enter into Joy! Sin, Death, and the Life of the World to Come." *The End of the World and the Ends of God: Science and Theology on Eschatology,* edited by John Polkinghorne and Michael Welker, 256–78. Theology for the Twenty-First Century. Harrisburg, PA: Trinity.

Whitehead, Alfred North. (1933) 1967. *Adventures of Ideas.* New York: Free Press.

———. 1978. *Process and Reality: An Essay in Cosmology.* Corrected ed. Edited by David Ray Griffin and Donald W. Sherburne. Gifford Lectures 1927–1928. New York: Free Press.

12

Can We Hack the Religious Mind?

The Interaction of Material Reality with
Ultimate Reality in the Human Self

TED PETERS

> Mapping the dimensions of our humanness in this way is not
> just an end in itself, but a prelude to a more radical inquiry:
> whether these deep structures of our humanness, as we have
> come to understand them, can guide us in our efforts to figure
> out the underlying deep structure of the universe—that we may
> symbolize using a word like 'God.'

—JAMES ASHBROOK AND CAROL ALBRIGHT,
    THE HUMANIZING BRAIN

CAN WE HACK THE religious mind? Can we hack any mind? Just what
is mind? What is the interactive relationship between our mind, our
mind's activity, our body, and our physical relationship to the world in
which we are embedded? Can one's intent to serve God actually restructure
the brain so as to serve this intended purpose? To develop answers to such
questions we must appeal to a cognitional theory.

In this position paper I provide the foundation and framework for
the cognitional theory with which I work when addressing issues regarding
human nature, selfhood, reason, and free will. Here I describe the cognitional architecture of human consciousness structured in consonance with
contemporary neuroscience, phenomenology of consciousness, material
engagement theory, and theological epistemology. Specifically, I attempt

to construct a coherent cognitional edifice while borrowing bricks from the work of Stanilas Dehaene and Walter Freeman in neuroscience, Dan Zahavi and the Husserlian tradition in phenomenology, and in theology Nancey Murphy along with Bernard Lonergan, S.J. In brief, I hypothesize that human consciousness is structured like a pyramid; and I wish to map the mental traffic that travels within the pyramid from the material base to the ethereal top and back down again.

This cognitional theory is important in two respects. First, it clarifies the complex scaffolding of human experience, thereby encouraging parallels to if not dependence on the non-linear dynamics of quantum physical activity within the brain. Given the current debate within neuroscience between the localizers, who search for local brain regions which correlate (if not cause) corresponding mental states, and the globalizers, who search for whole-part or top-down brain processing, I plan to draw more from the globalizers.[1] I rely on what I elsewhere describe as epigenetic or emergent *holism*, according to which the whole influences the parts. This non-reductionist assumption permits us to acknowledge that the person as a whole can, to some degree, influence through whole-part and top-down causation the activity of his or her body, brain included.

Second, this cognitional theory clarifies a misleading impression growing in the cognitive sciences as a byproduct to recent advances in neuroscience. The byproduct is a tendency to reduce conscious operations to preconscious or subconscious determinants.[2] Dehaene, for example, startles us by declaring that in everyday activity we fail to realize just how much of our activity is guided by "an unconscious automatic pilot. We constantly overestimate the power of our consciousness in making decisions—but,

---

1. Let's distinguish whole-part from top-down processing, then distinguish top-down from bottom-up processing. Whole-part causation reflects boundary conditions or initial conditions that shape internal activities. A cookie mold, for example, sets the boundary conditions for the dough that will become a baked cookie of a predetermined shape. Downward or top-down causation results when a higher-level dimension (mind, for example) acts on a lower-level dimension (body or even brain, for example). When the mind determines it's time to lift one's arm, up goes the arm. The mind determines top-down, so to speak, what the arm does. These two kinds of causality do not fit neatly into the category of efficient causation presupposed in methodological naturalism.

Neurotheologian Michael Spezio distinguishes top-down from bottom-up processing. "Top-down processes are those that formed during evolution or learning and that link stimulus processing to context, whereas bottom-up processes are those that depend primarily or wholly on basic stimulus properties, ignoring context. . . . Top-down processing is either explicit (conscious) or implicit (unconscious), controlled or automatic. Bottom-up processing is generally unconscious and automatic" (Spezio, "The Cognitive Sciences," 287).

2. I will employ the terms *preconscious* and *subconscious* interchangeably.

in truth, our capacity for conscious control is limited."[3] Many of today's neuroscientists so emphasize how the brain is on automatic pilot that the higher levels of consciousness drift to the margins if not off stage. Rightly or wrongly, one gets the impression that conscious activity is superfluous, because the unconscious brain takes charge of everything. I judge this to be misleading.[4] I would like to avoid beginning with a reductionist assumption as much as I would like to avoid the localization assumption. The entire scaffolding that builds on what is preconscious to structure consciousness belongs to this cognitional theory; and reducing the latter to the former is, in my judgment, premature.

Therefore, as a backdrop for other more specific studies, I offer a model of human cognition that places the automatic pilot within a more comprehensive framework that includes conscious mental processes. My conceptual model then opens the door of plausibility for studying the effect that symbolic and abstract thinking can have on both conscious and pre-conscious processes. More. Symbolic and abstract thinking—even thinking about God—can have an effect on the world around us. Quite specifically, I wish to examine how an individual's concept of ultimate reality (the divine) heuristically affects his or her sense of meaning in life and interpretations within experience; and this in turn leads to world altering activity. I surmise that the abstract idea of God remains in constant tension with resonant symbolic meanings while it restructures our conscious access to perception, restructures our world of meaning, and this in turn interacts with the material and social world through reciprocal activity.

One's abstract idea of God may derive from two sources. The first source is inter-subjectivity—that is, from the symbolic or linguistic life-world within which an individual consciousness swims. In short, whether each of us believes or doubts what we have been taught about the divine, what we have been taught directs the paths our thoughts follow. The second source is individual transcendental experience. This is an experience of what lies beyond both symbolic speech and abstract thinking. Yet, this experience conditions and re-orients both our symbolic and abstract thinking about reality, especially ultimate reality. The transcendental experience may affect our semantic and conceptual awareness like global brain activity affects its local regions.

Finally, the interaction we enjoy with God can be characterized as love. We love God. More importantly, we feel and we know that God loves us. From the top down our consciousness becomes restructured by this

---

3. Dehaene, *Consciousness and the Brain*, 47.

4. Peters, "Resurrection of the Very Embodied Soul," 305–26.

emanating field of love; and the world around us is affected by our loving action. This is not a delusion, I contend. It is real, just as real as antecedent physical causation is real.

Up and Down the Pyramid of Consciousness

We begin with human consciousness and the idea of God at work in that consciousness. When evolutionary virologist Martinez Hewlett asks, "What does it mean to be human?" the first thing he mentions is this: we are "self-conscious and self-reflective creatures."[5] What undergirds and supports this consciousness? Let's try on a conceptual model, namely, the Transamerica Tower.

The Transamerica Tower is shaped like a pyramid. At 853 feet high with 48 floors, it is the tallest of San Francisco's skyscrapers. With the Transamerica Tower as a visual simile, I contend that the architecture of human consciousness is similarly structured. At street level the building's occupants interact with their material environment just as each of us individually receives sense perceptions from the world around us (the hyletic or sensory level). By the time we rise above the four-story base to the fifth floor, we are engaged in *conscious access,* namely, selection and filtering of preconscious sense experience so that our consciousness can organize and manage what we are sensing. The brain is constantly processing a manifold of sense perceptions but selectively uploading only some percepts to conscious awareness. Only some first-floor interaction with the outside world takes the escalator to fifth floor of consciousness.

By the time we reach the 27th floor—originally the observation deck—we are engaged in symbolic discourse, both internal reflection and semantic meaning shared with our wider culture. Finally, when we reach the aluminum-paneled spire at the tower's top, we have arrived at reasoning and the abstract idea. Although the pinnacle of cognition—the abstract idea—is found at the very top, it is utterly dependent on our foundational interaction with the physical world—experienced through sense perception, conscious access, and symbolic discourse—for its content. The elevator does not speed directly upward from street level to the abstract idea; rather, it stops at each floor for a recursive rendezvous with as yet unidentified neuronal networks before proceeding upward.

5. Hewlett, "What Does It Mean to Be Human?," 147–64.

4. Abstract Idea, Knowledge

3. Symbolic Discourse

2. Conscious Access

1. Sensory Interaction

The Transamerica Tower © Ted Peters

One of my concerns as a theologian has to do with the abstract idea of God, an idea arrested by the reasoning mind from the symbolic level of linguistic discourse. We recognize that symbolic discourse as well as the highest level of abstract reasoning are dependent on the prior levels of pre-consciousness and consciousness. Even though an abstract idea lodging at the top of the pyramid is dependent on what is below; we still would like to ask whether that abstract idea can, in turn, influence what happens below. Does the stairway lead down as well as up? As I have mentioned, I surmise that the abstract idea of God remains in constant tension with resonant symbolic meanings while it restructures our conscious access to perception and restructures our world of meaning. In short, our abstract idea of God exerts a hermeneutical influence, so to speak, on new perceptual input as it rises from street level to the pinnacle.

The Pyramid's Foundation: Perception and Conscious Access

Please notice that I do not place the unqualified term *experience* at the foundational level of the cognitional pyramid. This is because human experience is always interpreted experience, even at the preconscious level prior to our conscious access to it. Raw sensory data are immediately processed, selected, organized, and packaged according to meaningful patterns. When we rise to the level of consciousness, symbolic language, and abstract reasoning, we rise as well to more complex and subtle mechanisms of interpretation. Human subjectivity is interpretation from bottom to top, and back down again.

Because each human person is being-in-the-world (*in-der-Welt-Sein*), to borrow a phrase from Martin Heidegger, I place perceptual interaction at this most fundamental level.[6] What neuroscientists are telling us is that only a fraction of our perceptual interaction with the world becomes admitted to consciousness. What occupies researchers such as Dehaene is the fascinating question of consciousness-access: just how does fundamental perception get filtered and selected and organized for conscious awareness? I follow Dehaene as he climbs the stairs from street level to the fifth floor.[7]

When our seeing and hearing climb the stairs toward consciousness we get an interpreted experience. "What we experience as a conscious visual scene is a highly processed image, quite different from the raw input that we receive from the eyes."[8] Yet, this interpretive operation, according to Dehaene, is still preconscious. "Behind the scenes, our brain acts as a clever sleuth that ponders all the separate pieces of sensory information we receive, weighs them according to their reliability, and binds them into a coherent whole. Subjectively, it does not feel like any of it is reconstructed."[9] Or, to say it another way, "all perceiving is a selecting and organizing."[10] We do not need full consciousness for interpretive movement to begin to select and organize our raw experience of being-in-the-world.[11] The interpretive

6 Neurobiologist Walter Freeman contends that each human brain is unique; nevertheless, already in the womb each brain is engaged with its environment, "growing from the genetically determined groundwork by the grasping for available sensory input from within and outside its own body" (Kaku, "The Future of the Mind," 52).

7. Although I follow Dehaene here, physicist Michio Kaku draws a parallel picture by distinguishing two levels of consciousness. "While Level I consciousness uses sensations to create a model of our physical location in space, Level II consciousness creates a model of our place in society" (Kaku, *The Future of the Mind*, 52). What Kaku emphasizes is the mental employment of modeling produced by as yet unidentified neuronal feedback loops. He attempts to explain self-awareness with his modeling model: "Self-awareness is creating a model of the world and simulating the future in which you appear" (ibid., 57).

8. Dehaene, *Consciousness and the Brain*, 60.

9. Ibid.

10 Lonergan, *Method in Theology*, 61.

11. In the Kantian philosophical tradition time and space were dubbed a priori categories that the mind superimposes on perceptions to organize them. Might these a priori categories be gifts of the brain to consciousness? Recent neuronal studies suggest that time and space are produced by the hippocampus to measure movement and location. "The activity of different neurons reflected integration over time and distance to varying extents, with most neurons strongly influenced by both factors and some significantly influenced by only time or distance. Thus, hippocampal neuronal networks captured both the organization of time and distance in a situation where these dimensions dominated an ongoing experience" (Kraus, "Hippocampal Time Cells," 1090). This makes the hippocampus our "resident search engine, which allows us to navigate in mental space when recalling memories or planning future actions" (Buzsáki, *Time, Space, and Memory*, 568). What seems to be happening in contemporary brain research is an increased reliance upon preconscious brain management of the parameters which

process starts from the first floor and ascends all the way to the top. Or, to repeat, human experience is always interpreted experience.

One of the melodies repeatedly sung by today's neuroscientific chorus is this: the brain-as-automatic-pilot has taken care of matters even before we become aware of it. I find this tune catchy, to be sure. But, I ask: is this the whole song? No. I forecast that future brain researchers will eventfully wend their way further up the pyramid's staircases toward linguistic symbolism and abstract reasoning. As they near the top, will the brain's song then become a multi-movement cantata? Or, to approach our basic surmise once again, will symbolic and abstract thinking have a supervening or downward effect on this interpretive process, even at the preconscious level?

Archaeologists imbibing material engagement theory provide support for the primordiality of material interaction and symbolic interpretation. Material Engagement Theory (MET) focuses "on the dense reciprocal causation and on the inseparable affective linkages that characterize the ontological compound of cognition and material culture."[12] The focus here is on the role of the material world—physical environments, objects, homes, tools, weapons—as it influences and is influenced by the symbolic domain of human consciousness. This applies to groups as well as individuals. Or, to reverse it, individual consciousness is largely structured by interaction with the more inclusive cultural consciousness. This symbolized structure, in turn, influences the meaning of human interaction with the material world. "While it can be said that material culture is actively involved in the adaptive strategies of groups, it is now clear that the explanation of those strategies and the way in which material culture is involved in them depend on internally generated symbolic schemes."[13]

By referencing the convergence of phenomenology with MET my point is this: the interaction of the human person with the material environment is mediated by symbolic thinking. As our physical perceptions rise up into awareness they are filtered, configured, and ordered by the symbolic world within which we live.

---

structure consciousness. Curiously, neurogenesis—the generation of new neural cells—contributes to forgetting; because time memories are associated with the cells being replaced by new ones. "Neurogenesis leads to degradation or forgetting of established memories" (Akers et al., Hippocampal Neurogenesis, 598). The brain is responsible for those "senior moments" with which we are familiar.

12. Malafouris, *How Things Shape the Mind*, 248.

13. Hodder, *Symbols in Action*, 186.

The Pyramid's Superstructure:
Symbolic Discourse and Abstract Thinking

Symbols are multivalent. They emit multiple levels of meaning. Although I do not exhaustively equate language and symbolic discourse, many symbols are linguistic constructions and most of ordinary language is multivalent as well. We are born into a language, a language that may be centuries if not millennia in the making. We inherit meanings that pre-date us, meanings we may not even be aware of but which influence the world of meaning within which we daily live. German hermeneutical philosopher Hans-Georg Gadamer spoke of the work of our inherited language as *Wirkungsgeschichte,* the effect that past history embedded in our language has on structuring today's consciousness.[14] French hermeneutical philosopher Paul Ricoeur observed that we are born into a linguistic world imbued with symbolic meaning, and symbolic meaning makes abstract thought possible. "The symbol gives rise to thought."[15] We do not own our own symbolic meaning. We share it intersubjectively with our contemporaries and with our ancestors. Language and symbol provide the stream of historically conditioned consciousness within which we swim and within which our own subjectivity takes form.

The pursuit of human reasoning requires abstracting concepts from the more primordial linguistic experience, assigning them univocal meaning, and then placing them in rational relationships with one another. Language in general and symbolic speech in particular carry multiple meanings, whereas abstract thought needs to focus on one and only one meaning for each term. Whereas symbolic speech is equivocal, abstract thought attempts to be univocal. The multivalent symbol gives rise to abstract thought; but abstract thought carries thinking beyond the textured meanings of the symbol. In time, an abstract concept can reenter the flowing stream of language and pick up multiple meanings once again, becoming a new symbol in its own right.

Language, according to evolutionary anthropologist Terrence Deacon, is "a mode of communication based upon symbolic reference (the way words refer to things) and involving combinatorial rules that comprise a system for representing synthetic logical relationships among these symbols."[16] Language is by no means a mere epiphenomenon to human consciousness. It is a force in its own right, an evolutionary force. "Language must be viewed as

14. Gademer, *Truth and Method.*

15. Ricoeur, *The Symbolism of Evil,* 237.

16. Deacon, *The Symbolic Species,* 41.

its own prime mover. It is the author of a co-evolved complex of adaptations arrayed around a single core semiotic innovation that was initially extremely difficult to acquire. Subsequent brain evolution was a response to this selection pressure and progressively made this symbolic threshold ever easier to cross. This has in turn opened the door for the evolution of ever greater language complexity."[17] This complexity includes multivalency, the dynamic of language to become richly symbolic and generate new meaning.[18]

Multivalency may be due either to multiple references or to feelings associated with a symbol. "A symbol is an image of a real or imaginary object that evokes a feeling or is evoked by a feeling," contends Jesuit theologian Bernard Lonergan.[19] Symbolic discourse is pre-logical (not irrational, but pre-logical). Lonergan recognizes this, but he is less than fully clear on an important point I wish to make, namely, univocity (a single univocal meaning) is an abstraction from symbolic discourse. Symbolic discourse is not a distortion of univocal discourse; rather, symbolic discourse provides a sea of multiple meanings within which univocity appears as an island.

Here is Lonergan's way of describing the situation: "Symbols obey the laws not of logic but of image and feeling . . . . For univocity [the symbol] substitutes a wealth of multiple meanings . . . . It does not bow to the principle of excluded middle but admits the *coincidentia oppositorum*, of love and hate, of courage and fear, and so on. It does not negate but overcomes what it rejects by heaping up all that is opposite to it. . . . The symbol, then, has the power of recognizing and expressing what logical discourse abhors: the existence of internal tensions, incompatibilities, conflicts, struggles, destructions"[20] (Lonergan, 1972, 66). What Lonergan contends is that symbolic speech messes up abstract ideas by adding unnecessary additional meanings. But, this is just backwards. What actually happens—and this is the important point I wish to make—is that we inherit a language with multiple meanings and, from within this reservoir of meanings, we single out only those we wish to assign to our abstract idea. Symbolic meaning gives rise to abstract thought, to

17. Ibid., 44.

18. Deacon belongs to the semiotics school of Charles Sanders Pierce, which tends to conflate rational rules with ordinary linguistic symbols. To fully understand the multivalency of symbolic discourse, we must turn to the continental hermeneutical philosophers such as Paul Ricoeur. "Unlike a comparison that we *look at* from the outside, symbol is the very movement of the primary meaning that makes us share in the latent meaning and thereby assimilates us to the symbolized, without our being able intellectually to dominate the similarity. This is the sense in which the symbol "gives": it gives because it is a primary intentionality, that gives the second meaning," Ricoeur, *The Conflict of Interpretations*, 290.

19. Lonergan, *Method in Theology*, 64.

20. Ibid., 66.

be sure; but abstract thought goes beyond symbolic equivocity to univocity. More. When abstract thinking posits a univocal proposition, the multiple meanings embedded within the linguistic reservoir remain co-present, providing contextual meaning for the univocal propositions.

For example, a linguistic *symbol* for God such as "Father" is multivalent. It can mean many things. However, an *abstract idea* of God the Father such as we find in monotheistic theology is intended to correspond to a single precisely formulated idea, such as Saint Anselm positing that God is that than which nothing greater can be conceived (*id quo maius cognitari nequit*). For Saint Anselm to posit this particular definition of God requires a level of specificity that excludes competing ideas about God. Many of the symbolic connotations of the word *Father*—God as a loving parent or God as a patriarchal despot—are shaved off when rendering a considered judgment such as this: God is that than which nothing greater can be conceived. In sum, linguistic or symbolic discourse provides an ocean of meanings at multiple levels (equivocity), within which we find an occasional island of rational or abstract concepts with only a single designated meaning (univocity).

To review: we as individuals do not invent our own language. Nor do we invent our own symbols. We inherit them. Oh, yes, we can witness changes in language along with the emergence of new symbolic configurations over time; but both the continuity and change in linguistic and related meaning inheres in our relationships, in our interactions with the culture enveloping us. Linguistic meaning belongs to the group, to intersubjectivity. "Meaning is embodied or carried in human *inter*subjectivity.[21] Even though we earlier placed our relationship to the world around us at the pyramid's ground level of perception, at the intersubjective level of semantic meaning our very consciousness is influenced significantly by what we share with others. We think first like the group talks; then we turn inward toward individuated thinking.

What Lonergan rightly understands is that symbolic meaning is holistic; it orients a person's entire existence at a pre-objectified yet comprehensive level. "It is through symbols that mind and body, mind and heart, heart and body communicate. In that communication symbols have their proper meaning. It is an elemental meaning, not yet objectified."[22] Might this holistic model of symbolic meaning point the way to a corresponding holistic model for comprehending brain activity? If we follow the localizers among the neuroscientists, the answer would be negative. If we follow the

21. Ibid., 57.
22. Ibid.

globalizers, the answer might be affirmative. More research is required to confirm this hypothesis.

The Explanatory Gap

I acknowledge that neuroscience and related enterprises are relatively new on the scientific landscape; and it is difficult to know how far the horizon of inquiry will stretch. Yet, I applaud the search for material explanations of what seem to be mental, psychological, and spiritual dimensions of human experience. Nevertheless, I ask a cautionary question: can we encourage such scientific progress without falling into eliminative reductionism, without exhaustively reducing conscious experience to unconscious brain processes?[23] This is where the explanatory gap—sometimes called the 'hard problem'—enters in.

A widely recognized *explanatory gap* exists in this field, a gap between what we experience subjectively in consciousness and materialist attempts to explain this experience. Theologian William Grassie identifies the hard problem.

> Our physical descriptions of the way the brain works at the level of neurons, brain anatomy, and neurological processes bear no resemblance to our subjective experience as people with brains having complex mental and emotional states. Nor is there any neurological definition of consciousness as such. We have no device that can measure presence or absence of consciousness.[24]

This is a hard problem, "for no matter how deeply we probe into the physical structure of neurons and the chemical transactions which occur when they fire, no matter how much objective information we come to acquire, we still seem to be left with something that we cannot explain, namely, why and how such-and-such objective, physical changes, whatever they might be, generate so-and-so subjective feeling, or any subjective feeling at all."[25] It is the assumption that creates the gap: if we assume that reality is limited to a closed causal nexus of physical events that are objectively

23. A false impression is widespread, namely, that scientists already possess evidence supporting neurodeterminism. "The media routinely report on scans showing that specific brain locations light up when we feel rejected or speak a foreign language. These news stories may give the impression that current technology provides fundamental insights into how the brain works, but that impression is deceiving" (Yuste, "The New Century of the Brain," 40).

24. Grassie, *The New Sciences of Religion*, 96.

25. Tye, "Qualia."

described in the third person, then how can we explain the existence of first-person subjectivity?

Some pretend that no gap exists. They pretend that everything you and I experience subjectively in the first person will eventually be reduced and explained objectively in the third person. The result is that the public is beset with claims suggesting that physical explanations may eventually reduce subjective experience to the status of a delusion. "Neuroscientists increasingly describe our behavior as the result of a chain of cause and effect, in which one physical brain state or pattern of neural activity inexorably leads to the next, culminating in a particular action or decision. With little space for free choice in this chain of causation, the conscious, deliberating self seems to be a fiction."[26] The pretenders belong to the club of mind-brain identity theorists. "The mind-brain identity theory states that mental states, qualia, are literally identical to specific neural states." Accordingly, our experience of conscious awareness and experience of creative action are reducible to antecedent physical causation. Consciousness with its mental causation has no life it can call its own.

Cambridge physicist Stephen Hawking slams the door shut on human consciousness and free will right along with it: "recent experiments in neuroscience support the view that it is our physical brain, following the known laws of science, that determines our actions, and not some agency that exists outside those laws . . . It is hard to imagine how free will can operate if our behavior is determined by physical law, so it seems that we are no more than biological machines and that free will is just an illusion."[27]

An illusion? How about a fiction? What we experience as one's self, according to Daniel Dennett, is merely the "fictional center of narrative gravity."[28] Also affirming this self-as-fiction position, neurophilosopher Thomas Metzinger pits the brain against subjectivity. "Subjective experience is a biological data format, a highly specific mode of presenting information about the world by letting it appear as if it were an Ego's knowledge. But, no such things as selves exist in this world."[29] If we would accept this set of determinist assumptions which eliminate the human self, we could hack into the religious mind by simply hacking into the religious brain with scalpels or fMRI scans.

Nonreductionists such as David Chalmers respond with a warning against reductive overreaching. "Experience may arise from the physical,

26. Jones, "The Free Will Delusion," 32.
27. Hawking and Mlodinow, *The Grand Design*, 32.
28. Dennett, *Consciousness Explained*, 418.
29. Metzinger, *The Science of the Mind and the Myth of the Self*, 8.

but it is not entailed by the physical. The moral of all this is that *you can't explain conscious experience on the cheap.*"[30] Similarly, Stuart Kauffman at the Santa Fe Institute refuses to allow consciousness with its accompanying creativity to be reduced to physical processes. "Consciousness is emergent and a real feature of the universe."[31] Finally, philosophical theologian Nancey Murphy and neurotheologian Warren Brown declare war against reductionism and plan to "defeat neurobiological reductionism."[32] In short, according to the anti-reductionists, consciousness is more than neuronal firings. And, I might add, consciousness of God is more than automatic neuronal firings. Consciousness of God consists of organized neuronal firings oriented around God as one's ultimate concern.

Reductionism, Determinism, and Anxiety

Determinist and reductionist neurophilosophy elicits public anxiety. Each of us feels at home in our subjectivity, in our consciousness. Subjectivity establishes who we are and where we are. It establishes who is the person experiencing oneself in the world. Subjectivity instantiates us in being. So, for the neurophilosopher—ostensibly relying on the science of the brain—to explain our subjective first-person self-understanding in terms of something else elicits the fear that our personhood will be explained away. The third-person scientific perspective appears as a threat to our interior first person self-understanding. This is an existential threat posed by an abstract discipline. We dare not underestimate the power of this existential sense of threat.

Like a leering Dracula darkening a room with his outstretched wings, some neurophilosophers and ride-along bioreductionists relish the terrified feeling prompted in us by the threat of losing the reality of our subjective selfhood. One intellectual vampire is sociobiologist E.O. Wilson. "It [free will] is a product of the subconscious decision-making center of the brain that gives the cerebral cortex the illusion of independent action."[33] The blood of life's meaning is sucked out of us when we are told that what we think is most real, our self, is an illusion.

Thomas Clark understands the existential anxiety the reductionist agenda prompts. "Involved here are fairly deep and emotional issues of human autonomy and specialness, especially the fear that if consciousness is

---

30. Chalmers, "The Hard Problem," 18 (italics original).

31. Kauffman, *Reinventing the Sacred*, 4.

32. Murphy and Brown, *Did My Neurons Make Me Do It?*, 305.

33. Wilson, *The Social Conquest of Earth*, 288.

nothing over and above physically instantiated function, then we lose our privileged status as rational agents riding above the flux of brute causality . . . . If it turns out that subjectivity and the sense of self are merely function, then it becomes terrifying (for some) that no principled distinction may exist between us and a very clever robot"[34]

But Clark has no intention of respecting this fear. He takes no prisoners. He presses forward with his task of finding a reductionist explanation. "But of course we must not let such fears prejudice our initial conception of consciousness or restrict our investigation . . . . As a scientific strategy for unifying knowledge, the reductionist impulse is hardly to be eschewed but rather to be encouraged . . . . To reduce mental phenomena to functional processes via some plausibly evidenced identification is, after all, not to eliminate them, but simply to redescribe them from a third-person perspective."[35] Clark supports the *"functional identity hypothesis,"* which makes a strong claim . . . that subjectivity is constituted by those central representational processes which transform and enhance sensory information to the point where it normally dominates in the control of behavior."[36] In sum, Clark will not eliminate our first-person perspective; he will simply redescribe our first-person perspective in third-person terms. Clark bridges the explanatory gap by shrinking the gap to a small jump from first-person consciousness to a third-person reduction.

Are there alternative ways to leap the explanatory gap? Yes. In an apparently nonreductionist manner, Chalmers attempts to bridge the explanatory gap. Because information is ubiquitously present in all physical reality, and because the human brain is an information processer, could physical information and subjective information become united into a single bridge? Could we hold that human consciousness based upon a physical substrate continues to bear this prior physical information? Yes, answers Chalmers. "Information is truly fundamental . . . information is everywhere."[37] The gap has now been closed, thinks Chalmers, by an information bridge.

34. Clark, "Function and Phenomenology," 50.

35. Ibid., 50–51.

36. Ibid., 52 (italics original).

37. Chalmers, "The Hard Problem," 27. Because Chalmers sees a "gap," he is attacked by his reductionist critics on the grounds that he harbors a disguised Cartesian dualism. "The resulting naturalistic dualism Chalmers defends is Cartesian at its core, and despite his claim that such a position is entirely compatible with the scientific view of the world, dualisms have fared badly as science proceeds to unify our conception of humankind in nature (Clark, "Function and Phenomenology," 48). "An imaginary dazzle in the eye of a Cartesian homunculus (Dennett, "Facing Backwards," 34).

Stuart Kauffman is not ready to cross Chalmers's information bridge from subjective mental activity to objective brain correlates. Why? Because a bridge constructed of information is too weak. "Information [is] a concept that manages to be both restrictive and unclear" complains Kauffman.[38] To simply assert that information is everywhere is not helpful, because the role of information in human subjectivity is so complex. In fact, the information hypothesis fails to acknowledge that the concept of information itself depends upon the very conscious agents it attempts to reduce. "Information requires an *agent, a nonequilibrium self-reproducing system doing work cycles,* to *receive* the information, *discriminate* it, and *interpret and act* on it."[39] In human subjectivity, information is pondered, considered, rearranged, evaluated, and judged by an agent who takes action. Much more than Chalmers, Kauffman is ready to expand the explanatory gap.

The explanatory gap problem leads us to ask: do we have a self at all? My own position will be that we must presuppose the self with our subjectivity and first-person perspective if we are to pursue our proposed research into human consciousness of ultimate reality.

From Quantum Consciousness to Classical Causation

Before turning to the question of the self's existence, let me offer a transitional hypothesis: the reductionist temptation derives from a worldview constructed solely by Newtonian or classical physics. This classical worldview presupposes a closed causal nexus, where every effect seems to require an antecedent efficient cause. "Causal closure asserts that everything that occurs has a sufficient antecedent condition or set of conditions."[40] With the closed causal nexus as an assumption, the temptation to reductionism is quite understandable. But, we must ask: what happens when we incorporate quantum physics—the indeterministic interpretation of quantum physics—into our analysis of self-organization, human selfhood, agency, free will, meaning, value, and moral behavior?[41]

38. Kauffman, *Reinventing the Sacred*, 89.

39 Ibid., 96 (italics original).

40. Ibid. (italics original).

41. If we drill down below the bottom of consciousness, we might strike oil at the level of quantum physical activity. Does indeterminism at the quantum level provide a necessary—even if not a sufficient—condition for the rise of human consciousness and subjectivity? Perhaps, yes. Nevertheless, no consensus exists that would permit reducing what happens in consciousness to what happens at the quantum level. Consciousness exhibits emergent properties. Physical mathematician Roger Penrose, for

This is the step taken by Stuart Kauffman. Kauffman ghettoizes reductionism within Newtonian or classical mechanics. The problem, he maintains, is that reductionists operate with an outdated pre-quantum worldview. What if instead the human mind begins with quantum activity, with *indeterministic* quantum activity? A quantum basis for the mind would fittingly describe the human person in terms of agency, selfhood, consciousness, free will, meaning, value, and social morality. Observing how quantum activity in the brain decoheres and becomes part of the mechanical nexus of the classical realm, we could solve Descartes' enigmatic puzzle: we could explain how mind could affect matter. We will have jumped the explanatory gap.

"The mind is more than a computational machine. Embodied in us, the human mind is a *meaning and doing organic system,*"[42] contends Kauffman. Our a-causal mental activity at the quantum level eventually expresses itself in everyday cause-and-effect action. He continues. "Consciousness is associated with a poised state between quantum *coherent* behavior and what is called *decoherence* of quantum possibilities to classical actual events . . . the immaterial—not objectively real—mind has consequences for the actual classical physical world."[43] Having posited the co-presence of both quantum and classical physical properties, Kauffman then addresses Descartes' puzzle: how can a non-extended mind (*res cogitans*) affect the extended material world (*res extensa*)? "*Here, mind—consciousness, res cogitans—is identical with quantum coherent immaterial possibilities, or with partially coherent quantum behavior, yet via decoherence, the quantum coherent mind has consequences that approach classical behavior so very closely that mind can have consequences that create actual physical events by the emergence of classicity. Thus, res cogitans has consequences*

---

example, suggests that quantum activity may affect what takes place in our subconscious, but there lies a huge gap between quantum mechanics and consciousness. There might even be a change in the computational rules of physical activity when it becomes biology (Penrose, "The Quantum Nature of Consciousness"). Brain researchers avoid reducing new properties emerging at the biological level to their underlying influence at the physical level. "To date, quantum interactions do not seem to bear robustly on the issue of consciousness 'as such.' The biological basis of consciousness has been acknowledged as one of the fundamental unsolved questions in science. The weight of evidence indicates that it is a major biological adaptation. We therefore need to understand its evolutionary, developmental, and experience-dependent foundations in the brain" (Baars and Edelman, "Consciousness, Biology, and Quantum Hypotheses," 203). In order to pursue the emergence of human subjectivity one must pursue history—history in the form of evolutionary history. The study of physics in abstraction from evolutionary history will not suffice.

42. Kauffman, *Reinventing the Sacred*, 177 (italics original).

43. Ibid., 197 (italics added).

for res extensa! Immaterial mind has consequences for matter."[44] Kauffman distinguishes a-causality at the quantum level from efficient causality at the classical level. "*The quantum coherent mind does not . . . act on matter causally at all. Rather, via decoherence, the quantum coherent state has consequences for the physical classical world.*"[45]

A kindred spirit on the relation of quantum activity to mental activity—including free will—would be physicist Henry Stapp. "Contemporary physical theory annuls the claim of mechanical determinism. In a profound reversal of the classical physical principles, its laws make your conscious choices causally effective in the physical world, while failing to determine, even statistically, what those choices will be."[46] In order to cede to human subjectivity the status in reality that it deserves, say both Kauffman and Stapp, we must move beyond classical physics and acknowledge quantum physics. The inclusion of quantum physics in explanations of human mental processes will avoid reductionism.

Still, I remain cautious. It would be too much to rely completely on the quantum foundation laid out by Kauffman or Stapp. The quantum theory of mental activity is a hypothesis awaiting future confirmation. Yet, when we compare it with the reductionist temptation, it fares no worse. The brain-mind identity theory relies on yesterday's physics and, more importantly, it has as yet no conclusive evidence that it is correct. Of the two approaches—classical physical reductionism or the quantum brain hypothesis—the second is by far the more promising even if still awaiting confirmation.

What we experience every day in our consciousness is this: each of us enjoys an interior life within which we realize we are a self, a valuing and acting agent that impacts the world around us. What we experience is free will: free will consisting of deliberation, decision, and action. The quantum hypothesis replete with indeterminism seems to be a better fit with our experience than is the brain-mind identity hypothesis. With this in mind, we turn to the question: Do we have a self?

Do We Have a Self?

I am working with a material and symbolic treatment of the brain-mind relationship. Within this nonreductionist yet physicalist framework, we can still identify a centering dynamic, the appearance of a self, a first-person orientation. When neuroscientists and neurophilosophers give focused attention

44. Ibid., 209 (italics original).

45. Ibid., 225 (italics original).

46 Stapp, *Mindful Universe*, vii.

to the accessing of perceptual data by our consciousness, they are climbing the internal staircase toward human meaning. According to Chalmers, for example, *structural coherence* provides human awareness with a centering or organizing architecture. "We can think of awareness as *direct availability for global control* . . . Awareness is a purely functional notion, but it is nevertheless intimately linked to conscious experience."[47]

For Chalmers, consciousness and awareness are not identical; rather, they are correlates. "It is this isomorphism between the structures of consciousness and awareness that constitutes the principle of structural coherence . . . . The mechanisms of awareness perform the function of making information directly available for global control."[48] To my reading, global control implies a center, a self, a first-person perspective. So, let us pose the questions:

Does global control require a controller, a self? Does such a thing as the human self exist? Does the human self account for instances of downward causation, of whole-part influence? If we climb the staircase that leads to the top of the Transamerica pyramid, must we retrace our path downward to see how the top influences the stages below?

Before pressing such questions, perhaps we should interpolate a caution. I am not attempting here to reify the self or to retrieve a dualistic version of soul. The self is not a thing. It is not independent, autonomous, isolated. Rather, the presence of the self, I hypothesize, is the product of interaction at multiple levels.

This acknowledgment is important for feminist philosophers. Some feminist thinkers hold that the self is merely the subject of enunciation—a speaker who can use the pronoun *I*. Further, such a speaker is neither unitary nor fully in control of what he or she says, because discourse is bifurcated. At one level, the self appears to be conscious, individuated and in control. At another more subterranean level, however, the language inherited by the self from the surrounding social setting works in the preconscious domain and, from there, invisibly structures the conscious domain. The conscious self unknowingly absorbs into the preconscious the semiotic dimension of language, which is characterized by figurative language, cadences, and intonations. Everything said depends on its context of what is unsaid.

Acknowledging this raises feminist concerns about gender and the self. Since the rational orderliness of the prevailing symbolic system is coded to serve masculine vested interests while the affect-laden allure of the semiotic connotation is culturally coded feminine, it follows that no

47. Chalmers, "The Hard Problem," 22.
48. Ibid., 23–24.

discourse is purely masculine or purely feminine. The speaking subject finds both the masculine symbolic and the feminine semiotic to be equally indispensable, regardless of which socially assigned gender he or she may be. Because of these two levels of symbolic discourse, it is impossible to be a purely masculine self or a purely feminine self. Every subject of enunciation—every self—amalgamates masculine and feminine discursive modalities.[49] In short, the consciousness of the self is by no means *sui generous*; it is shared by the culture which finds the symbolic field meaningful. The shared culture can tyrannize the self.

One more preliminary before moving on. Let's remind ourselves of those steps from the bottom upward. At the ladder's bottom, Dehaene steps up from our perception of everything in our immediate life-world toward consciousness-access. Chalmers takes us further up the staircase toward centering, toward the consolidation of the human self or person. The human self lives in a world of linguistic discourse and symbolic meaning. To the symbolic world of the self and to the production of abstract ideas we now turn.

As Dehaene climbs the staircase from street level to the fifth floor where consciousness accesses perception, he looks up. What he thinks he sees he calls the *Global Neuronal Workspace* (GNW). What is this GNW? "Consciousness is brain-wide information sharing . . . Consciousness is an evolved device that allows us to attend to a piece of information and keep it active within this broadcasting system. Once the information is conscious, it can be flexibly routed to other areas according to our current goals. Thus we can name it, evaluate it, memorize it, or use it to plan the future. Computer simulations of neural networks show that the global neuronal workspace hypothesis generates precisely the signatures that we see in experimental brain recordings."[50] Does the GNW include both what is conscious and what is preconscious or unconscious? It seems to, according to Dehaene. It borders on globalizing.

Can consciousness influence what is preconscious or subconscious? Yes. Consciousness can actively assign designated information patterns to a preconscious or unconscious status by establishing habits; and this maintains room in the active consciousness for keeping focus on what is new or important. "The more routine a behavior becomes, the less we are aware of it."[51] By establishing habits, our consciousness can shelve certain activities in the unconscious closet until it needs to draw them out and give

49. Willett and Meyers, "Feminist Perspectives on the Self."

50. Dehaene, *Consciousness and the Brain*, 161.

51. Graybiel and Smith, "Good Habits, Bad Habits," 40.

them renewed attention. Because consciousness is brain-wide, so to speak, it can temporarily consign habits to the unconscious in order to maintain workspace in what is immediately conscious. It appears that via downward causation—via supervenience or top-down or whole-part causation—our consciousness governs at least some of what is unconscious.

What Nancey Murphy would call *supervenience*,[52] Warren Brown explicates in terms of top-down agency. "*Top-down agency* refers to the ability to modulate behavior in relationship to conscious thought and intention."[53] In other words, our symbolic understanding and our abstract reasoning provide top-down influences on conscious access and, in addition, they direct our agency in the world. The self is an agent who takes action and causes changes in the material and cultural world.

When I characterize free will as self-determination—that is, deliberation, decision, and action—free will takes on a future orientation. To be a self and to act freely implies that we provide reasons for what we do; and what we do influences what happens in the future. "A *future orientation* is meant to denote the ability to run a conscious mental simulation or scenario of future possibilities for the actions of oneself and others, and to evaluate these scenarios in such a way as to regulate behavior and make decisions now with regard to desirable future events."[54] Self-determination produced by top-down agency is not reducible to antecedent physical causation. Rather, it is the product of a human self.

But we must keep asking: is this self merely a delusion? Among neurophilosophers we can find some who affirm that the self is a delusion along with others who deny the delusion premise. Whether the self is real or a delusion, each of us *believes* we have a self.[55] "The brain makes us think that we have a self," writes Patricia S. Churchland. "Does that mean that the self

52. Murphy and Brown, "Divine Action," 196–204.

53. Brown, "Cognitive Contributions to the Soul," 117.

54. Ibid.

55. Immanuel Kant alerts us to a temptation to think that what we can abstract from experience we can also separate. This applies to the human self, which, despite this mistake, cannot be separated from the synthetic a priori, from the interaction of consciousness with objects of consciousness. "I cogitate myself in behalf of a possible experience at the same time making abstraction of all actual experience; and infer therefrom that I can be conscious of myself apart from experience and its empirical conditions. I consequently confound the possible *abstraction* of my empirically determined existence with the supposed consciousness of a possible *separate* existence of my thinking self; and I believe that I cognize what is substantial in myself as a transcendental subject, when I have nothing more in thought than the unity of consciousness, which lies at the basis of all determination of cognition" (Kant, *Critique of Pure Reason*, 246–47). In short, no substantial or permanent self—soul—exists in a disembodied state.

I think I am is not real? No, it is as real as any activity of the brain. It does mean, however, that one's self is not an ethereal bit of soul stuff."[56] What is she saying? Churchland rejects classical or Cartesian dualism, according to which the self or the soul is made from an immortal substance. Yet, she says that our first-person perspective requires a self to see itself as a self right along with everything else we perceive in the world.[57]

Widely read German philosopher Ottfried Höffe draws the right conclusion, in my judgment. "The person thinks, to be sure, 'with' his central organ; he acts 'with' the brain, but it is the person, not the brain, that thinks or acts."[58] Similarly, St. Andrews University neuropsychologist Malcolm Jeeves commits himself to an ontology of the human person inclusive of mind, brain and body: "the ontological reality of 'person' is primary."[59] He adds, "A holistic model of the human person does most justice to the scientific understanding of ourselves. . . . Our unity is central. We know each

56. Churchland, *Brain-Wise*, 124.

57. When making a review of the options for modeling the self or ego or first-person perspective, I delineate five discrete models in contemporary discussion:

(1) *Ego Continuity*, according to which a persistent self-awareness or even an immortal soul inhabits an ever-changing physical body and physical environment. This would be the classic Platonic or Cartesian position.

(2) *Self as Confused Expression of a Higher Self*, according to which, our individual soul is but a manifestation of the over-soul, the spiritual reality that unites all things. We find this model in New Age Spirituality.

(3) *Self as Delusion*, the position taken by many philosophers who claim to base their cognitive theory on neuroscience. "The mind . . . is the brain" (Dennett, "Facing Backwards," 107) or "there is no such thing as a self" (Metzinger, *The Science of the Mind*, 1). This is the reductionist model according to which no substantial ego exists. The self is a fiction.

(4) *Self as Story or Narrative*, according to which the self is an evolving social construction whose identity is defined by our history, our story. Jennifer Ouellette belongs here in the self as narrative model (Ouellette, *Me, Myself, and Why*, 260). For a historical or biographical self to develop requires relationship. "The development of a sense of self relies on the regulating, reliable, and felt presence of the other" (Fisher, *Neurofeedback*, 21).

(5) *Self as Experiential Dimension*. Here, "the self is claimed to possess experiential reality, is taken to be closely linked to the first-person perspective, and is, in fact, identified with the very first-person *givenness* of the experiential phenomena," according to Dan Zahavi, who directs the Center for Subjectivity Research at the University of Copenhagen (Zahavi, *Subjectivity and Selfhood*, 106). My own position comes closest to the experiential dimension model with some sympathies toward the story or narrative model.

58. Höffe, *Can Virtue Make Us Happy?*, 245.

59. Jeeves, "Brains, Minds, Souls, and People," 107.

other, not as brains ensheathed in bodies, but as embodied persons"[60].This
leads theologian Philip Clayton to declare the following:

> I suggest that language of personhood or 'whole persons' serves
> an indispensable function in comprehending human actions
> and interactions . . . . Only explanations that include this emer-
> gent level of personal actions and intentions are in fact able
> to explain the data available to us, the data of introspection,
> the data of human behavior, and the data of human cultural
> production.[61]

The person is centered by the self. It is not my task in this chapter to
take up directly the question of the metaphysical status of the human self,
but I stipulate for the purposes of coherency in my proposed cognitional
model that a phenomenal self with a growing history or biographical narrative is present and operative with a first-person perspective and with agency
in the world.

Reports of the Death of Free Will Are Premature[62]

If the human self is a delusion, is free will also? If preconscious causes determine conscious decisions, does this eliminate what we assume to be free
will? Does saying, "don't blame me. My neurons made me do it," eliminate
our moral responsibility?

Here is my position: *free will* consists of deliberation, decision, and
action that exhibits self-determination. Free will is the self in action, both
as self-control and as affecting the environment. This is a nonreductionist
assessment that requires some level of indeterminism in the physics—will a
quantum theory of the brain supply sufficient indeterminism?—of mental
processes. Physical indeterminism provides a necessary condition for human free will; but it is not a sufficient condition. What else is needed? The
existence of the self as a determining agent.

The so-called free will debate is not the same as the debate between
determinism and indeterminism. Rather, the free will debate deals with this
question: is the human self a determinant? In my camp we answer yes, the
human self determines (at least in part) what will happen in our world. I
would like to invite Murphy and Brown into my camp. They contend that
free will should be "understood as being the primary cause of one's own

60. Jeeves, "Brains, Minds, Souls, and People," 107.

61. Clayton, "The Emergence of Spirit," 290–310.

62. Weissenbacher, "Ten Principles," 48.

actions; this is a holistic capacity of mature, self-reflective human organisms acting within suitable social contexts."[63]

Patricia Churchland wanders on the perimeter of my camp. "I am not a puppet; I could have done otherwise," she writes[64] "Neuroscientists know in a general way what structures are crucial for normal self-control . . . self-control depends on the connectivity patterns between neurons in a set of subareas of the prefrontal cortex (PFC) and subcortical structures, mainly the basal ganglia and nucleus acumbens."[65] As brain-mind identity theorists are inclined to do, Churchland eschews any contracausal attempts to explain free will. "The name *contracausal* reflects a philosophical theory that *really* free choices are not caused by anything, or at least by nothing physical such as activity in the brain." Churchland opposes contracausal accounts of free will. She affirms that the brain produces a self complete with free will and self-control. "If you are *intending* your action, *knowing* what you are doing, and are of sound mind, and if the decision is not coerced (no gun is pointed at your head), then you are exhibiting free will. This is about as good as it gets"[66] My way of putting the matter is this: there is such a thing as the self, and the self provides its own set of antecedent causes for both internal and external effects. According to Churchland, similarly, free will is not an illusion. The facts demonstrate that self-control and free will happen. "What is *not* illusory is self-control."[67]

Self-control or self-determination benefit from what we describe as holism, top-down causation, or supervenience. "The question is no longer whether processes at these lower levels are deterministic; but rather whether higher-level systems, in general, are entirely governed by the behavior of their parts," writes Murphy[68]. A whole cannot be reduced to its parts; and a human self is a whole whose symbolic and abstract thinking supervenes on his or her consciousness, deliberation, decision, and activity. This means human persons gain "a level of control over their bodies and behaviour."[69]

This understanding of freedom as self-determination does not require a blanket indeterminism in the physical nexus. Rather, it requires that the self as agent be thought of as one of the determining causes among others in the causal nexus. Philip Clayton contends that freedom is a property of biological

63. Murphy and Brown, *Did My Neurons Make Me Do It?*, 305.

64. Churchland, *Touching a Nerve*, 178.

65. Ibid., 176.

66. Ibid., 180.

67. Ibid., 185 (italics original).

68. Murphy, "Divine Action," 254.

69. Ibid.

organisms which gradually developed over evolutionary time scales as the degree of complexity increased. With complexity comes the emergence of new causes, one of which is the emergent human self as agent. "Emergence points toward continuously new forms of complexity and causality," he writes.[70] The complex human self has evolved into an agent in the physical world. James Haag reinforces this position: "I propose that the dynamic process occurring between representations, decisions, and actions, instigated by a tendency to change (the will), *is* the self."[71] In brief, what we know as free will is, in fact, the self as a subject deliberating, deciding, and taking action which has a cause-effect impact on the physical world.

The type of freedom at stake here we know as free will, otherwise described as subjective arbitrariness, freedom of choice, human agency, and such. What is not at stake in this discussion is distinctively *Christian* freedom. The two freedoms are not the same. Whereas the concept of the *free will* in popular usage denotes the opportunity of the self to choose between alternatives, the concept of *Christian Freedom* requires transcending one's self-interest and taking action on behalf of the needs of other selves. Whereas the first is a form of self-expression, the second requires self-transcendence. Whereas the first freedom is a human accomplishment, the second is a gift of divine grace. Martin Luther describes Christian Freedom paradoxically. "A Christian is a perfectly free lord of all, subject to none. A Christian is a perfectly dutiful servant of all, subject to all" in love.[72] Curiously, in this chapter I am trying to rescue the self from enslavement to neuro-reductionist accounts; but, theologically, Christian Freedom then requires giving that very self away in the service of love.

Even more paradoxically and even more curiously, what most of us accept as free will is, from a theological point of view, bondage. The will is bound to self-expression, to self-interest, sometimes even to self-aggrandizement. Metaphor theorist George Lakoff enunciates the secular understanding of free will as self-expression. "There is a simple understanding of freedom. Freedom is being able to do what you want to do, that is, being able to choose a goal, have access to that goal, pursue that goal without anyone purposely preventing you. It is having the capacity or power to achieve the goal and being able to exercise your free will to choose and achieve the goal."[73] Or, "Freedom requires government of the self, by the self, and for

70. Clayton,"The Emergence of Spirit," 141.

71. Haag, *Emergent Freedom,* 197 (italics original).

72. Luther, *Luther's Works,* 31:344.

73. Lakoff, *Whose Freedom?*, 225–26.

the self."[74] From a theological point of view, what Lakoff dubs freedom is, in fact, bondage to the self. For the human person to love as God loves it requires liberation from the self. "The bondage of the will calls, therefore, for a liberation and, in the radical sense, for a redemption that will establish the will's identity anew," writes theologian Wolfhart Pannenberg.[75]

Christian freedom is distinguished by its attunement with God, an attunement given to us by God as a gift of divine grace. As important as this attunement is to the person of faith, distinctively Christian freedom is not the focus of this exploration into cognitional theory. Rescuing human freedom as self-determination from the jaws of the reductionist dragon will suffice for this knight's errand.

The Cognitive Pinnacle: Abstract Knowledge

At the pyramid's pinnacle we locate knowledge, rationally produced concepts of the type neuroscientists along with all scientists, philosophers, engineers, and virtually everybody wants. Knowledge may be located within consciousness; but it is not in itself consciousness. Knowledge is the result of a process wherein a self assesses experience, engages in active understanding, and renders judgments about what can be known and not known. "Consciousness is just experience, but knowledge is a compound of experience, understanding, and judging."[76] This is so very important that it is worth repeating: "Consciousness is just experience, but knowledge is a compound of experience, understanding, and judging." Knowledge is consciousness with an object; and abstract knowledge is objective knowledge intended in subjective awareness.

Judgment leads to decision, the decision of a self to take action. According to the Lonergan scheme, the movement from judgment to decision and then to action constitutes a *moral conversion*. The moral conversion marks the move from abstract deliberation to value, ethics and self-constitution as a moral person.[77] The moral conversion begins with an objective idea and concludes with personal integration.

Now, just what do I mean by saying rational knowledge is objective? Dehaene offers a helpful distinction between transitive consciousness and intransitive consciousness. Transitive consciousness intends an object; whereas intransitive consciousness is simply a state of awareness, of

74. Lakoff, *Whose Freedom?*, 36.

75. Pannenberg, *Anthropology in Theological Perspective*, 119.

76. Lonergan, *Method in Theology*, 106.

77. Tracy, *The Achievement of Bernard Lonergan*, 20, 165.

wakefulness or vigilance.[78] When we become occupied with a toothache, we are experiencing transitive consciousness. We may so focus on the tooth-ache that all other items present to our perception recede to an invisible background. This is what the phenomenologists call *consciousness-of.* That which we are conscious-of is the object.

What then is intransitive consciousness? While waking up in the morning our inquisitive child with thumb in mouth might ask: "Are you awake?" We might moan in answer, "Yes, now I am." In the waking state we are intransitively aware; but when the child asks a question we focus transitively or objectively on our answer, "Yes, now I am, damit." Intransi-tive consciousness provides the backdrop or stage on which transitive con-sciousness engages in objective play.

This distinction between transitive and intransitive consciousness sets contemporary neuroscientific discussions apart from early twentieth-century phenomenology, where consciousness was necessarily conscious-ness-of, necessarily transitive. Employing the concept of intentionality, phenomenologist Edmund Husserl tied subject and object together within consciousness: the subject intends an object, so to speak. "The object of the presentation, of the intention, *is* and *means* what is presented, the intentional object."[79] This is not realism. It is phenomenology.[80] "Thus, in-tentionality does not presuppose the existence of two different entities—consciousness and the object. All that is needed for intentionality to occur is the existence of an experience with the appropriate internal structure of object-directedness."[81] Object directedness occurs within consciousness; it structures consciousness, according to Husserlian phenomenologists. My point here is this: as we move from traditional phenomenology into con-temporary neuroscience we bring along transitive consciousness with its concept of intentionality; and we supplement it with intransitive conscious-ness, the state of simply being awake or aware. In objectless intransitive con-sciousness, our being-in-the-world is present to our awareness even though it may not in itself be an object of our intentional thought.

We must now take a step beyond phenomenology toward realism, to-ward the reality of the object of human knowing. Deep within us we have

---

78. Dehaene, *Consciousness and the Brain*, 22.

79. Husserl, *Logical Investigations*, 596 (italics original).

80. "Phenomenology is not . . . just another name for a kind of psychological self-observation, rather, it is the name of a philosophical approach specifically interested in consciousness and experience inaugurated by Husserl and further developed and transformed by, among many others, Scheler, Heidegger, Gurwitsch, Sartre, Merleau-Ponty, Levinas, Henry, and Ricoeur" (Zahavi, *Husserl's Phenomenology*, 4–5).

81. Zahavie, *Subjectivity and Selfhood*, 21.

a yearning to know, to know what is real, to know what is ultimately real. "Ontological thirst" is what Mircea Eliade called this deep human yearning.[82] Learning to distinguish what is real from what is fictional, merely imaginary, or even false is a hurdle we jump on the way to the finish line: knowledge of reality. This takes thinking. "Thinking is for the purpose of determining whether or not what is thought does exist."[83] The human thirst for knowledge will not be quenched by anything less than reality, not by anything less than the truth of being that transcends the inquiring subject.

In order to jump the hurdle between falsity and truth we rely upon judgment. After our consciousness has accessed our perceptions and then filtered them through symbolic discourse, we pause just before we take a leap: the leap of intellectual judgment. It is the leap of judgment that moves experience toward knowledge. "Desiring to know is desiring to know being; but it is merely the desire and not yet knowing. Thinking is thinking being; it is not thinking nothing; but thinking being is not yet knowing it. Judging is a complete increment in knowing; if correct, it is a knowing of being; but it is not yet knowing being, for that is attained only through the totality of correct judgments." Knowledge is personally satis-fying only if it is true knowledge, true knowledge of one or another object. In other words, abstract thinking includes judgment before the mind can claim to have knowledge; and knowledge by definition is knowledge of what exists, of what really is. To know being in the capital 'B' sense of Being-itself, however, requires a comprehensive collection and melding of all our judgments, says Lonergan; but this is something to which we undoubtedly lack conscious access.

Knowledge is pursued through questioning. And this questioning can itself be subject to questioning. I call this capacity for recursive questioning, *critical consciousness*. The human mind is capable of critical thinking; and critical thinking spurs the process of making judgments within the pursuit of knowledge. Because critical thinking leads ineluctably toward big questions regarding the intelligibility of our world or the ground of all Being, the hu-man pursuit of knowledge leads eventually to the question of God. According to Lonergan, human consciousness is inclined to ask about the transcendent ground of reality, to ask about the divine reality. Questioning "rises out of our conscious intentionality, out of the *a priori* structured drive that promotes us from experiencing to the effort to understand, from understanding to the effort to judge truly, from judging to the effort to choose rightly . . . there is the same transcendental tendency of the human spirit that questions,

82. Eliade, *The Sacred and the Profane*, 64.
83. Lonergan, *Insight*, 354.

that questions without restriction, that questions the significance of its own questioning, and so comes to the question of God . . . [expressing] our native orientation to the divine."[84] The pursuit of knowledge opens the question of ultimate reality—the question of God—in human consciousness. In short, the question of the divine is native to human consciousness.

The place of ultimate reality in one's mind and in one's life cannot escape a paradoxical tension. On the one hand, we find ultimacy at the level of thought, abstract thought. On the other hand, the ultimate reality cannot be thought. The result is that the divine or the ultimate is a thought about what cannot be thought. If Anselm is correct that God must be that than which nothing greater can be conceived (*id quo maius cognitari nequit*), then a thought about the ultimate is a thought about what is beyond thought. The tension of the paradox is relieved by allowing it to remain while the person of faith lives a life of love. God "may be well be loved, but not thought," we find in medieval *The Cloud of Unknowing*. "By love may [God] be gotten and holden; but by thought, never."[85]

Summary Thus Far

What I have presented here is a foundation plus framework for a cognitional theory that attempts to map the scaffolding of human consciousness and locate human knowledge. I have placed the foundation—the ground floor of our cognitional pyramid—at street level where each person is inextricably related to the surrounding world and is continually perceiving the surrounding environment. As we climb through sense impressions to the fifth floor, we find consciousness at work accessing its perceptual intake. In the process of accessing this perceptual intake, our sense impressions become selected, organized, and packaged in order to permit conscious attention and understanding. Then, rising above bare intransitive consciousness to the observation deck on the 27th floor, linguistic consciousness structures our already filtered perceptions into meaningful objects, sometimes objects with multiple meanings. At the level of language, the world—our life-world or *Weltanschaung*—becomes structured in terms of a meaningful interaction between parts and whole. This linguistic life-world is intersubjective— that is, we individuals share it with our contemporaries as well as with our ancestors. We share centuries of tradition that lives on today embedded in the connotative meanings associated with the linguistic symbols we inherit. Out of this reservoir of linguistic and symbolic meaning we abstract

84. Lonergan, *Insight*, 103.
85. Underhill, trans., *The Cloud of Unknowing*, 14.

selected conceptual objects for judgment, for judging whether they exist or not, for judging claims of truth or falsity, for quenching our thirst for reality. We rely upon the abstract idea that has passed through the fires of judgment to connect us with what is real, with being, with the truth of being which transcends our subjective apprehension of it. Finally, it is only natural and normal that we ask questions about ultimate reality, about the intelligibility of the universe, about the divine.

This human questioning of reality knows virtually no limits, because the quest is aimed at the whole of reality. The religious mind of the whole person thirsts for the whole of reality, for grasping the deep structures of the universe. "A religious perspective claims to speak not of a part but of the whole," observes theologian David Tracy; "without the sense of that reality of the whole, I believe there is no religion."[86] The religious mind asks questions—even abstract questions—about the whole.

As human beings we do more than ask questions, however. We make decisions and take actions. The religious mind intends to serve God by loving the neighbor. When discerning whether or not to serve God by loving one's neighbor, the religious self relies upon linguistically derived concepts of God which are intelligible and which function in the abstract mind as knowledge. On the basis of this knowledge, the decision to serve God can be made and, in turn, this decision instructs the brain to get with the program, so to speak, and to orient one's entire life around this intention. How is this possible? Because neurons that fire together wire together.

Neurons That Fire Together Wire Together

The abstract idea of God in the mind has the potential to rewire the brain through free will, through self-determining decisions to love one's neighbor. If a person is convinced that God is love and that we humans should love as God does, that person will make the decision to develop daily habits which exhibit compassion and attend to the needs of those in need. Such a habit becomes reinforcing, so that over a period of time what was originally a conscious decision becomes a preconscious or even unconscious pattern of daily behavior. In sum, the abstract idea of God gains a causative influence on bodily functions, even brain functions.

How is this possible? Because of downward causation and because the brain is susceptible to alteration by decisions made by the self. In her writings on complex, dynamic systems, philosopher Alicia Juarerro explains how the effect of synaptic plasticity permits changes in potentiation.

86. Tracy, *The Analogical Imagination*, 159.

Learning induces structural brain changes that make it more or less likely that in a similar situation stimulation will cause a particular population of neurons to fire.[87] Carla Shatz, writing in *Scientific American,* reports memorably, *neurons that fire together, wire together.*[88]

Recall what we said earlier when referencing Dehaene. By establishing habits, our consciousness can shelve certain activities in the unconscious closet until it needs to draw them out and give them renewed attention. Because consciousness is brain-wide, so to speak, it can temporarily consign habits to the unconscious in order to maintain workspace in what is immediately conscious. It appears that via downward causation—via supervenience or top-down or whole-part causation—our consciousness governs at least some of what is unconscious. Or to say it another way, in the case of virtuous habits our conscious mind has instructed our automatic pilot where to fly.

Essential to this chapter's thesis is the observation that one's neurology becomes altered through thought leading to action, which in turn impacts future thought and action. This ongoing process of transformation—linking, unlinking, and potentiating various neural pathways—involves the interrelated aspects of action-oriented learning, imagination, emotion, and the development of automaticity. Virtue and morality are shaped by affective, imaginative, and interpersonal interactions with the material and social world feeding into symbolic understanding and self-determination. Having climbed to the very pinnacle of the Transamerica pyramid, the religious person reverses direction, so to speak, and restructures the entire complex on the trip back down to the symbolic and material foundations.

The implication for the religious mind is clear: loving actions, when performed repeatedly, could influence the morphology and potentiation of neural systems that support such loving actions, readying them so that they are available for activation in future circumstances. It further implies that a virtuous life requires one to continue to act accordingly, because failing to practice virtue can result in regression. The discipline of Virtue Ethics has long known what today's neuroscience only reinforces, namely, that as one develops in a virtue, there becomes less a need to consciously direct moral action. One acts preconsciously and spontaneously as virtue becomes an indelible part of one's character.[89]

87. Juarerro, *Dynamics in Action,* 53.

88. Shatz. *The Developing Brain,* 60–67.

89. For this discussion I am dependent on the research of Alan Weissenbacher, who is writing a doctoral dissertation, "The Born Again Brain: Neuroscience and Wesleyan Salvation," at the Graduate Theological Union.

Our Idea of God and the Reality of God

Can we hack the religious mind? Yes. What we find in the religious mind is likely to be a worldview filled with symbolic meaning plus, at least in some cases, an abstract idea of God. Does this abstract idea accompanied by its symbolic penumbra affect conscious access in order to structure experience, perhaps even perceptual experience? Yes. This structuring of experience is the product of top-down supervenience taking place within the consciousness of a human self.

I rely on supervenience, not supernaturalism. Theologian Klaus Nürnberger acknowledges that the religious mind amounts to the organization of the natural mind. "According to modern neurology, all human knowledge is located in synaptic networks and processes in our brain. God consciousness cannot possibly be an exception. Spirit is structured and oriented consciousness."[90]

Our natural cognitive faculties need no supernatural intervention. "Religious experiences do not depend on any special faculties over and above humans ordinary emotional and cognitive faculties," writes Nancey Murphy. "Their religiousness consists in (sometimes) their special content, but, more importantly, in their circumstances—circumstances that justify their being interpreted as acts of or encounters with the divine. In brief, religious experience supervenes on cognitive and/or affective experience in the context of an encounter with God."[91] The cognitional theory I hypothesize here does not require supranatural communication or even a mystical encounter with the *numinous* transcendent. Rather, the presence of the abstract idea of the divine in the human mind exhibits a top-down causative influence on ordinary everyday consciousness.

By abstract I mean cognitive, mental, ideational, rational. Some religious models of ultimate reality can be quite anthropomorphic, such as Hinduism's Krishna or the old man with a white beard in Christian art. Other models rank higher on the level of abstraction, such as Moses' experience with *YHWH* or mystical apprehensions of the divine in Brahman.[92] Whether as anthropomorphic projection or as radically transcendent, the abstract concept of the ultimate exerts downward causation on one's psychic activity and, eventually, on one's biological and social activity. More important than the mere concept of ultimacy is its effect, namely, does it inspire love? Does it radiate love like a soccer goal prompts a roar from

90. Nürnberger, *Faith in Christ Today*, 28.

91. Murphy, "Nonreductive Physicalism," 147.

92. Wildman, "Behind, Between, and Beyond Anthropomorphic Models," 885–906.

the stadium crowd? Key to the religious mind is the role the ultimate plays in structuring the worldview through supervenience, which in turn births faith, hope, and love.

The key is the role of the ultimate regardless of how the ultimate is symbolized. Whether this abstract idea takes the form of a monotheistic God, polytheistic gods and goddesses, Brahmanic fullness or Buddhist emptiness, what we refer to as the divine stands at the end of all rational questioning. "*The object of theology is what concerns us ultimately,*" writes theologian Paul Tillich; "*Only those propositions are theological which deal with their object in so far as it can become a matter of ultimate concern for us.*"[93]

The "object" language of Tillich here can be misleading. Ultimate reality turns out to be something non-objective. Ultimate reality is not one object among others, because it includes us as well. It includes both the object of our knowledge and our own subjectivity which has abstracted this object from the linguistic flow of meaning. Because ultimate reality is inclusive of both object and subject, it can no longer be represented merely as an abstract item of knowledge. Our relationship to ultimate reality—to God or the divine—is so self-involving that our subjectivity becomes a participant rather than an observer of what is ultimately real. The best term to use to describe this self-involving relationship is *love*. One cannot know God without loving God or, more precisely, without experiencing the love of God for us. In sum, our relationship with ultimate reality requires the totality of our consciousness, not merely abstract knowledge.

We have not here proven the existence of God. William Grassie reminds us: one "cannot prove or disprove the existence of God by studying someone's brain."[94] Though it has not been our task to prove or disprove the existence of a divine ultimate, we have, however, demonstrated the plausibility of a nonreductive account of human cognition that includes top-down agency wherein the idea of God affects our experience and influences our intentional action in the world. With this in hand, a worthy future task would be to add a theory of divine action within human consciousness. "The nonreductive physicalist account of nature needs to be complemented by a theological account in which descriptions of divine action supervene on descriptions of historical events, but without being reducible to them."[95]

93. Tillich, *Systematic Theology,* 1:12, (italics original).

94. Grassie, *The New Sciences of Religion,* 104.

95. Murphy, "Nonreductive Physicalism," 147.

Conclusion

In order to hack into the religious mind, we must rely upon a theological observation: one's relationship to the divine is much more than merely knowledge at the abstract level. Lonergan introduces the notion that the person of faith falls in love with God. The Christian will want to add: love should envelope one's total consciousness, not just abstract knowing. We experience our love relationship with the divine as fulfillment. "That fulfillment is not the product of our knowledge and choice. On the contrary, it dismantles and abolishes the horizon in which our knowing and choosing went on and it sets up a new horizon in which the love of God will transvalue our values and the eyes of that love will transform our knowing." The scope of fulfillment is inclusive and reorienting. "As the question of God is implicit in all our questioning, so being in love with God is the basic fulfillment of our conscious intentionality. That fulfillment brings a deep-set joy that can remain despite humiliation, failure, privation, pain, betrayal, desertion. That fulfillment brings a radical peace, the peace that the world cannot give. That fulfillment bears fruit in a love of one's neighbor that strives mightily to bring about the kingdom of God on this earth."[96]

Lonergan makes an additional point which flowers from the nourishment of his Christian roots, namely, our love relationship with God is a gift of divine grace. "In religious matters love precedes knowledge and, as that love is God's gift, the very beginning of faith is due to God's grace."[97] Paradoxically, what we pursue through questioning turns out to be something already given us by grace. Just how does a fulfilling love relationship with the divine go back down the stairs from abstract knowledge toward symbolic speech, conscious access, and perhaps temporal and spatial perception of the world around us?

The transcendental experience which some report in meditation or prayer can be described as mystical. Frequently, it is described as interactive love between one's self and the divine. And, more often than not, it is an experience of divine grace. Just how does a fulfilling transcendental relationship with the divine go back down the stairs via abstract knowledge toward symbolic speech, conscious access, and perhaps temporal and spatial perception of the world around us? Let's try to find out.

96. Lonergan, *Method in Theology*, 106.
97. Ibid., 105.

References

Akers, Katherine G. et al. 2014. "Hippocampal Neurogenesis Regulates Forgetting During Adulthood and Infancy." *Science* 344/6184, pp. 598–602.

Ashbrook, James B., and Carol Rausch Albright. 1997. *The Humanizing Brain: Where Religion and Neuroscience Meet.* Cleveland: Pilgrim.

Baars, Bernard G., and David B. Edelman. 2012. "Consciousness, Biology and Quantum Hypotheses," *Physics of Life Reviews.* 285–94; www.elsevier.com/locate/plrev/.

Bittner, Rüdiger. 2015. "What Is It to Be Free?" In *Quests for Freedom: Biblical–Historical–Contemporary,* edited by Michael Welker, 99–116. Neukirchen-Vluyn: Neukirchener Theologie.

Brown, Warren S. 1998. "Cognitive Contributions to the Soul." In *Whatever Happened to the Soul? Scientific and Theological Portraits of Human Nature,* edited by Warren S. Brown et al., 99–126. Theology and the Sciences. Minneapolis: Fortress.

Buzsáki, György. 2014. "Time, Space and Memory." *Nature* 497/7451, pp. 568–69.

Chalmers, David J. 1997. "The Hard Problem: Facing Up to the Problem of Consciousness." In *Explaining Consciousness: The "Hard Problem,"* edited by Jonathan Shear, 9–30. Cambridge: MIT Press.

Churchland, Patricia S. 2002. *Brain-Wise: Studies in Neurophilosophy.* Cambridge: MIT Press.

———. 2013. *Touching a Nerve: The Self as Brain.* New York: Norton.

Clark, Thomas W. 1997. "Function and Phenomenology: Closing the Explanatory Gap." In *Explaining Consciousness: The "Hard Problem,"* edited by Jonathan Shear, 45–60. Cambridge: MIT Press.

Clayton, Philip. 2006. "The Emergence of Spirit: From Complexity to Anthropology to Theology." *Theology and Science* 4/3, pp. 290–310.

Deacon, Terrence W. 1997. *The Symbolic Species: The Co-evolution of Language and the Brain.* New York: Norton.

———. 2012. *Incomplete Nature: How Mind Emerged from Matter.* New York: Norton.

Dehaene, Stanislas. 2014. *Consciousness and the Brain: Deciphering How the Brain Codes Our Thoughts.* New York: Viking.

Dennett, Daniel C. 1991. *Consciousness Explained.* Boston: Little, Brown.

———. 1997. "Facing Backwards on the Problem of Consciousness." In *Explaining Consciousness: The "Hard Problem,"* edited by Jonathan Shear, 33–36. Cambridge: MIT Press.

———. 2006. *Breaking the Spell.* New York: Viking.

D'Souza, Dinesh, 2009. *Life beyond Death: The Evidence.* Washington, DC: Regnery.

Eliade, Mircea. 1959. *The Sacred and the Profane: The Significance of Religious Myth, Symbolism, and Ritual within Life and Culture.* New York: Harcourt, Brace.

Fisher, Serbern F. 2014. *Neurofeedback in the Treatment of Developmental Trauma: Calming the Fear-Driven Brain.* New York: Norton.

Freeman, Walter. 1995. *Societies of Brains: A Study in the Neuroscience of Love and Hate.* The International Neural Networks Society Series. Hillsdale, NJ: Erlbaum.

Gadamer, Hans-Georg, 1994. *Truth and Method.* Translated by Joel Weinsheimer and Donald G. Marshall. 2nd rev. ed. New York: Continuum.

Grassie, William. 2010. *The New Sciences of Religion: Exploring Spirituality from the Outside In and Bottom Up.* New York: Palgrave Macmillan.

Graybiel, Ann M., and Kyle S. Smith. 2014. "Good Habits, Bad Habits." *Scientific American* 310/6, pp. 38–43.

Haag, James W. 2008. *Emergent Freedom: Naturalizing Free Will*. Religion, Theology, and Natural Science 17. Göttingen: Vandenhoeck & Ruprecht.

Hawking, Stephen, and Leonard Mlodinow. 2010. *The Grand Design*. New York: Bantam.

Hewlett, Martinez. 2010. "What Does It Mean to Be Human? Genetics and Human Identity." In *Human Identity at the Intersection of Science, Theology, and Religion*, edited by Nancey Murphy and Christopher C. Knight, 147–64 Ashgate Science and Religion Series. Aldershot, UK: Ashgate.

Hodder, Ian. 1982. *Symbols in Action: Ethnoarchaeological Studies of Material Culture*. New Studies in Archaeology. Cambridge: Cambridge University Press.

Höffe, Ottfried. 2010. *Can Virtue Make Us Happy? The Art of Living and Morality*. Translated by Douglas R. McGauhey and Aaron Bunch. Evanston IL: Northwestern University Press.

Husserl, Edmund. 1970. *Logical Investigations*. Translated by J. N. Findlay. 2 vols. International Library of Philosophy and Scientific Method. London: Routledge & Keegan Paul.

Jeeves, Malcolm, 2014. "Brains, Minds, Souls, and People." In *The Depth of the Human Person: A Multidisciplinary Approach,* edited by Michael Welker, 93–108. Grand Rapids: Eerdmans.

Jones, Dan. 2011. "The Free Will Delusion." *New Scientist* 210/2808, pp. 32–35.

Juarrero, Alicia. 1999. *Dynamics in Action: Intentional Behavior as a Complex System*. Cambridge: MIT Press.

Kant, Immanuel. 1934. *Critique of Pure Reason*. Translated by J. M. D. Meiklejohn. Everyman's Library. London: Dent.

Kauffman, Stuart A. 2008. *Reinventing the Sacred: A New View of Science, Reason, and Religion*. New York: Basic Books.

Kaku, Michio, 2014. *The Future of the Mind: The Scientific Quest to Understand, Enhance, and Empower the Mind*. New York: Doubleday.

Kraus, Benjamin J., John A. White, Howard Eichenbaum, Michael E. Hasselmo, 2013. "Hippocampal Time Cells: Time versus Path Integration." *Neuron* 78/6, pp. 1090–1101, http://www.cell.com/neuron/abstract/S0896-6273%2813%2900317-6/.

Lakoff, George. 2006. *Whose Freedom? The Battle over America's Most Important Idea*. New York: Farrar, Straus and Giroux.

Lonergan, Bernard J. F., SJ. 1958. *Insight: A Study of Human Understanding*. New York: Philosophical Library.

———. 1972. *Method in Theology*. New York: Herder.

Louchakova, Olga. 2008. "Reconstitution of the Self during the Study of Advaita Vedanta (Traditional Indian teachings of non-dual consciousness): Phenomenological Investigations." *Toward a Science of Consciousness: Consciousness Research Abstracts, 315*, p. 194.

———. 2007. "Spiritual Heart and Direct Knowing in the Prayer of the Heart." *Existential Analysis* 18/1, pp. 81–102.

Luther, Martin, 1955–1986. *Luther's Works*. American ed. Vols. 1–30, edited by Jaroslav Pelikan; St. Louis: Concordia, 1955–1967; vols. 31–55, edited by Helmut T. Lehmann; Minneapolis: Fortress, 1955–1986.

Malafouris, Lambros, 2013. *How Things Shape the Mind: A Theory of Material Engagement*. Cambridge: MIT Press.

Metzinger, Thomas. 2009. *The Science of the Mind and the Myth of the Self.* New York: Basic Books.

Murphy, Nancey. 2010. "Divine Action, Emergence and Scientific Explanation." In *The Cambridge Companion to Science and Religion,* edited by Peter Harrison, 244–59. Cambridge Companions to Religion. Cambridge: Cambridge University Press.

————. 1998. "Nonreductive Physicalism: Philosophical Issues." In *Whatever Happened to the Soul? Scientific and Theological Portraits of Human Nature,* edited by Warren S. Brown, et al. Theology and the Sciences. Minneapolis: Fortress.

Murphy, Nancey, and Warren S. Brown. 2007. *Did My Neurons Make Me Do It? Philosophical and Neurobiological Perspectives on Moral Responsibility and Free Will.* Oxford: Oxford University Press.

Nürnberger, Klaus. 2016. *Faith in Christ Today: Invitation to Systematic Theology.* 2 vols. London: Xlibris.

Ouellette, Jennifer. 2014. *Me, Myself, and Why: Searching for the Science of Self.* New York: Penguin.

Pannenberg, Wolfhart. 1985. *Anthropology in Theological Perspective.* Translated by Matthew J. O'Connell. Philadelphia: Westminster.

Penrose, Roger, 2014. "The Quantum Nature of Consciousness." https://www.youtube.com/watch?v=3WXTXoIUaOg.

Peters, Ted, 1999. "Resurrection of the Very Embodied Soul?" In *Neuroscience and the Person: Scientific Perspectives on Divine Action,* edited by R. J. Russell, et al., 305–26. Berkeley: Center for Theology and the Natural Sciences.

Ricoeur, Paul. 1969. *The Symbolism of Evil.* Translated by Emerson Buchanan. Beacon Paperbacks. Boston: Beacon.

————. 1974. *The Conflict of Interpretations: Essays in Hermeneutics.* Edited by Don Ihde. Northwestern University Studies in Phenomenology & Existential Philosophy. Evanston IL: Northwestern University Press.

Satel, Sally, and Scott O. Lilienfeld. 2013. "Losing Our Minds in the Age of Brain Science." *Skeptical Inquirer* 37/6, pp. 30–35

Shatz, Carla. 1992. "The Developing Brain." *Scientific American* 267/3, pp. 60–67.

Spezio, Michael. 2012. "The Cognitive Sciences." In *The Routledge Companion to Religion and Science,* edited by James W. Haag et al., 285–95. Routledge Companions. London: Routledge.

Stapp, Henry P. 2011. *Mindful Universe: Quantum Mechanics and the Participating Observer.* 2nd ed. Berlin: Springer.

Tillich, Paul. 1951–1963 *Systematic Theology.* 3 vols. Chicago: University of Chicago Press.

Tracy, David, 1970. *The Achievement of Bernard Lonergan.* New York: Herder.

————. 1981. *The Analogical Imagination.* New York: Crossroad.

Tye, Michael, 2015. "Qualia." In *Stanford Encyclopedia of Philosophy.* https://plato.stanford.edu/entries/qualia/.

Underhill, Evelyn, trans. 2007. *The Cloud of Unknowing.* New York: Cosimo.

Weissenbacher, A. C. 2017. "The Born Again Brain: Neuroscience and Wesleyan Salvation." PhD diss., Graduate Theological Union.

————. 2015. "Ten Principles for Interpreting Neuroscientific Pronouncements Regarding Human Nature." *Dialog* 54/1, pp. 41–51.

Wildman, Wesley J. 2013. "Behind, Between, and Beyond Anthropomorphic Models of Ultimate Reality." In *Models of God and Alternative Ultimate Realities,* edited by Jeanine Diller and Asa Kasher, 885–906. Dordrecht: Springer.

Willett, Cynthia, Ellie Anderson, and Diana Meyers, 1999. "Feminist Perspectives on the Self." http://plato.stanford.edu/entries/feminism-self/.

Wilson, Edward O. 2012. *The Social Conquest of Earth.* New York: Norton.

Yuste, Rafael, and George M. Church. 2014. "The New Century of the Brain." *Scientific American* 310/3, pp. 38–51.

Zahavi, Dan. 2003. *Husserl's Phenomenology.* Cultural Memory in the Present. Stanford: Stanford University Press.

———. 2008. *Subjectivity and Selfhood: Investigating the First-Person Perspective.* A Bradford Book. Cambridge: MIT Press.

Index

motion
  first law of, 18
  and force, 15
  Newton's laws of, 19–20
  Newton on, 16
  Newton *vs.* Leibniz, 21
multivalency, 215
Munchhausen trilemma, 164
Murphy, Nancey, 49, 191–92, 208, 219,
  226, 228
Muskhamel, C., 133
mutualism, 78
mystical experience, 182–85
  Einstein on, 186
mysticism, 9
  antipathy toward, 175
  historical and cultural variations,
    180–82
  and science, 174–75
mystics
  in all Christian traditions, 184
  versus mystification, 185–87

Napoleon, 155
Nardi, James B., 91, 96
National Aeronautics and Space
  Administration, 58–59
national parks, Brazil, 108
Natural History of Religion (Hume), 168
natural selection, 5, 84
Navier-Stokes equation, 50
nebula, 58
nebular hypothesis, 65–66
necessary constitutive interaction,
  122–23
nematodes, number of, 91
neo-Darwinism, 79
neoplatonism, 17
neo-vitalism, 149
nervous system, 6
Neuenschwander, Dwight, 22
neurology, 236
  and mysticism, 184
neurons, 6, 52, 54, 235–36
neuroscience
  explanatory gap, 217–19
  focus of, 114–15
neurotransmitters, 6
neutrinos, 33

new materialism, 149
Newton, Isaac, 35, 65
  on gravity, 20
  laws of motion, 19–20
  versus Leibniz, 21
  on motion, 16
  quantity of motion, 20
  on space, 62
19th century physics, 22–23
noble gases, 43
Noether, Emmy, 22
noninterventionist objective divine
  action, 8–9
Nürnberger, Klaus, 237

Oersted, Hans Christian, 2–24
old quantum theory, 27
Old Testament, on famine, 94
O'Malley, Maureen, 85
one-celled plants, 5
On the Origin of Species (Darwin), 65
ontological dualism, 191–92
ontological emergence, 155
ontology, 144
  of interaction, 187–89
operationalization, 120n
Orion Nebula, 64

Paley, William, 167
parallel endosymbiosis, 81
parasitism, 70, 78
particle physics, 3, 30–33
Pauli, Wolfgang, 31
  exclusion principle, 42–43
Payne-Gaposhkin, Cecilia, 60
Peacocke, Arthur, 49, 53
perceptual interaction, 211–12
Perlmutter, Saul, 67
person, 146
personal identity after death, 192
Peters, Ted, 10–11
phase, change of, 37–38
phenomenology, 213
philosophy
  and biology, 86–88
  linguistic turn in, 147–48
  ontology of interaction, 187–89
  problem in, 188
photoelectric effect, 26